The Cinema of Generation X

The Cinema of Generation X

A Critical Study of Films and Directors

by Peter Hanson

McFarland & Company, Inc., Publishers
Jefferson, North Carolina, and London

Library of Congress Cataloguing-in-Publication Data

Hanson, Peter, 1969–
    The cinema of Generation X: a critical study of films and
directors / by Peter Hanson.
       p.   cm.
    Includes bibliographical references and index.
    ISBN 0-7864-1334-4 (softcover : 50# alkaline paper) ∞
    1. Motion pictures— United States— History.   2. Motion
picture producers and directors— United States— Biography.
3. Generation X. I. Title.
PN1993.5.U6H34   2002
791.43'75'097309049 — dc21   2001008469

British Library cataloguing data are available

Manufactured in the United States of America

Cover photograph: Steven Soderbergh directing the 2000 film
Erin Brockovich

McFarland & Company, Inc., Publishers
  Box 611, Jefferson, North Carolina 28640
  www.mcfarlandpub.com

Acknowledgments

For her patience, support, insight, and clear-headed reactions throughout the various stages of this book's development, I am indebted to Leslie S. Connor, to whom this book is dedicated. Thanks also are due to Margaret Eck, Joe Masucci, Frank Mouris, the Clan Swierzewski, the New York State Archives Partnership Trust, the New York State Writers Institute, and the management of Hoyts Crossgates Cinemas and the Spectrum 7 Theatres, both in Albany, New York.

Table of Contents

Preface

Youth isn't always wasted on the young.

Beginning in the late 1980s and continuing through to the present day, a wave of youthful filmmakers—working in modalities ranging from the brazen to the austere—has infused both mainstream and independent American films with the vigor, the promise, the possibility, and even the foolhardiness of youth. And while it sometimes seems there is little order and unity among these wildly diverse artists, one essential fact joins them: They all are members of Generation X.

The tones wrought by Gen-X filmmakers are as varied as the directors themselves: Steven Soderbergh's provocative postmodernism, Quentin Tarantino's swaggering violence, Kevin Smith's philosophical ribaldry, David Fincher's seductive nihilism. And even individual directors from this unpredictable group have surprises up their sleeve: Soderbergh followed the straightforward drama *Erin Brockovich* with an experimental examination of America's war on drugs, *Traffic*, and a glossy caper film populated by several of Hollywood's biggest stars, *Ocean's Eleven*. Just as no one description captures the entirety of the cinema of Generation X, no one description captures the entirety of an important Gen-X filmmaker's body of work.

The reasons why directors born in the 1960s and 1970s are so hard to nail down are many and fascinating, but the enigma of the cinema of Generation X revolves around a few key facts: Gen Xers grew up during one of the most tumultuous periods of American history, were inundated with popular culture to an unprecedented degree, suffered through social changes such as a rash of divorces, and then created a youth culture anchored in irony, apathy, and disenfranchisement. Is it any wonder that the filmmakers who belong to this group send mixed messages?

This book explores how a difficult transition from childhood to maturity colored the sensibilities of Gen Xers who became filmmakers, and further details how those sensibilities inform such intriguing Gen-X commonalties as the obsession with pop-culture references, the willingness to embrace postmodern narrative techniques, and the telling aversion to moral absolutes. It says everything about the cinema of Generation X to note that this generation has produced such unconventional movies as *sex, lies, and videotape, Pi, Fight Club,* and *Memento.*

Yet Gen Xers also create unthreatening escapism, whether it's the superheroic action of *X-Men* or the supernatural adventure of *The Mummy Returns*. These pictures, and others like them, are as reflective of the character of Generation X as any others, however, for it follows that a generation raised on shallow popular culture would create their own disposable entertainment given the chance.

The disparities between the serious artists of this generation and their crowd-pleasing counterparts are important, but so too are the instances in which many facets of this peculiar generation's identity converge: Consider Larry and Andy Wachowski's *The Matrix*, a testosterone-laden action movie that's also a mind-bending exploration of whether the concept of reality still holds its meaning in an age defined by technology.

The hero of *The Matrix* is a definitive Gen-X figure, because like countless members of the generation to which the Wachowksi brothers belong, the hero is overwhelmed by the onslaught of sensation and information and misinformation that is life in the modern world. He is lost, and only others like him can help him find his way. Not all Gen Xers are lost, of course, but nearly all Gen-X filmmakers are on a quest not unlike that pursued by the hero of *The Matrix*. They want to make sense of a senseless world.

To understand how these directors use their work to further this quest is to gain insight into the collective soul of a generation, and to more deeply understand why the cinematic creations of that generation are far more than just movies. Taken together, they provide an illuminating interpretation of the culture in which we live.

1

The Arrival

In the last summer-movie orgy of the 1980s, Hollywood's propensity for high concepts and higher budgets reached an apex that epitomized the excesses of Greed Decade blockbusters, but also redefined the earning potential of such films. On June 23, 1989, months of savvy advertising and priceless word-of-mouth helped give the superhero adventure *Batman* a monstrous opening weekend, underlining mainstream Hollywood's ability to spin a masterful marketing campaign around a simplistic, youth-oriented idea.

Although critics were almost universally enthusiastic about the picture's state-of-the-art visuals and the appeal of director Tim Burton's dark wit, the movie's hackneyed story left all but the most undemanding viewers disappointed. So for observers who had lamented the steady evolution of the action-oriented blockbuster since Steven Spielberg's *Jaws* and George Lucas's *Star Wars* earned unheard-of revenues in the mid–1970s, the record-setting conquest of *Batman* was a nail in the grave of quality cinema. After all, *Batman* was merely the victor in a high-concept sweepstakes whose other entrants included *Indiana Jones and the Last Crusade*, the third installment in Spielberg's nostalgic adventure series; *Ghostbusters II*, a follow-up to the popular supernatural comedy starring Bill Murray; *Honey, I Shrunk the Kids*, a Disney-produced family adventure with a science-fiction premise; and *The Abyss*, director James Cameron's epic underwater drama.

Before the summer of 1989 drew to a close, however, a film hit theaters that had neither a high concept nor easily marketable youth appeal. The picture was psychological and erotic, making it a distinct alternative to the simple-minded, neutered entertainment of the year's blockbusters. And while the summer's big flicks all had some form of brand-name appeal — the Batman character had been popular, in various mediums, since before World War II; *Indiana Jones* and *Ghostbusters* were sequels;

3

and so on — the dark-horse movie that opened on August 2 was the first-time directorial effort of a little-known film editor, and it was released by a New York City–based boutique distributor best known for bringing European pictures to America. The movie's meatiest credentials, in fact, were a Palme d'Or prize from the Cannes Film Festival and a warm reception at the Sundance Film Festival. It hardly had the makings of a pop-culture sensation.

Yet as summer drifted into fall, that's exactly what *sex, lies, and videotape* became, in the process spurring a boom period for Miramax Films and launching the career of writer-director Steven Soderbergh.

sex, lies, and videotape wasn't a blockbuster on the order of *Batman*— the box-office take of Soderbergh's picture was smaller than the budget of Burton's — but the film's impact was, in a way, more powerful. For while *Batman*'s huge returns set the course for the next several years' worth of high-concept entertainment, the surprising manner in which *sex, lies, and videotape* escaped the art-house ghetto and found a niche in the nation's multiplexes reminded jaded cinephiles that bold cinema could still attract sizable audiences.

Boldness, though, wasn't the quality that made *sex, lies* unique; Spike Lee's controversial race-relations drama *Do the Right Thing*, released in that same eventful summer of 1989, had more brazen attitude in its libidinous, hiphop-driven opening sequence than Soderbergh packed into his entire debut feature.

So if *sex, lies* didn't make its mark by earning huge revenues or by filling the screen with unprecedented content, what made the picture so special? Was it the offbeat plot, about an impotent drifter who videotapes women discussing their sex lives so he can masturbate while watching the tapes? Was it the surprisingly mature performance by model-turned-actor Andie MacDowell, who just four years previous was humiliated by having her dialogue in *Greystoke: The Legend of Tarzan, Lord of the Apes* over-dubbed by Glenn Close? Was it the film's thoughtful approach to sensuality, in which shattering intimacy was communicated without the glamorously photographed nudity and histrionics of such 1980s sexfests as *9½ Weeks* and *Fatal Attraction*?

To understand what made *sex, lies, and videotape* significant, it's necessary to look back twenty years, to July 14, 1969. In the last days of the studios' tightfisted control over Hollywood's output, old-fashioned ideas about mainstream cinematic entertainment were being challenged by new voices. The studios were still manufacturing insipid comedies, bloated musicals, and formulaic star vehicles — 1969's two biggest box-office hits were *The Love Bug*, a farce starring a car, and *Funny Girl*, an adaptation of a Broadway hit — but the influence of the baby boomer–driven counterculture was seen in such progressive late–1960s films as *The Graduate*, *Bonnie and Clyde*, and *2001: A Space Odyssey*. By comparison to the movie that hit screens on July 14, however, the aforementioned pictures offered mere glimmers of counterculture attitude, for *Easy Rider* was a hippie film from top to bottom, oozing youthful style in everything from its sex-drugs-and-rock-and-roll story line to its brashly off-the-cuff cinematography.

The counterculture had made notable appearances on American screens prior to *Easy Rider*'s opening, but the arrival of the Dennis Hopper–directed motorcycle drama was an unmistakable omen that the filmmaking establishment was about to experience an upheaval as extreme as those shaking every other facet of American culture at the time. Despite its myriad flaws, *Easy Rider* symbolized the cinematic coming-of-age of a new generation.

Twenty years later, the arrival of Soderbergh's sexual-dysfunction drama symbolized the coming-of-age of another generation. The debut of Soderbergh's movie ushered in the cinema of Generation X.

Ennui Shall Overcome

Although Generation X has a soundbite-ready name — appropriated from the title of Canadian author Douglas Coupland's irony-laden 1991 novel about aimless, jaded youth, *Generation X: Tales for an Accelerated Culture* — the exact parameters of the generation are elusive. Pundits generally agree that Generation X succeeded the baby boomers. Admitting that setting such chronological borders is an inexact science, here are the dates that will be used to inform this book: Gen-X filmmakers are those directors born between 1961 and 1971, a ten-year period that falls well within the range given by most sociologists seeking to identify when Generation X was born. While ten years of births can't encompass an entire generation, the filmmakers born in these years were exposed to key social, political, and cultural factors. Therefore, their collective body of work can be analyzed as a reaction to the forces that shaped their generation as a whole.

Because setting the boundaries of a generation is an imperfect science, some might quibble with the dates chosen for this book, and with good reason: David O. Russell, the brash filmmaker behind *Three Kings*, has a distinctly Gen-X approach to cinema, but he's not included in this book's study group because he was born in 1958. Yet the giants of Gen-X

Auteur de force: Oscar-winning director Steven Soderbergh, arguably the most important Gen-X filmmaker, contemplates a scene on the set of *The Limey* (Artisan Entertainment).

cinema — including Soderbergh, born in 1963 — are. So the filmmakers in this book are a representative sampling, not an inclusive roster. In this case, however, a representative sampling is the best that one can offer: Given the youth of Generation X, many important filmmakers from this age group probably have yet to emerge or artistically mature. The youngest filmmaker included in this book is Sofia Coppola, who was born in 1971 and made her feature-film directorial debut with 2000's *The Virgin Suicides*, yet filmmakers younger than her surely will emerge in the coming years and still be legitimate representatives of Generation X. This book's scope falls short of prognostication.

Well within this book's scope, however, is the spiritual wanderlust that defines the cinema of Generation X, a body of work that includes such landmarks of contemporary filmmaking as *sex, lies, and videotape*, *Pulp Fiction*, *The Usual Suspects*, *The Sixth Sense*, and *American Beauty*. The great theme that permeates this body of work is one of the most basic questions of human existence: "Who am I, and where do I belong?" Whether it's a would-be filmmaker asking her friends where their lives are going in *Reality Bites*, passionately political lovers debating the best way to serve the human community in *Waking the Dead*, a troubled youth confronting her choice to commit herself to a psychiatric hospital in *Girl, Interrupted*, or a hacker risking his sanity by asking the question "What is the Matrix?" in *The Matrix*, nearly every protagonist in a notable Gen-X movie is on a quest to understand the meaning of his or her existence.

Similar quests appear to motivate the most interesting Gen-X filmmakers, suggesting that the members of this generation who express themselves cinematically use their work to ask the questions that mean most to them and their chronological peers. These searchers use a broad spectrum of characters as their onscreen alter egos, so while the protagonists in some Gen-X movies actually belong to other generations (such as Kevin Spacey's baby-boomer character in *American Beauty*), others personify the quintessential Gen-X archetype, the slacker.

In some pictures, the mystery of existence is explored through questions of work, love, and family, as in *Reality Bites* and *American Beauty*. In others, a statement about contemporary society is made by depicting how criminals interact with other segments of the population, as in the movies of Quentin Tarantino, including *Pulp Fiction*. And in some extreme cases, the disharmonies of modern life are exaggerated to hyperbolic and even nonsensical proportions, as in the anarchistic *Fight Club* and the surreal *Being John Malkovich*. These skewed fantasies are among the most telling Gen-X movies, because they illustrate that Gen Xers inherited a damaged society from those who came before.

And in *The Matrix*, arguably the ultimate expression of Generation X's collective identity, the abstract question of what makes today's society so disorienting is given a concrete, cynical answer. That picture dramatizes the disturbing concept that the cities and towns and patterns of modern life are just an illusion created by machines to placate humans, who are employed by the machines as soulless energy sources. If films such as *Reality Bites* ask how Gen Xers can find their way in a world that is not their own, *The Matrix* poses an even bigger question: How can Gen Xers overthrow the powers that be, then remake the world in their own image?

This book is an attempt to catalog the myriad ways in which Gen-X filmmakers illustrate their roles in society, their attempts to reshape society, and — particularly in the case of slackers — their frequent choice to drop out of society altogether. The foundation of this study will be a mixture of social and cinematic history, as well as close examinations of dozens of movies directed by Gen Xers. American filmmakers, ranging from Hollywood insiders to indie-cinema outsiders, comprise most of the group under examination; to keep the parameters of this study workable, and also to focus on the influence of several important evolutions in American culture, filmmakers born within this book's range of birth years but whose work has primarily been in non–English-language movies have been excluded.

It would be presumptuous to offer a single answer to the question burning in the hearts of this generation's filmmakers—"Who am I, and where do I belong?" Certainly one of the richest lessons gleaned from studying the cinema of Generation X is how inclusive a body of work it is: There are as many ideas about what role Gen Xers play in modern life as there are Gen-X filmmakers. But perhaps the act of identifying the question that motivates these directors, and of examining the tools they use to seek answers to that question, can give shape to the seemingly formless spiritual and societal malaise underlying some of the most exciting cinematic experimentation of the late twentieth century and the early twenty-first.

Based on the intriguing movies that Gen Xers already have made, and the promise of the ones that they have yet to make, the movement that reached prominence with the arrival of Soderbergh's *sex, lies, and videotape* promises to be one of the most revolutionary chapters in the history of American film. The story of that movement is the story of this book.

2

Born in the U.S.A.

Because Generation X grew up during a period of great tumult in American society, movies made by Gen Xers are filled with ambiguity and ambivalence. These directors use their work to look for a place of their own in a world defined by the preceding generation, and the frustrations, disappointments, and epiphanies inherent to such a quest provide the drama inherent to the best Gen-X movies.

In the early-to-mid–1970s, when the first wave of Gen-X filmmakers passed through or approached puberty, America suffered two of the most divisive upheavals in its history: the anticlimactic conclusion of the Vietnam War, the first major military action in United States history to end without any semblance of victory, and the unprecedented downfall of Richard Nixon, the first and, to date, only president to resign from the highest office in the land. The escalation of the Vietnam War had sparked years of fierce social unrest, which was matched by violent civil disobedience and police actions connected to the civil-rights movement.

Against the backdrop of Vietnam, Watergate, and civil-rights conflicts, the women's movement took center stage in the mid–1970s; combined with the ongoing sexual revolution and an astronomical rise in divorce rates, the gender-equality debate of the 1970s led to a new morality far different from that of the era during which the baby boom occurred. The fuzzy parameters of this new morality contributed to the confusing social climate into which Gen Xers were born, and goes a long way to explaining why so many Gen-X filmmakers seem obsessed with amorality — as seen in the senseless violence committed by characters in *Seven*, *Pulp Fiction*, and numerous other pictures.

The tragedy of America's losses in Vietnam, the shock of discovering that a sitting president was a criminal, and the drug-related deaths of such cultural icons as Jim Morrison, Janis Joplin, Jimi Hendrix, Lenny Bruce, and Elvis Presley all cast dark shadows across the idealism of the 1960s,

**Shadows and light: The stylish films of David Fincher, seen lining up a shot on
the set of *Seven*, are filled with such morbid themes as alienation and martyrdom (New Line Cinema).**

and there was more darkness to come. As the first waves of Gen Xers
entered their college years in the late 1970s and early 1980s, reports of ugly
violence filled the airwaves: a cult's mass suicide in Guyana, the murder
of rock and roll poet John Lennon, madmen's attempts to assassinate President Ronald Reagan and Pope John Paul II, the incomprehensible brutality of the Khmer Rouge in Cambodia. Suddenly, the air was thick with
the stench of death, and there wasn't anything that a protest or a love-in
could do to stem the devastating tide.

　　As countless observers have noted, a sizable contingent of boomers
responded to the darkening of modern society by retreating into the same
consumerist cocoons that had given their parents comfort; Lawrence Kas-
dan named this shift with the title of his poignant movie about 1960s
youths selling out their ideals, *The Big Chill*. And if the generation that
defined the 1960s felt the big chill, then it only follows that the next generation experienced the after-effects of that chill. By the time the blights
of AIDS, the Iran-Contra scandal, and the collapse of family farms and
savings-and-loan institutions arrived in the mid–1980s— the same time at
which the first waves of Gen Xers reached adulthood — the chill had become
a killing frost.

Furthermore, America was fast becoming a place in which the gap between the haves and the have-nots seemed almost insurmountable. Director Oliver Stone, that uncompromising and sometimes infuriating voice of 1960s-style idealism, captured the bleak mood perfectly with a line in his 1987 stock-exchange drama, *Wall Street*: "Greed, for lack of a better word, is good." That the line was uttered by the film's villain hardly seemed to matter. The point was made, with painful clarity, that the country's priorities had reverted back to what they were before the counterculture tried to force change.

Although this sketch of the 1970s and 1980s is necessarily oversimplified, it offers a rough picture of the forces at work during the years when Generation X came of age. Even the youngest Gen Xers were born too late to participate in the historical social unrest that reached its twilight in the mid–1970s, so all Gen Xers grew up in the aftermath of a beautiful but unrealized dream, and this sad fact informs their sensibility. Some wear this hand-me-down ennui as anger, some as cynicism, some as apathy. But all who belong to Generation X feel the after-effects of the big chill.

On a more immediate level, Gen Xers felt the repercussions of the dissipation of the American family. From 1965 to 1985, the number of U.S. divorces exploded from just over 300,000 to nearly 1.2 million, so an estimated 40 percent of Gen Xers are children of divorce, compared to 11 percent of boomers.[1] The rupture of home life was exacerbated by countless other travails, as author Geoffrey T. Holtz noted in his book *Welcome to the Jungle: The Why Behind "Generation X."* When boomers who spent their adolescence and young adulthood defying the values of their parents became parents themselves, they embraced laissez-faire ideas about parenting and education, forcing nascent Gen Xers to at least take an unprecedented role in their upbringing, and at worst parent themselves. The changing dynamics of American family life led vast numbers of Gen Xers into poverty, owing to such factors as the small percentage of fathers who fulfilled child-support commitments following divorces.

So in addition to seeing the previous generation's dream of a better world give way to cynicism and materialism, Gen Xers were, to varying degrees, given less support by parents and educators than any previous generation of American children. Cut from the tethers that grounded their predecessors to ideas of societal and familial security, these youths became adults who, unsurprisingly, question the virtue of pursuing traditional goals—and seethe with the frustration and resentment of the disenfranchised. These violent emotions don't fuel every member of Generation X, of course, but the quantity of disaffected characters in Gen-X movies strongly suggests that the filmmakers born in America between 1961 and 1971 bear the scars of collective separation trauma.

Reflecting the clash of idealism and cynicism that filled the popular culture of their youth, the cinema of Generation X is mired in mixed messages, undefined anger, inarticulate declarations, and visceral impact. While certain Gen-X filmmakers adhere closely enough to Hollywood traditions that their movies make social statements within the context of accessible narratives, others have tried — as did the most adventurous filmmakers of the previous generation — to find a cinematic equivalent to the punch-in-the-gut intensity of a great rock and roll song.

Pumping Irony

The most rebellious Gen-X filmmakers, provocateurs such as Darren Aronofsky (*Requiem for a Dream*) and Neil LaBute (*In the Company of Men*), make movies that shock viewers with explicit language, startling imagery, and scorching satire. At the other extreme are mainstream entertainers including Michael Bay (*Pearl Harbor*) and M. Night Shyamalan (*Unbreakable*), both of whom make slick, violent thrill rides. There's even room in the mix for filmmakers such as Edward Burns (*The Brothers McMullen*), whose character-driven pictures are so old-fashioned that they could have been made in the 1950s.

The filmmakers whose work is most reflective of their generation's collective identity, however, work neither on the fringes of the industry nor squarely within its mainstream. Quentin Tarantino (*Pulp Fiction*), Kevin Smith (*Dogma*), David Fincher (*Fight Club*), and Paul Thomas Anderson (*Magnolia*) stand alongside Steven Soderbergh as the most important filmmakers of their generation because they rarely homogenize their pictures to appease audiences or assault viewers so aggressively that their work is marginalized. By employing such devices as fractured narratives, ironic humor, coarse language, bracing violence, and heated discourse about social issues, these directors make extreme cinematic statements while addressing topics that are crucial to their chronological peers.

Yet the significance of Gen-X filmmakers disseminating their generational identity through motion pictures is more than a historical footnote about people capturing their collective experience on celluloid. Soderbergh and his contemporaries stand to replace the movie brats of the 1970s (and the empty stylists of the 1980s) as the world's most prominent filmmakers during the early decades of the twenty-first century. For while the careers of such 1970s wunderkinds as Spielberg and Lucas are still thriving, they and their peers slipped into the safe cocoon of respectability many years ago. Only Martin Scorsese, the most consistently experimental of the movie brats, still has a semblance of the youthful zest that made his early pictures so fresh and exciting.

The ascension of Gen Xers to dominance of the film industry is not entirely as promising, however, as was the process by which the movie brats brought their counterculture sensibility to Hollywood.

In the late 1960s and early 1970s, youth-oriented films such as *Bonnie and Clyde*, *The Graduate*, and *Easy Rider* gave a moribund art form a slap in the face. The intense violence and bleak morality of Scorsese's early movies, notably *Mean Streets* and *Taxi Driver*, brought new vitality to cinematic portrayals of urban life; similarly, Francis Ford Coppola's revisionist *Godfather* movies added bloody authenticity to crime films and depicted gangsters as living, breathing human beings. Cutting-edge filmmakers such as Hopper, Bob Rafelson (*Five Easy Pieces*), and Mike Nichols (*Catch-22*) explored topics pertaining to the counterculture, while classicists such as Peter Bogdanovich (*The Last Picture Show*) melded youth-oriented

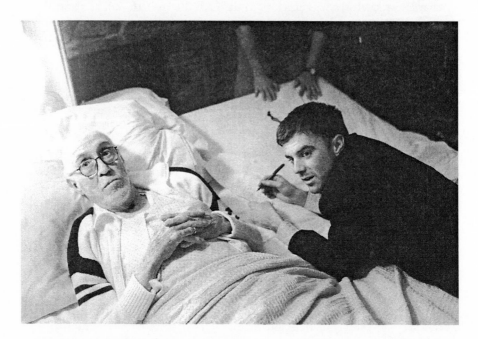

Bedside manner: Brash director Paul Thomas Anderson, who uses his films to explore the lives of lost souls, works with the late Jason Robards on the set of *Magnolia* (New Line Cinema).

themes with old-fashioned style. Collectively, the movie brats injected unprecedented realism, social consciousness, and invention into their work, thereby shaking American cinema free from the stifling constraints of the dying studio system.

Gen-X directors, however, seem more concerned with blending layers of fiction than with pursuing realism, and this tendency to employ ironic storytelling has everything to do with how Gen Xers have been bombarded with incessant information since their youth. The explosion of mass media in the 1980s, in addition to the emergence of around-the-clock news coverage, resulted in a new entity called "infotainment," which is alternately defined as news packaged as entertainment or entertainment packaged as news. Whatever the definition, the existence of infotainment reflects how the line separating reality and fiction blurred in the 1980s, and that blurred line crosses straight through the cinema of Generation X.

Characters in Tarantino's films often bond by discussing the ephemera of pop culture, as in the *Reservoir Dogs* scene of several crooks sitting around a diner table and discussing their varied interpretations of Madonna's song "Like a Virgin." In addition to forming a link between characters, such scenes gently reach through the "fourth wall" separating fiction from reality by forming a link between the characters and viewers from Tarantino's age group. Gen Xers who grew up listening to Madonna are intimately familiar with her work, so when it's debated onscreen, it's a conversation in which Gen-X audience members could easily participate. The insertion of pop-culture references into movie scenes was the logical next step from the way baby-boomer filmmakers used rock and roll to score films; it's a simple matter of speaking to viewers in their own idiom.

In actor-comedian Ben Stiller's first directorial effort, *Reality Bites*, he plays Michael, an ambitious professional who courts a woman named Lelaina (Winona Ryder). His competitor is Lelaina's ne'er-do-well friend Troy (Ethan Hawke), a young adult so aimless and unmotivated that Lelaina describes him as a master of "time suckage." In a crucial scene, Michael picks up Lelaina for a date while several of her friends, including Troy, watch a rerun of the 1970s program *Good Times* and challenge each other to remember sitcom arcana. When Michael tries to edge his way into the conversation by mentioning a *Good Times* episode costarring diminutive actor Gary Coleman, Troy rudely tells Michael that they've already been there, done that. At the end of the scene, Michael is embarrassed, Troy smugly triumphant. The content of the scene is traditional — two suitors clash in the presence of the woman for whose affections they are competing — but the idiom of the scene is pure Generation X. It is also, not coincidentally, purely superficial.

Unambitious, jaded layabouts like Troy recur throughout the cinema of Generation X. In the most pervasive stereotype, these "slackers" are the Gen-X equivalent of hippies: They withdraw from the rat race as a half-assed rebellion against dehumanizing cultural forces. Yet slackers seek no revolutionary means for overturning or even healing the culture that appalls them. Rebellious boomers hit the streets to demonstrate against misguided military actions, repressive politics, and other such ills, while slackers echo the previous generation's discontentment but have neither clearly defined antagonizing forces nor clearly defined reactions to such forces.

The nebulous ennui that informs the slacker stereotype is a powerful force in the cinema of Generation X. Tarantino, Smith, and other key filmmakers address this spiritual sadness directly through sociocultural dialogue exchanges and the portrayal of slacker characters, and indirectly by employing narrative structures that both reflect and deconstruct the conventions of mainstream cinema. These structures regard classic Hollywood through the same informed, skeptical gaze through which slackers regard American culture. The combination of pop-culture references, unconventional narrative structures, and the cynical, know-it-all posture that many Gen Xers wear as a status symbol produces a peculiar brand of reflective postmodernism, and this postmodernism is the modus operandi of many important Gen-X filmmakers.

The principal manifestation of Tarantino's postmodernism, for instance, is his affection for nonlinear storytelling. He deconstructs the timelines of story events so thoroughly that viewers often don't know how all the characters and events in a given movie relate to each other until well after the picture is over, by which point they've been able to reorder scenes in their minds. One possible explanation of why this kind of storytelling fascinates Gen-X directors is that because they've been exposed to junk narrative all their lives—via copycat movies, endlessly rerun sitcoms, and moronic music videos—conventional storytelling strikes them as mundane. They long for fresh ideas but habitually settle for clever spins on old ones.

Tarantino, Stiller, and many others deal with metafiction—fiction about fiction—while the more socially alert of their peers use postmodern approaches to dig beneath superficiality. Fincher's *Fight Club*, worlds removed from the sitcom-influenced cuteness of Stiller's debut feature, is an abrasive parable about young men waking themselves from society-induced slumber by using violence as a narcotic. The film is subversive on myriad levels: Gleaming actor Brad Pitt undercuts his heartthrob image by playing a slovenly anarchist; the principal characters express their hatred of consumer culture by blowing up buildings; and the picture depicts a twisted semi-reality in which neither characters within the movie nor viewers watching it can be absolutely sure what is supposed to be "real" and what is meant to be perceived as an artificial construct.

The picture's most audacious device is to suggest that Pitt's messianic character, Tyler Durden, may be a figment of another character's imagination. Because Tyler represents the psychological and sociological liberation of the character whom we're told may have imagined Tyler, the suggestion that he's not real implies that Gen Xers' boldest rebellions occur in their imaginations, not their lives. This provocative concept positions Tyler as a perfect symbol for a generation widely accused of political apathy: He represents the nihilistic social action that Gen Xers might take if they bothered to put down the remote control and get up off the couch.

Mixed Messages

Clever narrative structures, pop-culture references, and *Fight Club*-style edginess aren't the only tools that Gen-X directors have at their disposal. Texas-based filmmaker Richard Linklater, a crucial but comparatively obscure figure in the Gen-X firmament, scrupulously avoided such devices when he and Kim Krizan wrote *Before Sunrise*, a wonderfully thoughtful romance composed almost entirely of a single, far-reaching conversation. In the film, listless American Jesse (Ethan Hawke) meets a beautiful French student named Céline (Julie Delpy) on the last day of his trip through Europe. Jesse convinces Céline to explore Vienna with him, and during the course of a long day and evening, they chat, commiserate, debate, and, finally, become lovers.

By focusing on the way young people talk to each other — sometimes in grand, sweeping terms bloated by postadolescent arrogance, sometimes in fearful awe informed by the looming specter of adulthood — Linklater captured a vivid snapshot of the inspiring, terrifying transition made by young people on their way to becoming grownups. And even though Jesse is unmistakably a slacker with his fashionably trimmed goatee, shaggy hair, laundry-day wardrobe, and prematurely jaded attitude, he isn't limited by his generational identity. Other characters in slacker-themed movies — such as the one Hawke played in *Reality Bites* — are constructs used to represent Generation X as a whole. Jesse is a believable, complex character who happens to belong to Generation X.

The irony that one of the most mature Gen-X movies is about immaturity sends a mixed message that is typical of the murky sensibility shared by Generation X's most important cinematic representatives.

In the decade following Soderbergh's arrival on the scene, he and his peers made everything from vitriolic tracts to easygoing satires to old-fashioned character studies. But the most intriguing Gen-X movies are the hardest to categorize: What, for instance, is the best way to describe *Pulp Fiction* or *Fight Club*, two complex mixtures of action, comedy, sex, and violence? At the risk of being flip, the best way to define these pictures is to call them exercises in Gen-X style, because the speed and irony with which their makers blend pop culture, traditional narrative ideas, and postmodern storytelling is totally informed by the attitudes, experiences, and cultural savviness shared by *Pulp Fiction*'s Tarantino, *Fight Club*'s Fincher, and their myriad peers.

Although each Gen-X director has taken a different approach to content and style, the attributes that bind them are telling. Just as the tuned-in films of the late 1960s and early 1970s captured the identity of that era's counterculture, the Gen-X films of the 1990s and beyond reveal several intriguing things about their makers. Among the insights: Slackers do, in fact, perceive an antagonistic force in their lives, albeit an amorphous one; some Gen Xers carry the activism torch passed to them by the previous generation; and postmodern style, as practiced by Gen-X directors, is not style for style's sake, but rather a spirited, if not always prudent, attempt to seek new means of conveying thematic material.

3

Culture Vultures

Only slightly more than a decade has passed since *sex, lies, and video-tape* hit theaters, so it's necessary to regard the cinema of Generation X as a work in progress. Even though certain Gen-X filmmakers have earned grown-up accolades—including Soderbergh's 2001 Oscar for directing *Traffic*, following his historic twin nominations for *Traffic* and *Erin Brockovich*—the generation as a whole is far from reaching artistic maturity.

For that reason, this book is structured to reflect the different stages of Generation X's maturation. Beginning with the next chapter, this book will trace how Gen-X directors have documented their collective growth process: Chapter 4 deals with issues such as education and family; Chapter 5 examines topics related to work; and so on until the penultimate chapter, which deals in part with how Gen-X directors envision the future. Yet before any such issues can be explored, it's necessary to learn the language in which they are discussed.

As noted earlier, the idiom of Generation X is deeply informed by popular culture. While not every filmmaker born between 1961 and 1971 was raised in the same environment, pervasive social patterns during and after that period allow for some generalizations that will accurately characterize the upbringing of a large segment, if not a majority, of such filmmakers. The most important of these generalizations involves television. For the adolescents and preadolescents of the 1970s, television was a ubiquitous presence: part baby-sitter, part surrogate community, part entertainment. (The Internet appears to serve a similar role for Generation Y, which comprises youths born in the 1980s and 1990s.)

The role of television in American life changed dramatically during the period when Gen Xers were growing up. The Vietnam conflict, for instance, was called "the living-room war" because haunting combat stories were broadcast into American homes every day. And the explosion of cable vastly increased the number of channels that reached American homes. Previously, daytime and late-night television were ghettos for niche programming such as soap operas and rerun movies, respectively. But cable paved the way for competitive broadcasting around the clock. And while not every Gen-X filmmaker was raised with television as a constant companion, enough were — and enough have celebrated their relationship with television in their work — that it's informative to note the symbiotic relationship between 1970s youths and the boob tube.

As mentioned earlier, one important corollary of Gen Xers' bond with television is the emergence of infotainment. Movie fans have always enjoyed hearing about Hollywood's behind-the-scenes machinations, but the public's access to such information increased dramatically during the period of Gen Xers' youth and adolescence. In 1980, for instance, the nightly "news" program *Entertainment Tonight* emerged to satiate the public thirst for Hollywood gossip and trade secrets. The infotainment explosion is a crucial parallel to Gen Xers' television addiction, because in addition to being exposed to nonstop junk culture, Gen Xers were given countless opportunities to peer behind the curtain of said junk culture.

These opportunities helped produce unprecedented media-related savviness, which often manifests as cynicism (a been-there, done-that attitude toward entertainment) and/or fascination (an endless appetite for behind-the-scenes information). In fact, an ambivalent mixture of cynicism and fascination probably is the most prevalent attitude toward pop culture reflected in Gen-X cinema.

Hollywood was not the only subject area dissected in the mass media during the youth of Generation X, of course; the rise of entertainment-as-news dovetailed the rise of news-as-entertainment. Previously, news reports appeared on radio and television only in measured doses, or in rare wall-to-wall coverage of breaking stories. But with the emergence of Cable News Network (CNN), broadcast news became a nonstop enterprise. Suddenly, anyone interested in world events could tune into them at will and explore them in (comparative) depth, instead of waiting for a carefully doled-out soundbite on the evening news. CNN and the news-gathering organizations it influenced changed public discourse about world events, because the public went from receiving daily updates of important stories to receiving hourly updates of important — and not-so-important — stories. Just as the national conversation about entertainment was accelerated and deepened by the rise of entertainment-as-news, the national conversation about world events was changed by the rise of news-as-entertainment.

The relationship between Gen Xers and television grew even more symbiotic with the emergence of videocassette recorders, the importance of which to Gen-X filmmakers is monumental. Previous generations of would-be directors learned about movies by seeing them in theaters, catching them on television, or viewing them in film schools. Gen Xers grew up with the ability to study movies with the assistance of fast-forward, rewind, and pause buttons. Combined with their access to behind-the-scenes information, courtesy of outlets such as *Entertainment Tonight*, Gen Xers' VCR usage made them more knowledgeable about the elements of film than any previous generation. Christopher Nolan, director of the video-age mystery *Memento*, noted some after-effects of viewers' ability to take unprecedented control of the movie-watching experience.

> As soon as you can stop [a film] and control the timeline, then it becomes like a book on some level. People are more accepting of the idea of jumping around and putting the story together in a fresh way. The supreme example of that is the trailer: You take different scenes, chop them up, stick them together, and allow the audience to reassemble the linear narrative.[1]

The downside, of course, was that people other than would-be filmmakers became just as knowledgeable: Heightened audience awareness of how films are made led to heightened expectations on the part of general audiences. With everybody peering behind Hollywood's curtain, cinematic illusions had to become more and more elaborate.

A final noteworthy aspect of this generation's relationship with television involves a specific channel: Music Television, the music-video outlet launched in 1981.

During the many years in which its programming was dominated by music videos, MTV offered a huge exhibition venue for short films, similar to the venue offered by commercials but with greater opportunities for creative freedom. Just as commercials bred important directors in the previous generation — Brits Ridley Scott (*Blade Runner*) and Adrian Lyne (*Fatal Attraction*), among myriad others, cut their teeth filming TV spots — videos made for MTV comprise the apprenticeship of several important Gen-X directors. David Fincher helmed memorable, award-winning clips for artists including Madonna and Aerosmith prior to making feature films; Spike Jonze, the wizard behind *Being John Malkovich*, first made his mark with irreverent clips for the Beastie Boys and other artists.

However, the MTV aesthetic of quick cuts, flashy lighting, and sped-up narrative became a cliché so quickly that by the late 1980s, it was an insult to refer to a film's "MTV-style editing"— shorthand for style over substance. Nonetheless, Fincher, Jonze, and others have proven that directors can use MTV, commercials, and other nontheatrical venues as an extension of, or an alternative to, film school.

Yet the employment opportunities created by MTV's existence are of secondary importance to the channel's stylistic influence. The aforementioned MTV-style editing had a noticeable effect on audiences when it appeared in mainstream films of the 1980s, such as *Flashdance* and *Top Gun*. Filmmakers discovered that viewers were able to digest visual information more quickly than ever before. This paralleled a resurgence in the popularity of action films, so by the late 1980s, the ideal studio film was a fast-moving, violent thrill ride, preferably modeled on the hugely successful *Die Hard*.

All of these factors—Gen Xers' relationship with television; the emergence of VCRs, infotainment, CNN, and MTV; the speeding-up of cinematic storytelling—defined what Gen Xers brought to the table when they arrived in Hollywood. Baby-boom directors came to Tinseltown eager to update classical cinematic style. Gen Xers headed to Hollywood eager to replace classical cinematic style with something faster and fresher. That something, by and large, was cinematic postmodernism.

Postmodern Problems

Postmodernism itself, of course, is nothing new. Coined to define an architectural movement in the 1970s, and later appropriated as a catchall term for movements in other creative fields, postmodernism is loosely defined as the attempt to meld classicism with modernism; modernism, in turn, is the catchall term for expressionism, cubism, and other bracing art movements of the early twentieth century. Because cinematic postmodernism is such an abstract concept, however, it's difficult to pinpoint just when it began to manifest. Certainly the movies of David Lynch, particularly *Eraserhead* (1977) and *Blue Velvet* (1986), match the definition of postmodernism: Their stories are classical in structure, but their style is contemporary. Yet the fact that Lynch gained his greatest notoriety in 1986—just three years before Soderbergh entered the scene—is an indication of how closely the manifestation of cinematic postmodernism coincided with the arrival of Gen-X cinema.

The sticking point here, of course, is that postmodernism existed before it actually had a name. Since the expressionist movies of such 1920s German auteurs as F. W. Murnau (*Nosferatu*) are clearly modernist, aren't the avant-garde movies of 1960s French filmmakers including François Truffaut (*Breathless*) clearly postmodern? The answer is "yes," but that doesn't lessen the important connection between postmodernism and Gen-X cinema. The American filmmakers of the baby-boom generation appropriated some of the French New Wave's postmodern style — as seen, especially, in the most vital work of Scorsese and Coppola — but they also were deeply influenced by the Hollywood studio system. Scorsese's *Taxi Driver*, for instance, can rightly be described as having myriad postmodern elements, but its narrative structure is too classic for the film to be rightly described as pure postmodernism.

So if cinematic postmodernism in its purest form only entered the mainstream consciousness with the arrival of films such as Lynch's *Blue Velvet*— admittedly, an arguable assertion — then the crop of postmodern films that flourished in *Blue Velvet*'s wake could be described as the first mainstream American postmodernist films. These are fine, and perhaps even nitpicking, distinctions, but there's a reason for them. *Blue Velvet* was embraced by the public as a novelty. *sex, lies, and videotape* was embraced not as a novelty, but as a popular entertainment. It took Lynch, Scorsese, and others to prepare the public for serious cinematic post-modernism, so when Soderbergh, Tarantino and other Gen Xers began to employ postmodern techniques on a regular basis, audiences were recep-tive to such narrative experimentation. The important connection between Gen Xers and postmodernism, then, is that they took the stylistic move-ment out of the arthouse and into the multiplex.

That said, *sex, lies, and videotape* features only the most accessible kind of cinematic postmodernism: a fragmented narrative. The story begins in spurts, with active shots of handsome drifter Graham (James Spader) woven in with static images of housewife Ann (Andie MacDowell). Soderbergh, who edited the picture in addition to writing and directing it, weaves the lives of his four principal characters together so that audiences see connections of which the characters might not be aware. While at first glance his intercut-ting may seem nothing more than simple parallel action — the idea, developed by cinematic pioneer Edwin S. Porter (1869–1941), of shifting back and forth between related actions— Soderbergh's intercutting actually is more sublime.

He layers Ann's narration over shots of Graham driving in his car, so our curiosity about Graham is increased when we learn that Ann is anx-ious about his arrival. She's nervous because the current endeavors of Gra-ham, a college chum of her husband's, are shrouded in mystery. Instead of simply defining the relationship between disparate images, Soderbergh defines the relationship and also provides its subtext. That he additionally takes us inside each of the characters— by showing that Ann's narration is part of a therapy session, and by showing the simplicity of Graham's root-less lifestyle — accelerates the speed of his storytelling.

Such intricate juggling certainly had been done in previous films, but the significant aspect of Soderbergh's nonlinear approach is his presumption

Seeing is believing: The narrative trickery of Steven Soderbergh's *sex, lies, and videotape,* with Andie MacDowell as a woman who discovers her husband's adultery, exemplifies the use of postmodern concepts in Gen-X storytelling (Miramax Films).

that viewers can and will play along with his narrative game. He backs off a bit from his aggressive editing during certain extended dialogue scenes, but the concepts of layered narration and complex intercutting are crucial to the film's climax, during which Soderbergh also brings in the thorny issue of reality being witnessed through the remove of artifice.

The climax involves Ann's philandering husband, John (Peter Gallagher), viewing a videotape that Graham made of Ann. On it, she explains the void in her marriage, then prepares to consummate her flirtation with Graham. Soderbergh begins Ann's confessional by showing it as a grainy image on the video screen in front of John, then cuts to a clear film image, as if the scene is happening in the present. Then, to exit the confessional, Soderbergh cuts back to the grainy image on the video screen, allowing him to bring us back into the true present, so we can see John's reaction to the videotape. Combined with the narrative game he began in the first scene, the temporal shifts involved in the confession scene reveal that the idiom of the film is inherently, not superficially, postmodern.

sex, lies, and videotape did exceptionally well for an unheralded art film, but it never achieved blockbuster status, and scored only a token Academy Award nomination, for Best Original Screenplay. Yet just eleven years later, Soderbergh released a film as layered as *sex, lies, and videotape*: *Traffic*, his epic about America's war on drugs. The latter picture enjoyed tremendous box-office success and received a slew of Oscar nominations, including one for Best Picture. Soderbergh certainly evolved in the intervening period (so much so that his other 2000 film, *Erin Brockovich*, was as conventional as *Traffic* was unconventional), yet his evolution is an insufficient explanation for why *Traffic* enjoyed greater public acceptance than *sex, lies*. Perhaps the real reason behind the shift is that American audiences matured in step with Soderbergh: Viewers became acclimated to techniques that seemed bold or even off-putting in 1989, largely because of how those techniques were employed in successful films directed by Gen Xers.

Tom Tykwer, the young German director whose 1999 arthouse hit *Run Lola Run* exuded a vivacious energy that put some of his American contemporaries to shame, commented on the maturation of audience sensibilities.

> Everybody knows that we're hitting the limits of traditional filmmaking because it's becoming so perfectionistic. You are seeing films that are so perfect you don't even connect to them anymore. A film like [*Being John*] *Malkovich* is an invitation to do something different. Even *The Matrix*, because it serves all of our traditional desires in the cinema, but it plays with your mind in a very strange way. Ten years ago, I don't think people would have even been ready for it.[2]

The Man from Knoxville

Probably the most crucial juncture during the process of familiarizing American audiences with postmodernism was the release of Tarantino's *Pulp Fiction* in 1994. Just five years after Soderbergh's challenging narrative techniques paved the way, Tarantino arrived with a picture even more disjointed than Soderbergh's — yet *Pulp Fiction* became the blockbuster that *sex, lies, and videotape* did not, earning over $100 million at the box office and scoring an Oscar nod for Best Picture.

The unlikely success of *Pulp Fiction* made Tarantino the central figure of Gen-X cinema for much of the 1990s. While Soderbergh's prominence became clear once he had achieved numerous successes, Tarantino's became evident immediately, because a slew of copycat movies followed in *Pulp Fiction*'s wake — ironic, too-cool-for-school crime films such as *Things to Do in Denver When You're Dead* and *Eight Heads in a Duffel Bag*. With his wiseass erudition, funny pop-culture references, playful narrative splintering, and exploitation-movie sensationalism, Tarantino defined an idiom that was revisited by many of his peers, to say nothing of many shallow imitators.

Tarantino's personal history adds to his significance as a Gen-X exemplar, for he was raised by his mother following his parents' divorce. This connects him to the shifting family dynamics that had such an unsettling effect on Tarantino's generation. Filmmakers from previous generations had come from broken homes, but the issues of abandonment and gender identity sparked by familial schisms such as that which affected Tarantino's household recur in myriad Gen-X films, notably *Fight Club*.

Tarantino and his mother relocated from his native Knoxville, Tennessee, to Los Angeles when he was a child, and after the burgeoning filmmaker dropped out of high school, he got a job working at a video store. The importance of videocassettes to Gen-X filmmakers already has been noted, and the way that Tarantino reportedly immersed himself in movies while working at the store amplifies this point. During this ad hoc apprenticeship, Tarantino made connections with customers who were involved in the film business, leading to his discovery by enterprising producers. His plucked-from-nowhere ascension became Generation X's equivalent to the story about starlet Lana Turner getting discovered in a Hollywood drug store: After Tarantino hit, it became a cliché to say that tomorrow's great filmmakers aren't studying at film schools, but helping customers at video stores.

Tarantino's intimate familiarity with a variety of film styles — and, to a degree, the undisciplined manner in which he explored favorite genres, as opposed to studying a well-rounded curriculum, as he might have in film school — put him in a unique position to blaze a postmodern trail. He knew film inside and out, so it was no big deal for him to turn film inside-out.

He first did so with his remarkable debut film, 1992's *Reservoir Dogs*. Depicting the violent and fractious events occurring before and after a heist, the picture is as good an example of postmodern storytelling as Soderbergh's *sex, lies*. In both pictures, stories are told elliptically: Moments are plucked out of time and place, then reordered not to represent their chronological occurrence, but to accentuate connections that would not be clear were the moments presented chronologically.

In some bold cases, Tarantino even blends the present and the past in a single frame. The picture contains a bravura scene during which a robber code-named Mr. Orange (Tim Roth) describes encountering cops and a police dog in a bathroom while carrying drugs on his person. As the camera makes a 360-degree circle around Orange, who is telling the tale, the background shifts from the present to the past, so suddenly we're in the bathroom with Orange and the cops. Orange describes how he wriggled free of the situation, then the scene shifts back to the "present." Tarantino creates this illusion with blocking and lighting, not special effects, so the scene is postmodern in realization as well as intent: He uses classic techniques in the service of a fresh storytelling idea.

Were this the only temporal game that Tarantino played in *Reservoir Dogs*, it might be insignificant, because myriad stage and film dramatists used similar techniques previously. But because the bathroom scene is part of a fabric of temporal gamesmanship — a fabric so cleverly woven that the film's central event, the heist, is never shown — the bathroom scene identifies the mischief inherent in Tarantino's storytelling.

Honor among thieves: In Quentin Tarantino's *Reservoir Dogs*, with Harvey Keitel (standing) and Steve Buscemi, an offbeat story structure is used to dramatize the tale of a heist gone wrong (Miramax Films).

Pulp Fiction is even more brazen than Tarantino's debut film. The picture doesn't contain a traditional narrative, per se, but rather three interconnected narratives. An ambitious blend of gutter-level violence, witty romance, salacious humor, aching pathos, and macho posturing, the film thrives on the same confidence that powered *sex, lies, and videotape.* Tarantino doesn't spoon-feed his offbeat tale to viewers, but instead presumes that viewers have been exposed to enough of the same narrative as him that they can digest information in the disjointed way that he delivers it. It helps, of course, that he's an exquisite writer capable of making long stretches of dialogue as entertaining as fast-moving screen action, and it helps that he's a fine director with an eye for pleasing compositions and great taste in actors. Yet no matter how easily Tarantino's film goes down, it's still a bracing dose of experimentalism.

In a typically confrontational directorial choice, Tarantino puts a distracting postmodern touch into an important taxicab scene involving past-his-prime boxer Butch (Bruce Willis). Echoing the way he didn't show the heist in *Reservoir Dogs,* Tarantino shows us a prelude to Butch's big match, in which the boxer is told to throw the fight, but doesn't show the match. Instead, Tarantino cuts straight to the taxicab, in which Butch is driven by Esmeralda (Angela Jones). During their conversation, we learn that Butch not only reneged on his promise to throw the fight, but killed his opponent.

While viewers receive this startling information, however, some notice that the background of the scene seems odd. Although the scene is filmed in color, the rear projection illustrating the street behind the taxi is filmed in black-and-white. Is Tarantino winkingly reminding viewers that the story they're hearing is at least as old as the black-and-white boxing pictures of the 1930s? Or is he making a blunt, expressionistic statement about Butch's world not being "black and white" in moral terms? In a sense, this ambiguous imagery is one of Tarantino's most postmodern touches, for while he ties up most of his narrative threads in classical style, he allows viewers to interpret details such as the black-and-white background as they will. His style puts modernism and classicism side-by-side, pulling liberally from each school.

Violence is as important to Tarantino's movies as postmodernism, and there's a peculiar tension in the audience during a Tarantino movie. As an onscreen character slowly pulls out a knife — or a sword, or a syringe — viewers don't want to see the bloodshed that's coming, but they don't want to look away from the screen. Even when he's grossing viewers out, Tarantino provides surprising, magnetic drama that feels like nothing ever seen before.

It's only after one of his movies is over that it becomes clear how familiar the content really is, because Tarantino recycles plots and situations from countless B-movies and crime novels. He's not merely derivative, however, for he filters this second-hand narrative material through a distinct worldview. Lance (Eric Stoltz), the drug dealer in *Pulp Fiction*, is yet another onscreen dope-peddler, but Tarantino portrays him as an amiable slacker watching cartoons in his bathrobe, thereby humanizing an over-familiar archetype and adding gravity and credibility to Lance's scenes.

Another example of Tarantino grounding an audacious scene with real-life details involves Jules, the Bible-quoting hit man played by Samuel L. Jackson in *Pulp Fiction*. After surviving a near-death experience, Jules announces that he's having "what alcoholics refer to as 'a moment of clarity'," then vaults into a remarkable speech analyzing the pros and cons of his violent existence. In Tarantino's perspective, real life and reel life are so entwined that it's impossible to tell where one ends and the other begins, which is why he often is called the director who most epitomizes his generation.

Once they achieved prominence, Tarantino and Soderbergh drew from the postmodern well again and again. Tarantino's charming crime film *Jackie Brown* employed the same kind of temporal patchwork he used in his first two features, and Soderbergh played games with time and place in *The Underneath*, *Out of Sight*, *The Limey*, and *Traffic*. Yet these two are hardly the only Gen-X directors who use narrative trickery to amplify narrative content. David Fincher's *Fight Club* features not only a disjointed timeline, but also scenes that subversively blend reality, fantasy, and delusion; and Doug Liman's *Go* is the most entertaining of countless Tarantino homages.

Liman's breakthrough film, *Swingers*, contains overt references to Tarantino and his influence. In one scene, a *Reservoir Dogs* poster is visible; in another, dialogue about how Tarantino's style is ripped off from Martin Scorsese's is followed by a coy rip-off of a famous slow-motion shot from *Reservoir Dogs*, accompanied by the 1970s pop hit "Pick Up the Pieces"—a musical counterpoint that underlines how self-conscious an act pop-culture recycling has become. *Swingers*, while highly enjoyable and occasionally affecting, straddles the line separating pop-culture send-ups from pop-culture artifacts, because even while the film's young men on the prowl for sexual partners steep themselves in borrowed style — Rat Pack-style suits and decades-old swing music — they issue freshly minted catch phrases like the oft-quoted "You're money, baby." What's more, it's possible to see echoes of *Swingers'* pop-culture recycling in other Gen-X

Poker faces: Nineties attitude and sixties style intersect in Doug Liman's *Swingers*, which features (from left) Vince Vaughn, Jon Favreau, and Patrick Van Horn as buddies on the prowl for "beautiful babies" (Miramax Films).

movies. When one *Swingers* character compliments another's suaveness by saying "That was like the Jedi mind shit!," it recalls similar *Star Wars* references in Kevin Smith's *Mallrats*. And when a *Swingers* scene of a man charming a woman is underscored by the 1970s song "Magic Man," it resembles the use of the same song, for an almost identical effect, in Sofia Coppola's *The Virgin Suicides*.

The manner in which the hip postmodernism of Gen-X directors punctures sanctimonious ideas about society and storytelling contributes to the widely held sentiment that members of this generation hold nothing sacred, but author Geoffrey T. Holtz made a good point about the Gen-X predilection for black comedy:

> Satire and self-aware irony have replaced slapstick. Rather than using humor to escape the inanity and desperation that runs through so many aspects of late-twentieth-century America, [Gen Xers] often use it to confront these problems. Homelessness, suicide, murder, unemployment, even AIDS — all serious issues, but fodder for humor among a generation so well versed in societal problems large and small.[3]

Spike Jonze's *Being John Malkovich* is perhaps the most breathlessly postmodern Gen-X film yet. The outrageous story, about a puppeteer who finds a portal leading to the inside of real-life actor John Malkovich's brain, has as much fantastic invention as *The Wizard of Oz*, yet it is designed to deliver not a moral homily, but a scathing commentary on contemporary America's obsession with celebrity.

The Fame Game

Gen Xers' fascination with celebrity culture is an outgrowth of their immersion in pop culture. Their exposure to the infotainment explosion was explored earlier, but certain aspects of that explosion are worth highlighting. During the 1990s, when vast numbers of Gen-X directors began working steadily, the focus of American celebrity culture shifted from such traditional entertainment figures as musicians and actors to everyday people enjoying what Andy Warhol termed their "fifteen minutes" of notoriety. Confessional television and literature, as exemplified by talk shows such as *The Jerry Springer Show* and an endless parade of books about dysfunctional families, gave average Americans a chance to enjoy the spotlight of celebrity in exchange for sharing their tragedies, peccadilloes, and personal soap operas.

Some of these insta-celebrities were innocuous figures trying to spread socially significant messages, such as young men and women explaining how difficult it is to reveal one's homosexuality. Yet some insta-celebrities were marginal figures exploited for sensational appeal. In a notorious incident that underlined the lurid appeal of confessional talk shows, a group of white supremacists appearing on Geraldo Rivera's program got involved in a violent brawl with audience members. Rivera himself was wounded in the fray, and he played up the drama of his injury as if he had been on the front line of a war. Viewers ate up such brawls, which occurred on virtually every episode of Jerry Springer's program, and Americans' morbid fascination with the dark aspects of human behavior reached an apex with the so-called "trial of the century."

In 1994, former football star O. J. Simpson was accused of murdering his wife and a male friend of hers. Prime-time viewers were treated to an aerial shot of Simpson's Ford Bronco crawling down a California highway, with police in slow pursuit, and the Bronco chase was played for sensational spectacle, because newscasters prepared viewers for several possible outcomes: Simpson might kill himself, they said, or he might be struck by police gunfire. The Simpson drama continued when his case went to trial, and the televised announcement of his not guilty verdict scored ratings that rivaled prime-time programming.

Other trials, such as that of the murderous Menendez brothers, received similar front-page treatment. In the 1990s, notoriety and fame became interchangeable concepts, and this social shift was reflected in films made by Gen Xers.

Being John Malkovich is the wittiest such reflection. Through the fanciful premise of the portal into Malkovich's head, the filmmakers allow their characters to take celebrity worship to its logical extreme: The characters become celebrities not because of accomplishment, but because they invade an established celebrity's physical being. Given that Hollywood-related reportage has long lent the private lives of famous people at least as much import as their actual work, the conceit at the heart of *Being John Malkovich* seems a rational response to the public's appetite for gossip. If reading about stars' sex lives is exciting, the movie ponders, wouldn't it be doubly exciting to participate in such a sex life? The characters in *Being John Malkovich* are psychic stalkers who would rather have sex *as* Malkovich than have sex *with* Malkovich, because Malkovich — or any other celebrity — is interesting for his social stature, not for his identity as an individual.

Director Spike Jonze, writer Charlie Kaufman, and their cohorts take this whimsical vision of vicarious experience to a comical extreme by

Almost famous: The whimsical fantasy *Being John Malkovich* satirizes America's obsession with celebrity by penetrating the mind of actor John Malkovich, seen receiving instruction from director Spike Jonze before filming a unique point-of-view shot (USA Films/Gramercy Pictures).

having characters sell rides through Malkovich's brain like rides on a roller coaster. Then the filmmakers put a jovially postmodern twist on the material by having the "real" Malkovich enter the portal, thereby penetrating his own mind as a stranger. Once he's inside himself, Malkovich experiences a nightmare of celebrity narcissism — from his self-as-self perspective, every person he sees has his own face, and the only word they say is his name. Predictably, the visit to the land of unrestrained self-love is maddening.

The film backs off a bit from its celebrity commentary by revealing that the portal is part of a sci-fi scheme cooked up by folks seeking eternal life. But even relegated to the backseat during the story's conclusion, the film's entertainment-industry satire lingers after the movie's conclusion with a bitter, true resonance. As screenwriter Charlie Kaufman noted:

A lot of it comes from the idea of not wanting to be yourself and being envious of other people. There is for sure the idea of looking out in the world and feeling you don't deserve to be there. How do you come to feel that you have as much right as anyone else to be on this planet, when you have a barrage of information telling you that you don't have a right to be here, or that you have to change yourself to be allowed to be here? I took each character and on an instinctive level explored how they would react to that anxiety.[4]

Other films imagined by Gen Xers deal with the very 1990s idea of achieving celebrity for something other than talent. *Natural Born Killers*, which controversy-magnet Oliver Stone adapted from a screenplay by Tarantino, shows a pair of serial killers who become popular celebrities; while basically a modernization of ideas seen in 1967's *Bonnie and Clyde*, 1973's *Badlands*, and other films, *Natural Born Killers* features a contemporary element in the figure of a sensationalistic TV broadcaster who exploits the killers' lives for his own gain. And *The Truman Show*, a poignant drama written by Gen Xer Andrew Niccol, depicts an innocent who doesn't realize that his entire life is a fabrication broadcast into millions of homes as a nonstop reality-TV program. In a quintessential bit of Gen-X irony, Truman Burbank (Jim Carrey), is the star of his own top-rated show, but he's the only person who isn't in on the joke.

Paul Thomas Anderson's sprawling *Boogie Nights* tracks the rise and fall of Dirk Diggler (Mark Wahlberg), an otherwise average young man who achieves fame in the porn-movie industry because of his enormous penis. The film's sad commentary on exploitation is best summed up by its perfect final image: Dirk stands before a mirror, with his face hidden by the camera angle, then unzips his pants and reveals, for the first time, his mammoth member. "I am a star. I'm a big bright shining star," he says—ostensibly to himself, but really to his phallus. The idea that audiences have celebrated not whole people but just facets of them says volumes about how fame is achieved America today. Just as patrons line up to be Malkovich, and just as violence-hungry viewers make two natural born killers into media figures, porn fans deify Dirk not for his charm or personality, but for his abnormal appendage. The freak show must go on.

Another layer of Gen Xers' attitude toward celebrity is seen in Ben Stiller's underrated satire, *The Cable Guy*, and Neil LaBute's overrated fable, *Nurse Betty*. In Stiller's film, the titular cable-television installer (Jim Carrey) is such a TV addict that his entire personality is a composite of fictional personalities from sitcoms and other programs; in LaBute's movie, a waitress (Renée Zellweger) detaches from reality after witnessing her husband's murder, then ventures from Kansas to California so she can hook up with the fictional soap-opera doctor she adores. Both movies make obvious but poignant statements about the dangers of replacing reality with fiction.

It Pays to Recycle

There's a world of difference between the characters in *Being John Malkovich*, who risk everything to escape reality, and those in *Reality Bites*, who merely comment that, well, reality bites. The scene from Ben Stiller's film in which two characters duel over sitcom trivia said something about the history the characters share. It also reflected a commonplace screenwriting tack, which is to mask the true intentions of a scene by having characters talk around said intentions. So even though the dialogue is about which episode of *Good Times* featured Gary Coleman, viewers understand that the real meat of the scene is two men sparring over a woman.

Helen Childress's script for *Reality Bites* features numerous such pop-culture references, such as when Michael (Ben Stiller) woos Lelaina (Winona Ryder) while they listen to *Frampton Comes Alive*, a rock album that was popular when the characters were children. These references—as well as those in Tarantino's films, such as the Madonna-related conversation in *Reservoir Dogs*—are effective because they ground the cinematic characters in a reality that exists beyond the screen. But sometimes the pop-culture references obscure the weight of a scene, and drag movies into the morass of boob-tube superficiality that colors the shallowest conversations among real-life Gen Xers. Consider this scene from *Reality Bites*, in which Lelaina tries to comfort her friend Vickie (Janeane Garofalo), who believes she might have contracted AIDS.

> VICKIE: You don't understand — every day, all day, it's all that I think about. Every time I sneeze, it's like I'm four sneezes away from the hospice. And it's like it's not even happening to me. It's like I'm watching it on some crappy show like *Melrose Place* or some shit, right? And I'm like the new character: I'm the HIV/AIDS character and I live in the building and I teach everybody that it's okay to be near me, it's okay to talk to me, and then I die. And there's everybody at my funeral, wearing halter tops or chokers or some shit like that.
>
> LELAINA: ...You're freaking out. And you know what? You're gonna have to deal with the results whatever they are.... It's gonna be okay. [Pause.] *Melrose Place* is a really good show.

Tarantino uses pop-culture references so masterfully that they are virtually his trademark. Viewers watching *Pulp Fiction* related to the way that hit man Vincent Vega (John Travolta) described his experience of eating a Quarter Pounder sandwich in France, where it is called a "Royale with Cheese"; the McDonald's product is such a ubiquitous item in American life that when viewers learn Vincent is a Quarter Pounder eater, they accept him as one of their real-life number.

Even films that Tarantino wrote but did not direct are filled with effective pop-culture references. In the crime story *True Romance*, a shy twentysomething courts a young woman by taking her to a comic-book store and offering to show her a vintage copy of *Spider-Man*'s first issue; in the submarine thriller *Crimson Tide*, to which Tarantino made uncredited screenplay contributions, two characters connect by discussing a comic titled *The Silver Surfer*. The specifics of these references are lost on viewers unfamiliar with comic books, but the thrust of the references—the scenes beneath the scenes—resonate with the credibility created by Tarantino's allusions to real life.

Again, the danger with excessive pop-culture referencing is that the real content of a scene can get buried beneath the ephemera. Tarantino generally is disciplined enough to avoid this trap, but he fell right into it during a notorious cameo appearance in the 1994 romantic comedy *Sleep With Me*. Re-creating a bit with which he reportedly entertains friends, Tarantino identifies why he believes the ultra-macho action movie *Top Gun* is filled with veiled homoerotica. His proof is little more than dialogue such as "Watch my tail, Maverick!" (which sounds provocative when taken out of context), but his enthusiasm and conviction are persuasive. The trouble is that Tarantino's scene stops the movie dead, setting narrative thrust aside for the cheap thrill of a hipster's entertaining self-indulgence.

It is possible, however, to be self-indulgent and still propel narrative. Kevin Smith — the verbose, crude, and occasionally brilliant writer-director of *Clerks*— has declared on many occasions that the *Star Wars* films were a crucial influence on his creative life. He reveals the depth of his affection for George Lucas's space opera in a *Clerks* scene featuring convenience-store cashier Dante (Brian O'Halloran) and video-store clerk Randal (Jeff Anderson).

Killing time between customers, the two debate the relative virtues of *The Empire Strikes Back* and *Return of the Jedi*, the second and third *Star Wars* flicks. At one point, Randal fires off a rant about *Jedi*, explaining that he dislikes how the film's heroes destroyed their enemies' incomplete space station oblivious to the possibility that "contractors" might be aboard the station. While the moment at first sounds like unrestrained geekiness, the sort of talk one might overhear at a *Star Wars* convention, the conversation actually reveals something about Randal. Despite the cynicism he displays throughout the movie, he has a conscience as well as social consciousness; the fact that these qualities primarily manifest when describing lightweight entertainment tells us, additionally, that Randal lacks the ambition to do much with his admirable qualities. This very funny scene allows Smith to vent his aggression about *Jedi* through Randal, but also to make insightful observations about the sort of person whom Randal represents.

Just as Tarantino did, however, Smith eventually fell off the high wire of pop-culture referencing. His follow-up to *Clerks*, the amateurish *Mallrats*, drowns in cheeky allusions to comic books and *Star Wars*. While the romantic story lines that ostensibly drive the movie are underdeveloped to the point of anemia, Smith devotes endless screen time to vignettes in which the character Silent Bob (played by Smith himself) attempts to master the "Jedi mind trick" that figures prominently in *Star Wars* mythology. The closest that Smith comes in *Mallrats* to balancing narrative concerns with pop-culture self-indulgence is giving a voice-of-reason cameo to comic-book titan Stan Lee. Lee's presence and some of his lines are inside jokes, but his role at least serves a significant dramatic purpose.

While using cameos such as Lee's to wink at audiences is nothing new — the technique dates back at least to Alfred Hitchcock's appearances in his own films— Gen-X directors often cast major roles ironically. Tarantino's casting of John Travolta in *Pulp Fiction* is the most successful example. The actor-dancer was in a career slump, having wasted the opportunities won by past successes, but Tarantino felt Travolta had lost none of the charm, swagger, and charisma he brought to such Me Decade hits as *Saturday Night Fever*. The director has said he wrote the Vincent Vega role as a tribute to the actor's past accomplishments, and Tarantino included actions, such as dancing, that echoed Travolta's previous screen appearances. So even though Vincent was a new screen commodity, he felt like an old one. The gimmick worked beautifully, adding a pop-culture echo to Travolta's performance — and, incidentally, spurring the most lucrative period of Travolta's career.

Tarantino tried the same trick by casting two other 1970s figures— blaxploitation star Pam Grier and B-movie regular Robert Forster — in *Jackie Brown*, but this time the gimmick worked half as well. Grier and Forster brought a wealth of experience to the movie, and gave gorgeously fresh performances, but because they never had been as familiar as Travolta, they didn't bring the same entertaining baggage. Viewers who knew the performers' histories got the joke; viewers who didn't merely discovered Grier and Forster as if they were new actors.

Making sure audiences are in on pop-culture jokes is a delicate art at which only a few filmmakers excel. Kevin Williamson showed his mastery in the script for *Scream*, a 1996 horror satire directed by slasher-flick veteran Wes Craven. Williamson brought a young, snide sensibility to the script, which simultaneously sent up and adhered to conventions of the then-tired serial-killer genre. Characters in *Scream* talked about having seen so many horror movies—*Halloween, Friday the 13th, A Nightmare on Elm Street*, and so on—that the narrative devices used in those films were clichés. Yet the characters tolerated the clichés as they might the bad table manners of a favorite uncle. So when a real killer starts stalking the characters, à la the murderers in slasher movies, the movie-savvy characters ironically telegraph their own demises.

Scream and its inferior sequels probably represent the apex of pop-culture referencing, because they are nothing *but* pop-culture referencing. The first film's nods to the audience include a cameo by 1970s TV star Henry Winkler as a high school principal, and, for those paying close attention, the behind-the-camera presence of Craven, director of the aforementioned *Nightmare on Elm Street*. Yet the speed with which the *Scream* series ran out of steam revealed the dryness of the well from which pop-culture references are drawn.

An interesting offshoot of *Scream*'s success was that it sparked a new cycle of slasher movies, including the Williamson-scripted *I Know What You Did Last Summer*. These movies offered exactly the kind of formulaic, insipid escapism that *Scream* satirized. So if the smothering irony of *Scream* was a kind of postmodernism, then the irony-free horror movies it inspired were a kind of post-postmodernism. The mere citation of such an unwieldy term reveals why the cycle of pop-culture referencing and re-referencing grew so dizzying during the 1990s.

The success of *Scream* redoubled Hollywood studios' efforts to court the youth market, and also revealed that enough new moviegoers had entered the marketplace that even very recent trends could be recycled. Therefore, a new wave of teen comedies appeared in tandem with the revived slasher genre. Inspired by the lascivious coming-of-age comedies (*Fast Times at Ridgemont High, Porky's*) and teen-empowerment dramedies (*Sixteen Candles, The Breakfast Club*) that flourished in the early 1980s, the new teen comedies included such Gen-X directed pictures as *Can't Hardly Wait* and *American Pie*. While these pictures possess a certain unpretentious charm, their fixation on breasts and bodily fluids mostly reflects the immaturity of their makers—and offers proof that the desire for friendship and fornication is universal to the adolescents of every generation.

The '70s Connection

The irreverent manner in which pop culture is used as a kind of short-hand in Gen-X flicks, however, isn't the most interesting manifestation of this generation's infatuation with mass media. By casting actors who achieved iconic status in the 1970s, revisiting themes that suffused the cinema of that era, and aping stylistic touches perfected by the movie brats, Gen-X directors built a crucial connection to the previous cinematic generation.

This connection can be seen most clearly in Gen-X films about the 1970s. Sofia Coppola's dreamlike tale about a group of sisters doomed to die at their own hands, *The Virgin Suicides*, is set in an affluent Michigan suburb circa the mid–1970s, so the film's costumes feature polyester pants and hippie-ish dresses. The clothing is complemented by subtler visual signifiers: Coppola's film is shot in a soft camera style that approximates the feel of natural light, recalling the self-consciously unvarnished photography of the movie brats' movies. Amplifying these connections is the fact that the *Virgin Suicides* director is the daughter of Francis Ford Coppola, whose *Godfather* pictures featured scenes so underlit that actors' eyes were hidden in shadow.

Other Gen-X pictures set in the 1970s include *Dazed and Confused*, Richard Linklater's shaggy comedy about drug-addled high schoolers; *Waking the Dead*, Keith Gordon's heartfelt exploration of the relationship between activism and politics; and *54*, Mark Christopher's inept attempt to re-create the heyday of New York City's most infamous discotheque/pleasure palace, Studio 54. The connection Gen-X directors feel to the 1970s is about more than respect for previous filmmakers, of course: For the segment of Generation X under discussion in this book, the 1970s were a time of adolescence and childhood. Their nostalgia for the period, therefore, is both personal and professional.

A handful of Gen-X films echo 1970s style without actually being set in the period. Steven Soderbergh's *Erin Brockovich*, a rabble-rousing drama about a law-firm secretary trying to expose corporate-sanctioned pollution, has the same scrappy, procedural feel as *Norma Rae* and *The China Syndrome*, two earlier films about crusading women. *8mm*, a gruesome story about snuff films that was written by Gen Xer Andrew Kevin Walker, is a sister film to *Hardcore*, the porn-industry drama written and directed by 1970s stalwart Paul Schrader. Tarantino's *Reservoir Dogs*, *Pulp Fiction*, and *Jackie Brown* all feature music and actors from the 1970s, as well as stylistic touches recalling crime films of the period.

Some Gen-X films have a 1970s feel that can't be traced to a particular influence. *The Yards*, James Gray's unoriginal but engrossing drama about corruption among contractors serving New York City's subway system, has photography as dark and moody as *The Godfather*'s, features a story line as intimate and oppressive as any that Martin Scorsese ever directed, and includes performances by three 1970s giants: Faye Dunaway, James Caan, and Ellen Burstyn. Burstyn also appears in Darren Aronofsky's viscerally overwhelming *Requiem for a Dream*, a painful parable about drug use. Aronofsky, incidentally, is such a child of the 1970s that when he was hired in 2000 to reinvigorate the moribund *Batman* franchise, he told interviewers that he wanted to set his Bat-flick in the 1970s, and give it the gritty, documentary-style feel of William Friedkin's 1971 Oscar-winner, *The French Connection*.

Ultimately, finding connections to *The French Connection* and other films is just a parlor game unless a deeper reason than nostalgia can be found for links between Gen Xers' work and the culture of their youth. That deeper reason has to do with what the arrival of baby boomers meant in Hollywood. As noted earlier, the studio system was dying when counterculture hits such as *Easy Rider* revealed the earning potential of catering to the youth market. Writ large, the studios gave the keys to their kids, and for a handful of glorious years, the kids took their beloved medium for a wild ride.

By the end of the 1970s, the ride was mostly over, because the success of mass-appeal hits such as *Jaws* and *Star Wars* gave the studios a new formula to copy. So when Gen Xers began to enter the film industry en masse in the late 1980s and early 1990s, mainstream American cinema had become almost as stagnant as it was when the boomers arrived.

It took them a few years to do it, but by 1999, Gen Xers shook up the industry as greatly as their predecessors had. That year, the irreverent domestic drama *American Beauty*, the startling no-budget horror movie *The Blair Witch Project*, the playful freakout *Being John Malkovich*, the ambitious multi-character story *Magnolia*, and the masterfully constructed ghost story *The Sixth Sense*—all directed by Gen Xers—proved that there was room in cineplexes for bold, brash ideas as well as corporate product.

Therefore, the deeper connection between the 1970s and Gen-X directors is that the brash auteurs of the Me Decade blazed the trail that Gen Xers followed. Just as the activists of the earlier generation proved that it was possible to force sweeping social change, the filmmakers of that generation proved that it was possible to force sweeping artistic change.

Biting the Hand That Feeds

A final level to this long discussion of Gen Xers' relationship with pop culture has to do with their most insular storytelling habit: making movies about movies. Because of the reasons cited earlier (television, info-tainment, and so on), Generation X grew up with a greater awareness about how entertainment is made than any previous generation. This per-haps explains their interest in subject matter that has marginal appeal to those outside Hollywood.

Paul Thomas Anderson veiled his movie about movies, *Boogie Nights*, by telling a story not about mainstream filmmaking, but about the porn industry. His picture addresses issues such as the inherent artifice of motion pictures, the dichotomy between screen personas and the actors who create them, and the intoxicating appeal of fame. Yet because he deals with a marginal subdivision of the film industry, his picture doesn't have the narcissistic feel of a movie that is only about Hollywood. Watching *Boogie Nights*, viewers learn about cinema while taking an anthropological journey into a subculture.

Phil Joanou, a former Spielberg protégé whose films are flashy to a fault, took a more direct approach in his movie about movies, *Entropy*. The picture is unwatchable for several reasons, but it's fascinating to see how a filmmaker who once was handed a career on a silver platter chose to fictionalize his professional life.

After making a slick thesis film at the University of Southern Califor-nia, Joanou was recruited by Steven Spielberg to direct an episode of the short-lived anthology series *Amazing Stories*. Joanou graduated to features with *Three O'Clock High*, a stylish but empty blend of *High Noon* and high school. He then directed *State of Grace*, a drama about the Irish mob in New York City. Featuring powerhouse actors Sean Penn and Gary Oldman, plus a violent script in the style of *The Godfather*, the film was rife with possi-bilities for memorable drama and visual action. Joanou quickly established a signature style with an MTV feel, so he became the symbol of a new wave of film-school brats— moviemakers whose only frame of reference is movies. The same criticism had been leveled at Lucas and his peers, but at least the movie brats of the 1970s were weaned on classic cinema. The movie brats of the late 1980s and early 1990s, critics crowed, were weaned on junk.

Joanou validated many criticisms of his work with the enervated *Entropy*, the story of a young director, Jake (Stephen Dorff), given the job of directing a multimillion-dollar period picture. Jake threatens to halt production when his backers strong-arm him into including gratuitous nudity, and while the character's essential dilemma of balancing art and commerce is a valid topic for discussion, Jake is presented as such a vapid sort that his thoughts on art — and, by extension, Joanou's— lack credi-bility. *Entropy* is the worst kind of self-reflexive filmmaking, because it's metafiction that talks the talk of introspection, but doesn't walk the walk.

Kevin Smith had the savvy to wrap his exercise in cinematic self-indulgence, *Jay and Silent Bob Strike Back*, in the kind of sexual and scatological humor that guaranteed at least a lucrative opening weekend for comedies early in the twenty-first century. The picture, a silly gaze behind the bright lights of the movie industry, concerns New Jersey marijuana dealers Jay (Jason Mewes) and Silent Bob (Smith), who appeared in all of the director's previous films. They discover that a movie is to be made from *Bluntman and Chronic*, the pot-themed comic book for which they were the inspiration.

The duo set out to derail the production, and amid myriad gross references to bodily functions and oral sex, Smith lets loose several cutting jokes at the expense of notable filmmakers and studios. Gus Van Sant, a director who shifted from independent films to studio projects, plays himself as being too busy counting money to actually direct; a gag about Miramax states that the company known for distributing arthouse movies went downhill after releasing the teen comedy *She's All That*; and Jay and Silent Bob beat the tar out of a detractor whose online handle is "*Magnolia* fan," a device that allows Smith to spew venom at the Paul Thomas Anderson

Alter egomaniac: Writer-director-actor Kevin Smith's weakness for lowbrow irony led him to make the farcical *Jay and Silent Bob Strike Back*, featuring Smith (with beard) and Jason Mewes (Dimension Films).

film of which he is a vocal critic. *Jay and Silent Bob* suggests that Smith wants it both ways: He wants viewers to accompany him on the ride of his movie, but he wants them to step outside the movie to laugh at the ludicrous aspects of filmmaking. This is Gen-X irony at its most mundane.

Only slightly more ambitious is *Josie and the Pussycats*, Harry Elfont's and Deborah Kaplan's tedious update of the 1970s cartoon show. The picture fails on nearly every level, but the filmmakers' apparent lifelong immersion in popular culture led them to create a funny story line about subliminal messages being placed in songs, movies, and television shows. The film's villains insert the illicit advertising without informing the entertainers they manage, then kill singers and actors who get wise to the scheme. When Elfont and Kaplan concentrate on imagining how peer pressure and salesmanship intersect in hidden slogans, the movie generates pointed laughter, but this choice material is accompanied by paper-thin characters, horrible dialogue, and a laborious narrative. *Josie and the Pussycats* suffers from the same problem as *Jay and Silent Bob Strike Back*: The people behind both films want to be taken seriously while doing exactly the thing they're satirizing, but they spend so much time winking at the audience that they often forget to entertain.

While not primarily concerned with filmmaking, *Pulp Fiction* and Wes Anderson's wryly satirical *Rushmore* both offer commentary that puts the weak efforts of Joanou, Smith, and others to shame. In *Pulp Fiction*, gangster's moll Mia Wallace (Uma Thurman) entertainingly recounts her experience of acting in the pilot for a TV series; in *Rushmore*, overachieving teenager Max Fischer (Jason Schwartzman) mounts preposterous stage versions of films such as *Serpico*. The Tarantino bit is like a casual acknowledgment that entertainment is all around us, and the Anderson bit is a winking jab at excess in entertainment. Yet even while providing amusing, insidery moments, these scenes run dangerously close to the nether world of movies that only make sense in the context of other movies.

At their best, Gen Xers create interesting new artifacts of pop culture. At their worst, they create disposable artifacts about pop culture. Because this is a trap into which so many of their number fall, it's heartening to note the power of the entertainment that Gen Xers create when they set popular culture aside and tell stories about genuine culture — specifically, the American society that bred them.

4

Growing Pains

Although it has been rightly criticized as the truest evidence of their collective inclination toward superficiality, Generation X's obsession with popular culture, at least as seen in films made by members of their number, really is a manifestation of the great theme that runs through the cinema of Generation X. Knowing some of the economic and cultural factors that make these people feel disconnected from society, it follows that they might feel a collective desire for escape into a made-up society of their own — hence the use of pop-culture references as a coded form of language. Because Gen Xers, speaking in the most general terms, aren't tethered to family and other institutions in the ways that their predecessors were, they create a comforting cocoon of artifice.

They also, interestingly, create other replacements for the warmth and security of family life, even as they exhibit deep ambivalence for the traditional concept of what an American household should look like. Specifically, Gen-X filmmakers have made a handful of disturbing observations about the dynamics of American families, with a particular concentration on what happens in the nation's suburbs. The fixation on the 'burbs is telling, because a fair number of this generation's filmmakers seem to have emerged from the affluent milieu of America's middle class. Just as they sometimes display an insular affection for pop culture, they sometimes betray a sheltered perspective of what constitutes hardship.

The characters in Sam Mendes's *American Beauty*, for instance, have it rough not because they're poor, starving, or diseased, but because they're not "fulfilled." While it would be wrong to belittle the need for personal fulfillment, creative release, and professional satisfaction, the manner in which some Gen-X filmmakers treat the petty crises of the privileged as high drama is occasionally distasteful. (This trend reached an apex in *The Game*, David Fincher's movie about a rich man who gets thrown into a life-or-death role-playing game because his brother thinks the protagonist needs to be shaken free of his constricting lifestyle.) Given the depth of need in countless parts of America and the rest of the world, films that portray comfortable, affluent lifestyles as oppressive are themselves oppressive, because of their tunnel-visioned perspectives.

Several interesting ideas emerge in these navel-gazing studies of suburbia, but some of the most resonant Gen-X films about family involve characters from further down the economic ladder. For instance, Jodie Foster — the exquisite screen actress who has been a familiar presence in American cinemas for so long that it seems odd to include her in a group so new to sociological discourse as Generation X, but who nonetheless fits in with that group chronologically — directed two thoughtful films about the issues facing blue-collar families. Her directorial debut, *Little Man Tate*, explored the peculiar quandaries facing the working-class mother of a genius child, and her follow-up, the mostly disappointing *Home for the Holidays*, looked at a less unusual, but more dysfunctional, nuclear family.

Both films make statements about the power of individualism and the need for family members to help loved ones unfurl their wings instead of clipping them, but perhaps the most important link between the movies is Foster's strong assertion that family takes many forms: The unit formed by the genius and his mother in *Little Man Tate* is as enduring as that formed by the extended nuclear family in *Home for the Holidays*.

The ability to draw strength from unconventional family units is a key topic for Gen-X filmmakers. This is unsurprising, given the number of Gen Xers whose homes were cleaved by divorce, and given how many were raised by two working parents— meaning that as children, these Gen Xers often were left to fend for themselves or commiserate with peers while mom and dad were at the office. Sometimes, the shift from the traditional family unit is depicted as a tragedy (the protagonist of *Fight Club* suggests that men raised by women are by definition emasculated), and sometimes, the shift is reflected hopefully, as in stories about surrogate families. Such tales illustrate that love can create bonds as deep as those created by blood.

All Gen-X stories about family, however, need to be examined through the prism of the question that drives the generation: "Who am I, and where do I belong?" As so many societal factors made vast numbers of Gen Xers feel unwanted — they were abandoned, actually or metaphorically, by parents who left the home following a divorce; changes in schools and the workplace forced them to grow up fast, in effect truncating their childhoods; the corporatization of America made huge numbers of workers feel disposable; and so on — the ache that drives many Gen-X stories about family is poignant and sometimes heartbreaking.

The caveat to all this talk of profundity, of course, is that family is one of the basic themes of American popular culture, particularly television. Even if attention is focused solely on movies and TV shows of the 1970s, for instance, there is plenty of iconography related to that most crucial of issues, divorce. *The Brady Bunch* depicted a "blended" family created by the second marriages of a father and a mother; *Alice*, and the movie from which the sitcom was derived, *Alice Doesn't Live Here Anymore*, showed a woman and her young son venturing out into the world following a failed marriage; the acclaimed feature *Kramer vs. Kramer* dramatized the effect that a divorce and its pursuant squabbles has on a young boy. This body of films and TV shows about new types of American families represented a substantial leap from the happy homes portrayed in such 1950s sitcoms as *Father Knows Best* and *Leave It to Beaver*. However, allowing that Generation X's exploration of family isn't an unprecedented foray into a new social frontier doesn't diminish what the filmmakers belonging to this generation have to say. Quite to the contrary, this contextualization allows viewers to see how Gen-X movies about family deepen the discourse that came before.

Love the Ones You're With

Offering a tonal contrast to the cynicism that oozes through his films, Paul Thomas Anderson uses hopeful surrogate-family imagery to great effect in *Hard Eight*, *Boogie Nights*, and *Magnolia*. In *Hard Eight*, ne'er-do-well John (John C. Reilly) gets taken under the wing of veteran gambler Sydney (Philip Baker Hall); Sydney steers John through dangerous adventures in a casino and even facilitates his young charge's romance with waitress Clementine (Gwyneth Paltrow). The older man's altruism seems at odds with his hardened character, so it's no great surprise at the end of the film to learn that Sydney actually is John's father, protecting the younger man to atone for abandoning him years before. In this case, what seems to be a surrogate family is revealed to be an actual family, suggesting that fate sometimes offers opportunities for the rebuilding of severed bonds. This material is especially poignant for Gen Xers raised by "deadbeat dads," fathers who mostly avoided their parental chores following divorces.

Severed bonds are a recurring theme in *Magnolia*, Anderson's multi-character epic about people suffering from emotional, mental, and physical decay in contemporary Los Angeles. In one story line, a dying patriarch (Jason Robards) is brought together with the estranged son (Tom Cruise) who despises him; in another, a lonely policeman (John C. Reilly) stumbles into a haphazard romance with a drug abuser (Melora Waters); in a third, a pathetic former quiz-show champ (William H. Macy) timidly courts a studly, unreceptive bartender. These plot lines, and the others with which they intertwine, all dramatize the human need for connection, so the very fact that Anderson connects them as intricately as he does is a statement in itself: These people who crave connection are tethered to others, even if they don't realize it.

Magnolia offers a complex vision of family, because it shows that traditional bonds can be infuriating — the patriarch's trophy wife (Julianne Moore) numbs herself with sex and drugs to wash away the taste of marrying for money — while showing that nontraditional bonds can be empowering. The patriarch's male nurse (Philip Seymour Hoffman) feels such empathy for his dying charge that he runs a gauntlet of red tape to arrange the father-son reunion. *Magnolia* is filled with little epiphanies and catastrophes, and the cycle of recrimination and redemption seems endless until a supernatural occurrence forces the characters to step out of their bubbles — in Gen-X terms, their insular perspectives — and see what's right in front of them. The narrative problem with Anderson's approach, and the aspect of the film that made it a love-hate proposition for audiences, is that the supernatural occurrence — a Biblical shower of frogs cascading down from the sky — is so freakish that it clashes with the intense credibility created by Anderson's mesmerizing dialogue and forceful camerawork, and the luminous contributions of his actors. Still, Anderson's point about the way people simultaneously crave and repel inclusion in the human community is touchingly made.

A similar statement is presented in *Boogie Nights*, the most accomplished of Anderson's early films. A sprawling epic about two decades of pornographic filmmaking, *Boogie Nights* depicts how well-endowed Dirk Diggler (Mark Wahlberg) gets taken under the wing of skin-flick mogul Jack Horner (Burt Reynolds) — shades of the patriarchal altruism in *Hard Eight*. Dirk is accepted into the community that makes Jack's films, which includes the director's coke-addicted wife, Amber Waves (Julianne Moore), seemingly airheaded starlet Rollergirl (Heather Graham), ambitious porn actor Reed Rothchild (John C. Reilly), and others. The ironies of this family portrait are myriad. First, and most obvious, is that these people converge not to create real emotional intimacy, but to fabricate and exploit sexual intimacy: They are bonded not by love, but by lovemaking in its crudest incarnation. Another layer of irony is that people in this clique, excepting the technicians, are accepted not for their personalities but for their physicality: Dirk fits into the group because his large penis makes him a valuable commodity, Rollergirl fits in because her girl-next-door looks enable her to enact widespread sexual fantasies, and so on.

The horrific obstacles he lays in front of his *Magnolia* characters comprise a kind of narrative overkill, but Anderson lets a sensible, if hyperbolic, narrative guide his hand in *Boogie Nights*. Cultural shifts such as the transition in the porn industry from shooting on film to shooting on video force characters to adjust their trajectories, which allows Anderson to illustrate how this particular "family" reacts to hardship. The Dirk character is used to dramatize the journey undertaken by nearly every adolescent who breaks from his or her family to pursue an individual path, only to find that walking away from "home" leads to loneliness. Even worse, in Dirk's case, leaving the nest leads to impotence. His virility stems from the connection he feels to his surrogate family.

The surrogate family also cushions the blow that Amber feels when she fails to win visitation rights to her actual child. The powerful sequence depicting Amber's courtroom hearing and its aftermath adds another layer of irony to the film, for while Amber comfortably inhabits her role as a "mother" to the members of the filmmaking collective, she's unable to mother her true offspring.

The final level of irony to *Boogie Nights* is seen in context of Anderson's career, because he employs the same actors from film to film: His movies about surrogate families are made by a surrogate family. Yet while he has run further with this particular subject matter than any other of his peers, Anderson isn't the only Gen Xer to illustrate the poignancy of people simulating familial love instead of inheriting it.

Morgan J. Freeman's affecting *Desert Blue* depicts how the denizens of a tiny desert town in California bond with a father and daughter from Los Angeles who get stranded in the town. Echoing the lyrical tone of Scottish director Bill Forsyth's *Local Hero*, Freeman's movie uses oddball scenes and unexpected conversations to show that people have the ability to connect with strangers when their souls are in sync even if their lifestyles are not. The movie ultimately is as bright as Anderson's are dark, so its mellow tone might be an acquired taste, but the message of inclusion and open-mindedness that Freeman puts across is universal.

The movie begins with cable-TV starlet Skye (Kate Hudson) reluctantly touring remote regions with her dad (John Heard), a professor who studies kitschy roadside attractions. They hit the town of Baxter to see the world's largest ice-cream cone, but get stuck there when a chemical spill outside town forces a quarantine. As hesitantly as she accompanied her father to Baxter, Skye befriends young townies including Blue (Brendan Sexton III), a shy, haunted sort trying to realize the dreams of his late

Adventures in the skin trade: Gen-X movies such as Paul Thomas Anderson's *Boogie Nights,* with Mark Wahlberg (left) and Burt Reynolds as partners in pornography, depict characters from disparate backgrounds forming surrogate families (New Line Cinema).

father; Ely (Christina Ricci), a doom-and-gloom type who gets her kicks by setting explosions; and all-terrain-vehicle nut Pete (Casey Affleck), whose prizes in local races make him the town hotshot.

These characters comprise a surrogate family demonized by Empire Cola, a conglomerate that built an ugly factory outside of Baxter but didn't hire any locals to work there. Prior to the factory's construction, Blue's father tried to develop Baxter as a tourist destination by constructing an "ocean park" with water from an aqueduct that runs through town, but when water was appropriated for the Empire factory, construction of the park stopped. This turn of events led, in part, to the demise of Blue's father, and one of the most resonant aspects of the film is the way that Blue's friends nurture him through the pain, confusion, and angst that have consumed him since his tragedy. This familial imagery is a powerful representation of the manner in which Gen Xers often became each other's stand-in relatives during times when parents were nowhere to be found and educators failed to provide adequate guidance.

Moreover, *Desert Blue* is a celebration of Generation X's inclusive attitude toward different ethnicities, sexual preferences, and religions. Minorities, both racial and sexual, made tremendous progress toward gaining public acceptance during the years when Generation X matured, so the various Gen-X movies in which surrogate families are melting pots of different personality types reflect the tolerance that, while not reflected in every member of the generation, is one of Generation X's most progressive attitudes. *Desert Blue* illustrates the ability that people have to see past how others present themselves— the townies, for instance, see the soulful person beneath Skye's bitchy facade — so by the end of the film, even seemingly demented characters are sympathetic because we see the pain in their souls, their deep connection to other people, or both.

The surrogate-family imagery of *Desert Blue* and Anderson's films recurs in various Gen-X movies, from *Reality Bites* (about a clique of twentysomethings joined by their postadolescent malaise) to *Reservoir Dogs* (in which hoods played by Harvey Keitel and Tim Roth develop something akin to the bond between a father and son) to *X-Men* (about freakish "mutants," cast out by society, forming a team to serve the greater good) to *Girl, Interrupted* (in which the female patients in a psychiatric-care ward bond by sharing their dysfunctions).

One interesting twist on the prevalent surrogate-family imagery is found in *You Can Count on Me*, Kenneth Lonergan's Oscar-nominated directorial debut. The film explores the relationship between Sammy Prescott (Laura Linney), a single mother living with her son in a small town, and Terry Prescott (Mark Ruffalo), her directionless brother. The two were orphaned during childhood when their parents died in an auto accident, so they have a special link: Notwithstanding Sammy's son, they are each other's only family. So when Terry drifts into his hometown for an extended visit with his sister, only to reveal that he's caught in a cycle of self-destructive behavior, Lonergan makes some pointed statements about the ways in which a surrogate family can be deficient.

Sammy is the authority figure in this relationship because her life is on track, but her authority is diminished by her failures (including her marriage), and by the fact that she's Terry's sibling, not his parent. Terry resents her attempts at control and guidance, and dislikes that she judges him, so the sibling rivalry between the characters is exacerbated by Sammy's endeavors to take on the surrogate-parent role. Yet for all his angst, Terry musters the strength at the end of the movie to declare what his sister's love means to him: "It's always really good to know that wherever I am, whatever stupid shit I'm doing, you're back at home, rooting for me." This confused young man has serious issues with the hand life dealt him, but in one of his clearest moments, he acknowledges that a having a surrogate family is better than having none at all.

Nuclear Meltdowns

One of the key factors behind Generation X's collective makeup is the transformation of the traditional American family, and the ennui that consumed the millions of children who grew up feeling abandoned by their parents — and, by extension — by society at large. This ennui is given form in a memorable speech from Helen Childress's script of *Reality Bites*, as spoken by quintessential slacker Troy (Ethan Hawke):

> TROY: My parents got divorced when I was five years old, and I saw my father about three times a year after that. And when he found out that he had cancer, he decided to bring me here [to Texas], and he gives me this big pink sea shell, and he says to me "Son, the answers are all inside of this." And I'm, like, "What?" And then I realize ... the shell is empty. There's no point to any of this. It's all just a random lottery of meaningless tragedy, and a series of near-escapes. So I take pleasure in the details: a Quarter-Pounder with cheese ... the sky ... and I sit back and I smoke my Camel straights and I ride my own mount.

As Troy's lament suggests, the dominant tone in Gen-X discussions of traditional families is cynicism, and the dominant family model featured in Gen-X movies is the dysfunctional nuclear clan infested with bitterness and resentment. The overrated, but nonetheless significant, *American Beauty* features perhaps the quintessential example of this skewed portrayal of family life in the United States.

Much of the attention earned by this Oscar-winning film was heaped on director Sam Mendes, a wunderkind Brit who secured his reputation with successful stage productions of *Cabaret* and *The Blue Room*. Both were sexed-up controversy magnets, and *The Blue Room* became a sensation in part because star Nicole Kidman briefly flashed her naked figure during each performance. Mendes therefore brought familiarity with handling stars and conjuring sensationalism to *American Beauty*, which was written by former sitcom scribe Alan Ball. Fitting his past employment, Ball brought superficiality and a penchant for one-liners. Together, the men crafted a breezily entertaining but insultingly obvious parable about the American middle class.

The story's central character is Lester Burnham (Kevin Spacey), who loathes his job as a writer for *Media Monthly* magazine, and who is so devoid of hope that his long marriage to Carolyn (Annette Bening) will find new life that he masturbates in the shower every morning instead of trying to get intimate with his wife. Lester feels humiliated by everything about his existence, and wants badly to recover the hopefulness of his youth. He finds a possible mechanism for that recovery when he meets Angela Hayes (Mena Suvari), a pretty cheerleader friend of Lester's daughter, Jane (Thora Birch). Emboldened by his flirtation with the precocious teenager, Lester quits his job, blackmails his employer, and even starts buying pot from Ricky Fitts (Wes Bentley), the haunted boy who lives next door. Meanwhile, Carolyn finds liberation of her own. Her career as a real-estate agent is stagnant, so she asks smooth-talking, handsome, successful homeseller Buddy Kane (Peter Gallagher) for advice. Her request eventually leads to a wild lovemaking session in a hotel room with her would-be mentor.

All of the story's elements are clichés familiar from decades of soap operas, pulp novels, and disposable films: Lester pursues the tired midlife fantasy of courting a cheerleader, then turns out to have a stronger conscience than expected; his would-be lover talks a tough line about sexual experience, but actually is a virgin; the pot dealer seems to be a burnout, but is in reality a soulful artist who finds transcendent beauty in the way a plastic bag gets caught in the wind. And Ricky's father (Chris Cooper) is portrayed as a militaristic dictator with violent homophobia, so, naturally, he's later revealed as a closeted homosexual.

Ball's script deals almost exclusively in archetypes, then twists the archetypes predictably. The film's limp message seems to be that true beauty is found in unexpected places, and that the sterile comforts of the American suburban lifestyle are truly ugly. The film's final twist is that Lester, after throwing off his societal shackles and then proving his moral integrity by refusing to consummate his relationship with the Lolita cheerleader, gets killed by the homophobe whose same-sex advances he spurned. Lester isn't punished for anything he did, but for something he didn't do. The gimmick of the movie, which was used much more strikingly in David Lynch's *Blue Velvet*, is peeling back the plastic surface of suburbia to reveal festering dysfunction, but everything the film reveals is familiar and tame.

American Beauty is worth discussing in detail not because it makes a powerful statement about American life, but because it has been celebrated for doing so when in fact it does exactly the opposite. Ironically, the least profound of the Gen-X films that depict family issues has a reputation as the most profound.

Troy's *Reality Bites* monologue about his father is not the only poignant commentary on nuclear families in the film about disaffected twentysomethings. A fair amount of discussion in the film is devoted to

Dysfunction junction: An illusion of happy domesticity is shattered in Sam Mendes's *American Beauty*, with (from left) Annette Bening, Thora Birch, and Kevin Spacey (DreamWorks Pictures).

how shy homosexual Sammy Gray (Steve Zahn) will reveal his sexual identity to his conservative mother, a quandary faced by vast numbers of Gen Xers who tested their parents' acceptance of alternative lifestyles. Viewers don't see the revelation scene, but they do see its aftermath: Sammy speaks directly to the camera, which director Ben Stiller uses to represent the camera of fledgling documentarian Lelaina (Winona Ryder), and nervously explains that his announcement was met with anger, not acceptance.

> SAMMY: I came out to her. She's still a little bit upset. But you know, I think the real reason I've been celibate for so long isn't really because I'm that terrified of the big "A" [AIDS]. I can't really start my life without being honest about who I am.... I want to feel miserable and happy and I mean and I want — I want to be let back in the house.

Sammy is shunned because he's different, and his pain echoes the feelings of abandonment that any child distanced from his or her parent feels. This feeling of familial disenfranchisement reverberates throughout Jodie Foster's *Little Man Tate*, during which a genius child is separated from his mother, and *Home for the Holidays*, which depicts a gay character as the black sheep of his family. Films such as Foster's and *Reality Bites* explore what happens when a child is cleaved from his or her family, and generally offer the homily that perseverance and love can nurture acceptance. For all their images of dysfunction, these films convey a vision of familial love conquering all — or at least surmounting the biggest obstacles separating relatives.

Stephen Soderbergh offered a unique take on the forces that bind and sever family members in his gorgeously realized period piece, *King of the Hill*. Adapted from A. E. Hotchner's memoir of growing up in Depression-era St. Louis, the picture concerns a resourceful youth named Aaron Kurlander (Jesse Bradford). In quick succession, his tight but struggling family is divided: His mother (Lisa Eichorn), develops tuberculosis and is sent to higher ground for a cure; his younger brother (Cameron Boyd) is sent to live with relatives because the family can't afford to feed two children; and finally his father (Jeroen Krabbé) departs to work as a traveling salesman. Aaron's reaction upon being left alone is utterly credible: He approaches his solitude as an adventure, even as sadness about being abandoned rises in his soul.

Joining forces with his older friend, Lester (Adrien Brody), Aaron enjoys a series of exploits that make him feel like a young outlaw, but soon even Lester is separated from Aaron. While these events are germane within the Depression-era story line — and are in fact fictionalizations of Hotchner's own youth — they have a special meaning within the context of Gen-X cinema. The rifts that split Aaron's family have the same effect that divorce, war deaths, and other misfortunes had on families throughout the 1960s and 1970s, so Aaron's reactions resonate with the unwelcome leaps into maturity that so many Gen Xers were forced to take during their youths. Little short of death and disease makes a kid grow up faster than a divorce, because the shock of losing the security of family, combined with the horror of seeing parents fight, often forcibly transforms children from the nurtured to the nurturing.

Therefore, the manner in which Aaron becomes his own parent, albeit only for a time, can be seen as a metaphor for any child shunted into premature adulthood. Accordingly, the ingenuity that he displays in bringing his family back together at the end of the film is a powerful illustration of how even the youngest members of a family can have a potent effect on their home environment. The fact that Aaron never truly entertains notions of living on his own, but rather keeps his eyes on the prize of rebuilding his nuclear family, accentuates the timeless concept that individuals draw their strength from the warmth of family. The film also speaks to the essential Gen-X concept of the importance of surrogate families. During the stretch of the picture that Aaron spends totally separated from his real family, he develops a support group including Lester, a sympathetic teacher, and colorful neighbors living in his building.

King of the Hill is about family, but even more than that, it's about imagination. The film's first image shows Aaron spinning a fantastic tale about a friendship with legendary aviator Charles Lindbergh. His deadpan fabrication flies over the heads of his classmates, but enchants his teacher; later, Aaron's ability to imagine a world that's brighter and more comforting than the real one is the skill that helps him survive his darkest moments. Key scenes show that his mother nurtures Aaron's imagination by listening to stories he makes up at night, and this idea — of how children, and by extension adults, grow by applying their creativity to work, play, and life in general — is another one that has received memorable treatment by Gen-X directors.

Themes pertaining to the family have received significant treatment in numerous other Gen-X films, of course. Edward Burns's gentle character pictures, including the well-received indie film *The Brothers McMullen*, are old-fashioned stories revolving around the trials and tribulations of such conventional units as an Irish-Catholic family. Ted Demme's *Beautiful Girls* depicts how a young adult raised among blue-collar friends reacts to his old gang when he returns to his hometown older and wiser. John Singleton's morality tale about life in South Central Los Angeles, *Boyz N the Hood*, shows a character caught between the conflicting guidance of a strong father and the surrogate unit comprising his friends.

Despite the turmoil that beset the family throughout Generation X's formative years, some filmmakers from this generation have made loving odes to the power of blood ties: Robert Rodriguez's popular fantasy *Spy Kids*, about a pair of preteens who use James Bond-style gadgets to rescue their loving parents from a criminal mastermind, puts forth such an unquestioning picture of familial devotion that it's a bracing alternative to the pain that characterizes most Gen-X depictions of home life.

School Daze

Movies about education become cloying when filmmakers hammer viewers with the same lessons that characters in the picture are learning, and an example of this pitfall is John Singleton's ambitious sophomore film, *Higher Learning*. After making a splash with *Boyz N the Hood*, a smartly constructed parable, the gifted young director tackled the amorphous subject of the changes people experience in college. While his choice to treat the subject matter seriously was a welcome change of pace after years of insulting *Animal House* knock-offs, Singleton filled *Higher Learning* with suffocating piousness.

All by myself: Given the number of Gen Xers touched by divorce, movies such as Steven Soderbergh's *King of the Hill*, with Jesse Bradford as a Depression-era youth who has to fend for himself, are especially poignant (Gramercy Pictures).

The picture follows three archetypal undergraduates during their first year at college, when each encounters a crisis. The black track star (Omar Epps) discovers that African-American athletes are treated like commodities by college sports programs; the pretty blonde from the suburbs (Kristy Swanson) dabbles in sexual experimentation with male and female partners; the impressionable white misfit (Michael Rappaport) gets recruited into a group of racist skinheads. In some of the story lines, an adult mentor provides portentous commentary at various steps along the journey; in others, contemporaries speak with precocious maturity. All of the vignettes are weighted down with the maddeningly obvious assertion that true learning often occurs outside the classroom, as well as the message that learning tolerance is among the most important steps in becoming a responsible adult.

A more effective movie about education, Jodie Foster's *Little Man Tate*, depicts a troubled time in the relationship between young genius Fred Tate (Adam Hann-Byrd) and his working-class mother, Dede Tate (played by Foster). The third important figure in this dynamic is educator Jane Grierson (Dianne Wiest), who persuades Dede that her son should be put in a special environment that stimulates his precocious intellect. The most heartbreaking stretch of the film occurs when Fred moves in with his educational benefactor, leaving his mother alone; the subtext to this sequence is that Jane thinks Dede isn't intelligent enough to guide a genius's education. Despite Jane's valiant attempt to provide a comfortable home for her young charge, she only knows how to nurture the boy's brain, not his heart. The separation wreaks havoc on the boy, who intentionally subverts his education to force a reunion with his mother, so the film's ultimate message is that a loving environment stimulates greater growth than a purely intellectual one. (The film also is a rare example of a Gen-X director depicting a failed attempt to create a surrogate family.)

A similar message is put across in *Good Will Hunting*, written by and starring Gen Xers Matt Damon and Ben Affleck. The Oscar-winning picture follows Will Hunting (Damon), an angry, working-class Boston youth, through the journey that begins when Harvard math professor Gerald Lambeau (Stellan Skarsgård) discovers the boy's mathematical genius. The prodigy just wants to enjoy an average life with his drinking buddies, but trouble with the law forces him to accept Gerald's tutelage — and to undergo therapy sessions with gruff but empathetic shrink Sean Maguire (Robin Williams). The entertaining, sentimental picture examines whether Will is better served by a life of the mind or the humbler life he desires, and after much onscreen soul-searching, Will makes a choice that echoes the end of *Little Man Tate*: He abandons a lucrative opportunity to exploit his intelligence, instead choosing to pursue human warmth, specifically the love of a pretty Harvard coed.

Both *Little Man Tate* and *Good Will Hunting* offer the crowd-pleasing idea that love has a stronger pull than intellectualism, and though *Tate* tries to present a balance in which the title character is nurtured both emotionally and intellectually, the films can be read broadly as criticisms of excessive education. While neither picture goes so far as to say that education harms people, both make the somewhat obvious assertion that people need to find which level of education suits them as individuals. This assertion is interesting for two reasons.

First is the fact that Gen Xers are often referred to as a generation with too much education in impractical matters and not enough in practical ones. This widespread stereotype is rooted in facts that bear upon only an affluent, entitled segment of Generation X — those members of the generation who can spend several comfortable years in the womb of college because they don't need to hurry into the workplace — but it is propagated by the images of Gen Xers shown in films and television. These fictional Gen Xers speak, as has been shown, in an idiom informed by over-saturation in popular culture, a form of excessive education.

All about my mother: Celebrated actress Jodie Foster's directorial efforts include *Little Man Tate*, featuring Foster as the mother of a young genius (Adam Hann-Byrd) (Orion Pictures).

Therefore, if Gen Xers Foster, Damon, and Affleck indeed meant to put across a cautionary message about education, that message could be interpreted as a reaction to the information with which Gen Xers have been bombarded since youth. In that case, the message common to *Little Man Tate* and *Good Will Hunting* is more interesting than a knee-jerk condemnation of soul-numbing educators and soulless educational institutions. It is a pained cry for relief from the hurricane of soundbites, infotainment, and junk culture in which Gen Xers have been swept up since childhood.

Interestingly, author Geoffrey T. Holtz noted that educational standards suffered a marked decline during key years of Generation X's youth. In *Welcome to the Jungle*, he reported that experiments with hands-off teaching (in which students were given greater authority to determine their own curriculum) and changes in grading policies (in which failing grades were eliminated, or at least used sparingly, to nurture students' feelings of self-worth) compromised the quality of schooling that Gen Xers received. Additionally, Holtz noted, the parents of Gen Xers experienced a dangerous shift in attitudes that led them to fight school funding more vigorously in the 1970s and beyond than in any previous time. As Holtz wrote:

> One paradox of stressing self-esteem came to light in an international math test given to thirteen-year-olds in 1988. American students were dead last among the nations who took the test, yet they led the pack in considering themselves "good at mathematics." Korean children, only 23 percent of whom judged themselves good math students, also happened to be the highest-scoring students. [Gen Xers] may have developed some of that high self-esteem — perhaps arrogance is a more appropriate term — in school. Unfortunately, what they needed to learn may have been a little humility, and a lot more math.[1]

Such trends created an atmosphere in which respect for schools was greatly lessened, as seen in the contempt for educators and educational institutions that permeates such youth films as *Animal House*, *Fast Times at Ridgemont High*, *The Breakfast Club*, and *Revenge of the Nerds*, all of which became hits thanks to the buying power of Gen-X moviegoers. The anti-teacher attitude also appeared in such popular rock songs as Alice Cooper's "School's Out" and Pink Floyd's "Another Brick in the Wall," both of which were radio staples during Generation X's youth. This metaphor of classroom-as-battleground was the inspiration for several Gen-X pictures, beginning with Keith Gordon's 1988 drama *The Chocolate War*, in which a strong-willed student and the inflexible headmaster of a private school challenged each other throughout a vigorous battle for dominance over their shared environs.

Probably the most entertaining Gen-X spin on educational issues is Wes Anderson's *Rushmore*, a satire so cheeky that it almost drowns in its own self-satisfied wit. Set at the prestigious Rushmore Academy, the picture tracks the exploits of one Max Fischer (Jason Schwartzman), a parody of every overachiever ever encountered in fiction and reality. The high schooler participates in a ridiculous number of extracurricular activities, but not because he excels in them; in fact, he's stretched so far past his intellectual capacity that he's in danger of flunking out of school.

Max isn't daunted by his academic problems, however. During the course of the movie, he plunges deep into work with groups including the Max Fischer Players, a pompously named theater troupe that makes overblown stage productions such as a Vietnam drama complete with faux helicopters and explosions. Max also attempts to spark a romance with a pretty young teacher, Rosemary Cross (Olivia Williams). His rival for her affections is Herman Blume (Bill Murray), a school benefactor as cynical as Max is optimistic. Just as Max lives beyond his means academically and artistically, he tries to inhabit a romantic identity beyond his years. He overreaches in every possible way, and his occasional successes owe more to perseverance and dirty tricks than aptitude.

Therefore, it's possible to interpret Max as the ultimate manifestation of the animosity toward education that recurs in several Gen-X films. Max benefits not from traditional education, but from creating his own educational opportunities. Seen through conventional eyes, Max is a failure: His grades are poor, he doesn't blend into the mainstream of the student body, and he doesn't respect authority. But from a nonconventional standpoint, Max is a smashing success: He expresses himself without inhibition, is on his way to becoming a fully realized individual, and thinks for himself. Like the geniuses in *Little Man Tate* and *Good Will Hunting*, faux genius Max defies the stagnant, cold ideals of traditional education and makes his own path.

Yet on a poignant level, Max's academic shortcomings amplify the danger of unchecked freethinking: By choosing to disregard the mainstream, Max diminishes his social opportunities and alienates many of his peers. The price for his individualism is isolation. The makers of *Rushmore* find a way to let Max have his cake and eat it too, albeit with a bittersweet aftertaste: Max loses Rosemary to Herman, but forms a romantic bond with a geeky schoolmate, essentially lowering his expectations sufficiently to embrace reality.

Max closely resembles another memorable Gen-X protagonist, Nebraska high schooler Tracy Flick, played to perfection by Reese Witherspoon in Alexander Payne's scathing *Election*. Tracy is an intense overachiever who joins every organization, has an answer for every question in every class, and, despite being almost pathologically upbeat, never seems to have any fun. Most of the people in Tracy's school pay her no mind, accepting her as part of the scenery. But one of her teachers, Jim McAllister (Matthew Broderick), finds her relentless ambition distasteful. And when it seems that Tracy is poised to coast past another obstacle by running unopposed for student-body president, he decides to take her down a peg — a biting dramatization of the antagonism that many Gen Xers perceive in their relationship with educators.

Payne uses a fittingly brash storytelling style throughout *Election*. During Tracy's first scene, he freezes a close-up so that her face is contorted in mid-speech, then leaves the unflattering shot onscreen while Jim's voice-over describes Tracy's history. The director's funniest touch is employing tribal voices as a musical leitmotif whenever Tracy fears that events are spinning beyond her control, a neat trick revealing the animal instincts burning beneath her cool demeanor. Tracy represents ambition unaccompanied by compassion (and, by extension, education unaccompanied by compassion), so she's part of the wonderfully dark skewering of "heartland values" that distinguishes Omaha-born Payne's work.

A final, albeit much more superficial, Gen-X reaction to education is seen in the films written and/or directed by Kevin Williamson. In *The Faculty*, which Williamson wrote, and *Teaching Mrs. Tingle*, which he wrote and directed, high school educators are depicted as monstrous villains. Both are escapist fantasies designed to help youths purge the angst they feel about their daily "tormentors," and both are aftershocks of the high school films that were popular in the 1980s. Unfortunately, *The Faculty* and *Teaching Mrs. Tingle* are silly, bloody thrill rides, featuring little of lasting substance.

5

To Slack or
Not to Slack

Although the word *slacker* was around long before the first members of Generation X were born — it was used primarily to describe soldiers who put forth the minimum acceptable effort or conspired to do even less than that, like classic comic-strip character Beetle Bailey — the emergence of a generation inclined toward epic sloth provided a new application for an old word.

At some point in the late 1980s or early 1990s, when people first began identifying and studying Generation X, the popular stereotype of the contemporary slacker emerged. As depicted in entertainment and news, slackers were educated youths weaned on popular culture and disenfranchised from mainstream American because of social, familial, and economic reasons. These pseudo-existentialists were different from commonplace layabouts, the stereotype established, because they extracted themselves from mainstream society not out of laziness but to stay true to a philosophical idea. That idea went something like this: Contemporary American society had become so dehumanized, corporatized, and homogenized that to participate in it was to contribute to dehumanization, corporatization, and homogenization. Or something like that. The forces against which slackers rebelled were so numerous and nebulous that to list just a few of them does a disservice to the vastness of the ennui that prompted the emergence of slackerdom.

Gen Xers were not the first filmmakers to put slackers, or slacker-like characters, onscreen. As far back as the early 1980s, well before *slacker* entered common parlance, Cameron Crowe devoted himself to understanding the issues of confused modern youths. (Born in 1957, Crowe is either a very young boomer or a very old Gen Xer, depending on which parameters are used.) The 1982 comedy *Fast Times at Ridgemont High*, which Crowe wrote but did not direct, gave viewers a beloved "stoner" icon named Jeff Spicoli (Sean Penn), whose fun-before-responsibility attitude can be read as a precursor to slackerdom. Crowe's directorial debut, the 1989 romantic comedy *Say Anything...*, introduced a quintessential Gen-X character named Lloyd Dobler (John Cusack), who tries to decide what path to take after graduating from high school. This young man's singular attitude is captured in this monologue, prompted when the father of his girlfriend asks Lloyd about his plans for the future:

> LLOYD: I've thought about this quite a bit, sir, and considering what's waiting out there for me, I don't want to sell anything, buy anything, or process anything as a career. I don't sell anything bought or processed or buy anything sold or processed or process anything sold, bought or processed or ... My father's in the Army. He wants me to join, but I can't work for that corporation. Um, so what I've been doing lately is kickboxing.... I don't know. I can't figure it all out tonight, sir. I'm just kinda hangin' with your daughter.

Crowe's films are the most articulate of many pictures made by non-Gen Xers that address important Gen-X issues, and the dreams and desires of this generation also have been addressed on television, particularly on the popular sitcom *Friends*. Yet in most Hollywood stories about Gen Xers but not by Gen Xers, a happy glow is cast upon young characters that isn't present in real life: The titular characters of *Friends*, for instance, get through all their travails by relying on humor and the bond created by their unshakable surrogate family. Notwithstanding Crowe's sensitive portrayals, the bogus nature of Hollywood's take on Generation X — and particularly the most misunderstood segment of that generation, slackers— underscores why it's crucial to look at stories of these people, by these people, and for these people. As Edward Norton, star of the Gen-X film *Fight Club* and a promising director in his own right, said:

> So much of what's been represented about my generation has been done by the baby boomers. They dismiss us: the word *slacker*, the oversimplification of the Gen-X mentality as one of hesitancy or negativity. It isn't just aimlessness we feel; it's deep skepticism. It's not slackerdom; it's profound cynicism, even despair, even paralysis, in the face of an onslaught of information and technology.[1]

Masters of Time Suckage

Three years before slackers received the glossy Hollywood treatment in Ben Stiller's *Reality Bites*, Richard Linklater presented a movie that was pure Generation X in style as well as content. For while Stiller effectively employed conventional narrative devices and appealing actors to make Gen-X issues accessible to both youthful and older audiences, it could be argued that using slick storytelling to discuss slackers was as crass as, say, making an expensive movie about hippies. Stiller's best defenses to such criticisms probably are that he belongs to the generation that *Reality Bites* is about, and that even within the confines of a slick story, *Reality Bites* has plenty of loose, seemingly off-the-cuff interaction. Nonetheless, Linklater has to be considered the pioneer in this cinematic territory, not only because he got there first, but because his slacker movie is fully infused with slacker spirit.

Set in Austin, Texas, Linklater's *Slacker* is a simple idea dragged out to feature length: Characters are introduced, shown moving from one place to the next and/or interracting with other characters, and after a moment or a few moments, the film drifts away to follow a character or characters who have wandered into the scene. It's like a narrative relay race, only without any semblance of a goal or of dramatic tension. While the film is in many ways affected and dull, it also is filled with provocative ideas that rise and fall based on the strength of their execution: Linklater's best vignettes feature truthful acting and spot-on dialogue, and the worst suffer from amateurism on every level. The personal quality of the film is visible from the first frame, because the character who begins the succession of vignettes is a laconic drifter played by Linklater himself.

The people of *Slacker* are layabouts, conspiracy theorists, media junkies, paranoids, eccentrics, lost souls, and so on. The only ones who seem the least bit fulfilled are those who have replaced conventional goals with their own strange pursuits, such as a cheerful anarchist and a demented fellow whose cramped apartment is filled with stolen televisions. Most of the characters are given opportunities to explain themselves, and most of the explanations say something about the generation to which their intellectually curious creator belongs. Consider, for instance, these words spoken by a philosopher (Brecht Andersch) in a coffee shop: "Who's ever written a great work about the immense effort required *not* to create? ... The obsessiveness of the utterly passive. And could it be that in this passivity, I shall find my freedom?"

Even more telling is a presumably autobiographical essay written by a fellow named Paul on a series of postcards, then discovered by his roommates after Paul inexplicably disappears from his apartment:

> All his days are about the same. He wakes up at 11 or 12, eats cereal or toast, reads the newspaper or looks out the front door, takes a walk, goes to a

movie matinee, listens to the radio, watches sitcom reruns till 1, and usually falls asleep around 2. He likes to sleep. Sometimes he has good dreams.

That this monologue is read aloud at a snail's pace, with only the images on successive postcards providing visual interest, indicates why *Slacker* is a tough sell for viewers indoctrinated into the cult of narrative momentum: Literary and languid and self-indulgent, the movie doesn't have a point, per se, and therefore doesn't make haste to get there. In a word, the movie slacks. Linklater casually introduces such peculiar characters as a young woman trying to sell a pap smear containing biological residue from pop star Madonna, and as an "anti-artist" whose creative expression is destroying and belittling things created by others, before the film trudges to a halt with final vignettes including a scene of an old man (Joseph Jones) walking down the street and speaking his thoughts into a tape recorder. His words echo the vibrant spirit burning within the seemingly disenchanted soul of Generation X: "The more the pain grows, the more the instinct for life somehow asserts itself."

The most fundamental disparity between *Slacker* and *Reality Bites* grows out of their stylistic differences. The vignettes in Linklater's picture accumulate into a statement from which viewers can choose to extract meaning if they so desire. Conversely, the very nature of Stiller's film is about putting across a point, in the moralistic sense of the word: While not an outright homily, the movie uses a conventional Hollywood narrative storytelling model, in which experiences hammer at a protagonist until he or she is forced to undergo a change or make a difficult choice.

The choice in this instance is made by Lelaina, who has to decide whether to pursue careerism, as represented by ambitious suitor Michael (Stiller), or individualism, as represented by unabashed slacker Troy (Ethan Hawke). In the muddy logic of Hollywood films created for mass consumption, Lelaina elects a compromise — she accepts Troy as her lover, thereby embracing slackerdom, but remains devoted to her career, thereby embracing traditional goals. The point is that Lelaina finds a way to grow up without totally betraying her generational identity.

Yet the presence of a moral lesson weakens *Reality Bites*'s credibility as a slacker film. One truth that binds vast segments of Generation X is the idea that youths who don't trust institutions lack the spiritual security that previous generations drew from their belief in God, country, or whatever. Furthermore, the idea of Gen Xers drawing strength from generational identity is laughable: People who don't believe in societal movements or institutions don't necessarily believe in each other. So saying in 1994 that different segments of Generation X can learn from and love each other,

Junk food and junk culture: A trip to a convenience store turns into a frivolous adventure in Ben Stiller's *Reality Bites*, with (from left) Ethan Hawke, Winona Ryder, Janeane Garofalo, and Steve Zahn (Universal Pictures).

as *Reality Bites* did, is as wide-eyed as suggesting in 1969 that the hawks and doves of the Vietnam era could live in peace. It wasn't accidental that the finale of *Easy Rider*, in which rednecks cheerfully assassinated hippies, caught the zeitgeist of the day. During times of generational upheaval, the tectonic plates of society clash before they merge.

Another factor worth considering is that *Reality Bites* was an attempt to document a generation that had yet to mature. In that light, it makes sense that some conjecture was required, and that some wishful thinking manifested onscreen. Just as Linklater walked on virgin terrain in 1991 when he made *Slacker*, Stiller and his collaborators had to think ahead of societal curves in order to give their story closure. And who knows? When *Reality Bites* celebrates its twentieth anniversary in 2014, perhaps the film's vision of a tentative solidarity among the divergent factions of Generation X will seem prescient.

Setting the issue of its larger statements aside, it's enjoyable to revisit the details that Stiller's movie got right. The language of the movie captures a moment when a TV generation developed its own vernacular, as seen in a vivid moment involving Lelaina and Troy. The slacker seductively invites his female friend to sit with him on the couch — for TV babies, the adult equivalent of a womb. But he isn't motivated by the desire for a little hanky-panky. Instead, he wants company while he channel-surfs. Lelaina declines, warning that her day will disappear if she parks next to Troy, whom she calls a "master of time suckage."

Another memorable bit of slackage in *Reality Bites* is the scene in which Lelaina and three friends venture from their living room to a convenience store so they can stock up on junk food with the credit card Lelaina just received from her dad. As the quartet of twentysomethings gather Pringles and Diet Coke and other goodies, they hear the Knack's nonsense song "My Sharona," which would have been a hit when these characters were children, on the radio to which the store clerk is listening. Lelaina and Vickie (Janeane Garofalo) pester the clerk to turn up the radio, promising that he "won't be sorry," then reward him by dancing foolishly to the amped-up rock music. The moment is a celebration of doing nothing — the characters bond over disposable pop culture, and turn a functional trip to a bland destination into an effervescent adventure. The vaguely depressing implication of the scene is that acting like idiots in a convenience store might end up being the highlight of the characters' evening, but such are the delights of slackers.

Linklater elevated slackerdom to poetry in *Before Sunrise*, his glorious romance about American twentysomething Jesse (Ethan Hawke), who meets young Frenchwoman Céline (Julie Delpy) on the last day of his trip through Europe. As noted earlier, Jesse is an unusual Gen-X protagonist in that he superficially resembles a slacker, but has a timeless quality seen in his refusal to spout cheap pop-culture references and his disdain for societal institutions.

Jesse is more representative of a moment common to every young life than one common exclusively to youths of his generation. The moment isn't exactly a coming-of-age, and it certainly isn't a loss of innocence, but it has elements of both of those landmark experiences. The moment that Jesse finds himself in during *Before Sunrise* is the frightening, intoxicating surprise of his first mature relationship. That the relationship begins and ends in the course of one day is among the several subtle nuances that make Jesse a quintessential Gen Xer; just as others of his generation rush through life on warp speed because of their short attention spans and/or abilities to process information briskly, Jesse has an Information Age epiphany through his love affair with Céline.

And while it's true that countless previous fictional characters have undergone major psychological changes because of brief encounters, the combination of the brevity of Jesse's affair with Céline, their over-intellectualized discourse, and the hesitancy that they both exhibit about becoming grown-ups brands the characters as youths on the verge of joining a society they don't understand. As Linklater's *Before Sunrise* cowriter, Kim Krizan, noted:

> Ours is certainly a disillusioned generation. Born into the slow-motion explosion of everything our parents believed in, we found ourselves coming of age in the social wreckage, then trying to transcend that dark mire by laughing at all things sacred. It seems that we've all nearly succeeded in postponing maturity, extending adolescence, and giving ourselves over to cynicism and detachment — a very romantic pose, really.... Ultimately, love is an exquisite mess, one that is safer to avoid than to indulge in. So what? Dive in anyway.[2]

If Jesse and Céline are symbolic of their generation, the actions they take also are symbolic, and one such action is among the first to bond the couple. They notice each other while seated in a train passenger car, then start chatting because a couple near them is arguing loudly. Jesse and Céline quickly suss out each other's nationalities, and she asks him if he speaks anything other than English. Jesse defensively explains that he took four years of French lessons, but once the moment came for him to speak French to a railway clerk in Paris, he blanked and spoke English. "No more French for me," he adds.

Jesse took four years of classes to learn the Gallic tongue, then tossed those years away in the moment when he should have reaped the rewards of his education. So Jesse apparently didn't learn the language with the intent of using it in later life; had that been the case, he could have cheated with a translation guide and forced the words to come out. Instead, he learned for the sake of learning. This passive approach to intellectual endeavor isn't unique to Gen Xers, of course; Beatniks and hippies predated slackers in the far-reaching way they drank from the fountain of knowledge. But the ease with which Jesse casually discards four years of education is a poignant depiction of how Gen Xers deal with all that bombards them.

From birth, Americans born in the Gen-X era were subjected to nonstop cultural and societal stimulus, and the speed with which information seeped into their brains accelerated throughout their maturation. So in a sense, it's only natural that Gen Xers can toss away knowledge as if it were garbage. In fact, doing so may be a survival skill: If Jesse and his peers don't shed the knowledge they're not going to use, they risk tumbling into madness like computers crashing from a data overload. Still, it's understandable that casual observers might characterize actions like Jesse's refusal to speak French in France as arrogance or laziness.

The arrogance interpretation has a lot of validity, in that Gen Xers who don't employ their education waste a commodity that less-privileged individuals would treasure. Yet the laziness interpretation — which is at the very heart of how the slacker stereotype emerged — actually is false. The key? Jesse completed his four years of French classes. He didn't give up because the classes were too much work or because he couldn't grasp the concepts. He gave up because when the moment came to speak French in France, he felt false. His action is one of misguided integrity, not contemptuous laziness.

That distinction may, in fact, be an essential insight into the character of Generation X, or at least into how that character is represented in cinematic fiction. Gen Xers may seem to value nothing, including their own generational identity, but perhaps they actually value that identity more than they know or acknowledge. The identity that these people value is, in part, a refusal to value anything, so the decision of whether to slack or not to slack tests how deeply each Gen Xer subscribes to beliefs shared by peers. When conundrums such as this one are considered, the confusion at the heart of Generation X quickly comes into focus.

Rebels with a Cause

Every generation's films offer a different take on the eternal issues facing youths who reject their parents' values— the 1950s James Dean classic, *Rebel Without a Cause*, remains the sine qua non of this genre — and the Gen-X pictures that map this emotional terrain range from the docile to the furious. Moreover, the turmoil within them offers yet another manifestation of the central thrust of Gen-X cinema, the quest for meaning. As so much of this generation's ennui stems from the chaotic social climate they inherited from their peers, watching Gen-X characters slam against — and burst through — the parameters of existing society is highly informative.

On the tame end of this spectrum are pictures such as *Reality Bites*, in which the schism between parents and their children is painted in broad strokes: A son shocks his mother by revealing his homosexuality, et cetera. Pictures that address the difference between generations timidly traffic in timeless, universal themes, so the coming-out story line, with its variables altered, could play in a 1950s story as viably as it does in a 1990s story line. Thus, the most interesting pictures in this area reside on the extreme end of the spectrum, and the most extreme is David Fincher's *Fight Club*, adapted by Jim Uhls from Chuck Palahniuk's novel. The pitch-black comedy features Gen Xers engaging in a violent, anarchistic revolt against contemporary American society, particularly the numbing sameness of consumer culture.

Early in *Fight Club*, the nondescript office drone played by Edward Norton (the character's name is never revealed) retires to his nondescript apartment after a day of nondescript work. His leisure activity is consumption. He sits in his bathroom and flips through a mail-order catalog labeled "Fürni," but clearly modeled on Ikea. ("I had become a slave to the Ikea nesting instinct," he notes in voice-over. "I'd flip through catalogs and wonder what kind of dining set defines me as a person.") The character fixates on a particular dust ruffle, then glances at a photo of an empty apartment while ordering a ruffle over the phone. The camera tracks across the empty apartment, and Ikea-like items appear alongside superimposed prices and product descriptions, a catalog's contents come to life. Then Norton's character walks through the scene — it turns out that we've been looking at his apartment, which now seems more like a showroom than a home.

Chaos theorist: David Fincher's provocative *Fight Club* stars Edward Norton (left) as an office drone who becomes enmeshed in the life of a charismatic anarchist (Brad Pitt) (Twentieth Century–Fox).

This arch device identifies that Norton's character is obsessed with consumer goods not for their utility, but because mass marketing has convinced him that his disposable income is burning a hole in his pockets. The early scenes of *Fight Club* (which depict the protagonist's empty lifestyle) are filmed in bleached-out color, and often feature unflattering overhead lighting, making Norton's character look like a bloodless cipher wandering through his half-life.

It takes a massive shock to free this protagonist from his insular bubble, and that shock is provided by one Tyler Durden (Brad Pitt), a straight-talking soap manufacturer clothed in kitschy, thrift-store clothes. After the two men share drinks and lament the inanity of modern existence — unsurprisingly, a common subject of Gen-X discourse — Tyler asks Norton's character to hit him as hard as he can. Our "hero" protests before obliging, but soon the men beat each other bloody. They find a release in violence akin to that found in sex, and eventually develop a cult around Fight Club, an illegal organization in which men escape the emasculation of consumer culture by pummeling themselves back to "reality." The dark edge to this metaphor — that the action reviving these men also destroys them — is never far from the surface of the movie, perhaps the most subversive of all Gen-X films.

The rebellion of Fight Club's members is in several important ways a rebellion against the people who brought Generation X into the world. Tyler, who laments that "We're a generation of men raised by women," confronts Norton's character early in the movie with this pointed dialogue:

> TYLER: Why do guys like you and I know what a duvet is? Is this essential to our survival in the hunter-gatherer sense of the word? No.... We are consumers. We are byproducts of a lifestyle obsession. Murder, crime, poverty — these things don't concern me. What concerns me are celebrity magazines, television with 500 channels, some guy's name on my underwear, Rogaine, Viagra, Olestra ... Fuck Martha Stewart! Martha's polishing the brass on the *Titanic*. It's all going down.... I say "Stop being perfect." I say "Let's evolve." Things you own end up owning you.

Tyler soon welcomes Norton's character into his dark, disturbing world. Tyler works as a projectionist and splices frames of pornography into family films; he waits tables and urinates into lobster bisques at lush banquets; he lives in a condemned building where the faucets spit brown water and the walls and furniture are coated in grease and filth. Norton's character quickly becomes an accomplice in such missions as stealing bags of biological waste from dumpsters behind a liposuction clinic so it can be mixed into Tyler's soap. ("We were selling rich women their own fat asses back to them," Norton's character observes.) Yet there's a decidedly postmodern wrinkle to the misadventures of these two characters, because late in the movie we learn that Tyler (probably) is a figment of his friend's imagination. Norton's character let his id manifest as a cocksure rebel so he could escape his numbing life, and once Norton's character realizes what he's done, he's shocked to discover how deep a hole he's dug for himself through the actions he took as Tyler.

By the end of the movie, which loops back to the scene that opened the story, Norton's character is driven to kill himself as a way of stopping Tyler's rampage. So the last scene of the picture features Norton's character with a gaping wound on the side of his head reflecting his suicide attempt. As bombs that he/Tyler set topple skyscrapers, Norton's character holds the hand of his demented girlfriend Marla (Helena Bonham Carter) to watch the carnage as if it were a movie. The myriad metaphors of this moment are composed of pure Gen-X malaise and attitude: The wound reflects either the self-inflicted misery of modern consumer culture, or the shock needed to extract oneself from such culture, or both; the emotional connection with Marla suggests that people who share contempt for contemporary society can only truly bond with their own kind; and the vision of an apocalypse as entertainment underlines the morbid, ironic perspective through which the most outrageous Gen-X characters watch America succumb to its excesses.

Adding extra fuel to this metaphorical fire is the fact that at the end of the scene, the image shimmers as if the projector is breaking, and then a subliminal cut of a shot from a porn film intrudes at lightning speed. So the final wrinkle to *Fight Club* is an instruction to do what the characters in the film do: Look for the messages beneath the messages, then do with that information what you will. Or, as Tyler says in one of his most impassioned monologues, delivered while watching Norton's character writhe in pain from a vicious chemical burn:

> TYLER: Stay with the pain! ... This is the greatest moment of your life and you're off somewhere missing it. You have to consider the possibility that God does not like you, never wanted you. In all probability, he hates you. It's not the worst thing that could happen.... We don't need him. Fuck damnation, man. Fuck redemption. We are God's unwanted children — so be it.... It's only after we've lost everything that we're free to do anything.

6

Take This McJob
and Shove It

Quentin Tarantino got his start in a video store. Kevin Smith got his in a convenience store. Screenwriter Andrew Kevin Walker got his in a record store. But the significance of this peculiar pattern is not how three famous Gen-X filmmakers, to say nothing of others whose stories haven't become entertainment-industry mythology, ascended from such humble settings to the height of success and notoriety. No, the noteworthy aspect of the background shared by these three artists is that before they realized their celluloid dreams, they were stuck in the drudgery of McJobs. As massive numbers of their peers were stuck in such drudgery alongside them, and are still to this day, it's necessary to understand the vicious cycle of McJobs if one is to understand the character of Generation X.

Although it's unclear whether he coined the term, Canadian author Douglas Coupland helped *McJob* penetrate popular usage by defining it in his influential novel *Generation X*. A McJob, readers learned, is a soul-numbing position with a low salary, generally in the service industry, taken by a Gen Xer in lieu of something more demanding — so a McJob is, say, working in a video store, a convenience store, or a record store. While Coupland wrote that McJobs usually are held by people whose opportunities are limited by economic factors, his definition should have been amended to acknowledge the myriad Gen Xers who take dead-end positions to avoid the stress and competition associated with following a traditional career trajectory.

For just as changes in education made many Gen Xers feel as if they were products being moved through schools on an assembly line, changes in the workplace owing to the emergence of monolithic multinational corporations — and the emergence of machines that made some jobs obsolete and others monotonous — made it difficult for Gen Xers entering the workplace to develop loyalty for employers or respect for the goals that previous generations pursued. In work, as in so many other aspects of life, Gen Xers found themselves asking what role they were expected to play, and whether they could invent a new role more suited to their unique generational identity.

In *Fight Club*, the violent nocturnal activities of Edward Norton's character make it increasingly difficult for him to take his daylight hours in the working world seriously. The more liberated he becomes by unleashing his malevolent id during off-hours, the less concerned he becomes with hiding his true self during work hours. He starts showing up to the office with ugly bruises and bloodied clothes, stops wearing a tie, starts smoking at his desk, and becomes confrontational with his coworkers. At one point, Norton's character is confronted by his boss, who has just connected Norton's character with a Fight Club flyer found in an office copier. The boss asks his underling what should be done about the document, and Norton's character thinks a moment before launching into this creepy oratory:

> The person who wrote that is dangerous, and this button-down, Oxford-cloth psycho might just snap and then stalk from office to office with an Armolite AR-10 carbine gas-powered semi-automatic weapon, pumping round after round into colleagues and coworkers. This might be someone you've known for years— someone very, very close to you.... Maybe you shouldn't just bring me every little piece of trash you happen to pick up.

This venomous speech exemplifies Generation X's predilection for black humor, because while the scene is rooted in a fantasy familiar to anyone who has ever worked for someone else — the dream of telling off an unctuous superior — the violence suggested by the words goes way beyond pent-up office frustration. This frightening scene also sets the tone for a handful of bitter moments in work-related Gen-X movies. Although few other such scenes are so edgy as to include death threats, many capture other manifestations of the disdain felt by those who punch a time clock.

Revenge of the Drones

Office Space, the first live-action feature directed by *Beavis & Butthead* creator Mike Judge, is arguably the sharpest expression of Gen Xers' resentment of conventional workplaces. The occasionally dry, occasionally outrageous comedy about drones throwing off the shackles of dead-end careerism traffics in somewhat familiar themes (comedies ranging from 1960's *The Apartment* to 1980's *9 to 5* and beyond explore the dehumanizing nature of office politics), but Judge attacks his material with such vigor that his film leaves a uniquely credible aftertaste. Even though the picture uses hyperbole to inflate its principal story elements to larger-than-life proportions, several aspects of the picture are as closely observed and true-to-life as the details in subtle journalism.

The hero/antihero of the piece is Peter Gibbons (Ron Livingston), a technology company employee who, like Norton's *Fight Club* character, is anesthetized by the sameness of his days. He lets his job get to him so badly that he's on track for ulcers and heart attacks until he visits a hypnotist, whose therapy frees Peter from his troubling concerns. At the end of the hypnosis session, Peter has settled into such a casual come-what-may attitude that it doesn't faze him when the hypnotist suddenly croaks from a heart attack.

Peter takes his new mindset out for a spin at his workplace, and in the picture's most arch satirical statement, his cavalier attitude is mistaken for ruthless upward mobility. The unsubtle implication is that Peter's employers distinguish him from his coworkers only when he starts acting in what appears to be a Machiavellian fashion, in effect making him more like a member of the ruling class than one of the working class. Beneath this misunderstanding is the sharp irony that Peter actually has become the exact opposite of the ruling class: He's an empowered member of the working class. But the idea of an underling becoming empowered is so foreign to administrators including Bill Lumbergh (Gary Cole) that they see their own heartlessness in Peter's carefree demeanor.

In one of the movie's funniest scenes, Peter gets called into a meeting with two efficiency experts, both named Bob, who explain that they're about to lay off Peter's closest friends in the office. They then ask him to describe an average workday, with the underlying threat that if his description doesn't pass muster, his will be the next job eliminated. Embracing the fact that he has nothing to lose, Peter launches into a monologue about corporate life as embittered as that delivered by Norton's character in *Fight Club*, but with deadpan humor in place of the homicidal rage in *Fight Club*.

> PETER: I come in at least fifteen minutes late. I use the side door — that way, Lumbergh can't see me. After that I just sort of space out for about an hour.... I just stare at my desk, but it looks like I'm working. I do that for probably another hour after lunch, too. I'd say in a given week, I probably only do about fifteen minutes of real, actual work.... The thing is, Bob, it's not that I'm lazy. It's that I just don't care.... It's a problem of motivation, all right? Now if I work my ass off and Initech ships a few more units, I don't

see another dime. So where's the motivation? ... I have eight different bosses right now, so that means when I make a mistake, I have eight different people coming by to tell me about it. That's my only real motivation, is to not be hassled. That and the fear of losing my job. But you know, Bob, that'll only make someone work just hard enough not to get fired.

While *Office Space* is rewarding as a compendium of effective running gags, it also builds to a potent climax. Peter's freewheeling attitude makes him something of a hero in the eyes of his coworkers, who still cower in fear of losing their insignificant jobs, so it makes sense when he becomes the ringleader of a gang who scheme to rip off their employer, Initech Corporation. Their justification, which is a twisted manifestation of the frustration to which anyone who has had McJobs can relate, is that the company deserves to be screwed in exchange for the way it regularly screws its employees.

The scheme backfires, however: The friends' cyber-age plan to drain money via computer trickery unexpectedly pilfers a huge amount of money at once, instead of the easily missed trickle of small amounts the crew

Management material: Ron Livingston (left), the worry-free protagonist of Mike Judge's biting satire *Office Space*, gives a pair of efficiency experts (John C. McGinley, center, and Paul Wilson) a piece of his mind (Twentieth Century–Fox).

meant to purloin. The coworkers' aghast reaction to their mistake is a telling comment on modern attitudes, because the shock doesn't make them regret their embezzlement. Instead, it makes them regret that they didn't come up with a foolproof means of stealing. Their contempt for their employers is absolute, and their respect for the employer-employee relationship is absolutely nil.

So when Peter decides to return the money and accept responsibility for spearheading the scheme, it's less about a criminal feeling guilty than it is about a man throwing himself onto a grenade to protect his buddies. These characters are in a war to save their own dignity, and if one of them has to go down so the rest can fight another day, so be it. That Judge finds a wry way to extricate Peter from his dire straits, while still sticking it to the inhuman company, suggests that the director's contempt for this sort of corporate culture is as deeply rooted as his characters'.

Judge's satire manifests in aspects of the film other than the main plot, often with greater subtlety. One of the funniest subplots involves Peter's love interest, Joanna (Jennifer Aniston), who waits tables at a homogenized chain eatery modeled on T.G.I. Friday's. The uniforms of the wait staff in the restaurant are festooned with pins that the manager (played by Judge) refers to as "flair," and on a couple of occasions, Joanna is criticized for not wearing enough flair. She asks how many pins she's supposed to wear, and is fed a line of nonsensical corporate-speak about how the company shouldn't tell her what to do — instead, she should want what the company wants, even if she's never told what that is.

Joanna's consternation is palpable when she tries to decipher this nonsense (all so she can retain a job she dislikes), and the thrust of the flair debate — that the company is forcing her to act in an individualistic fashion, then putting incomprehensible restrictions on how her individualism should manifest — is instantly familiar to anyone who has gotten a brainless directive from a work superior. So it's both amusing and poignant when, after Peter asks for an explanation of his girlfriend's work worries, she makes this strained utterance: "I don't really like to talk about my flair."

Probably the most famous exercise in Gen-X workplace wish-fulfillment occurs in *American Beauty*, during which pent-up magazine writer Lester Burnham (Kevin Spacey) releases his tension by blackmailing his employer with the threat of revealing the infidelity and embezzlement of one of his superiors.

Lester is so empowered by his devious activities that he bleats the acclaimed film's oft-cited soundbite: "I rule!" Aside from providing the cheap laugh of a grown man speaking in youthful vernacular, the line puts across an idea that's essential to Gen-X movies about work, and Gen-X movies in general. By saying "I rule" upon taking control of his own life, Lester underlines that previously he didn't rule. He neither dominated his own life nor held power over other people. Because Gen Xers have such an acrimonious relationship with societal institutions, the need that they and the characters they create have to exert control over their worlds is a crucial recurring theme.

After Lester extricates himself from his job and takes with him a substantial severance package, he gets new employment at a burger joint, explaining to the restaurant's befuddled manager that "I'm looking for the least possible amount of responsibility." These changes help Lester reclaim some of the virility he had when he was younger, but they shock the other members of his nuclear family, wife Carolyn (Annette Bening) and teenage daughter Janie (Thora Birch), as seen in this pointed dinner-table exchange:

> LESTER: Janie, today I quit my job and then I told my boss to go fuck himself. Then I blackmailed him for almost $60,0000. Pass the asparagus.
> CAROLYN: Your father seems to think this kind of behavior is something to be proud of.
> LESTER: And your mother seems to prefer that I go through life like a fucking prisoner, with my dick in a mason jar under the sink.

The idea running through all of these scenes, from *Fight Club* to *American Beauty* and beyond, is that forcing workers to conform to dehumanized corporate agendas stifles their souls. The edgy implication is that some oppressed workers will snap under the pressure and become violent, while others will subvert their oppression by taking power away from their "captors." This subject matter is consistent with the fact that Gen-X cinema — and Generation X itself — are still young. Adjusting to the demands of the workplace is an important process in the beginning of every person's professional life. In fact, finding a professional identity is often as trying, if not more so, than finding a personal identity.

Entertaining evidence of how deeply personal and professional evolution can be entwined is found in Kenneth Lonergan's *You Can Count on Me*, which in part tracks the workplace travails of Sammy Prescott (Laura Linney), a single mother who works as the lending officer of a small-town bank. The bank's manager, Brian Everett (Matthew Broderick), is a tightly wound company man with such a skewed idea of how to exert control that he chides one of his employees for adding garish colors to the display of her computer monitor. Sammy and Brian clash because she frequently leaves work during the day to attend to her young son, but beneath their quarreling is lust, which is consummated in a hotel-room tryst.

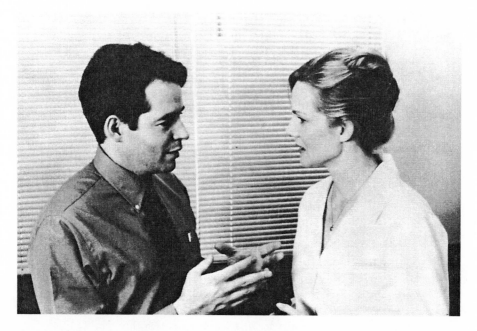

A matter of tryst: The intricacies of workplace relationships are captured in Kenneth Lonergan's *You Can Count on Me*, with Matthew Broderick as a bank manager sleeping with one of his employees (Laura Linney) (Paramount Classics).

Brian, who is married, predictably abandons the affair when Sammy starts to want more than frivolous sex, and the relationship comes to a head during a tense showdown in the bank manager's office: Brian suggests that Sammy should quit, and she fires back that she could easily reveal their affair and cause much more havoc in his life than he could in hers. Sammy's feeling of empowerment and righteous indignation is given extra weight by Brian's off-handed comment as she leaves the room: "Yeah. Fine. Why don't you just take over the whole bank?" From the look on her face, viewers can tell she might do that very thing.

Fringe Benefits

Reacting to the claustrophobia of life in a "cubicle farm" (the pervasive slang term for offices comprising square cages) is a uniquely contemporary issue. The corporate consolidation facilitated by the electronic conveyance of information, to say nothing of deregulation of major industries and the ascendance of monopolistic megacorporations, led to a radical shift in how workplaces were imagined in the last part of the twentieth century. Yet the reaction to burdensome indentured servitude also is a timeless theme, because the frustrations felt by the characters in *Fight Club*, *American Beauty*, and *Office Space* have precedents dating back at least as far as Charles Dickens's immortal *A Christmas Carol*, originally published in 1843. For isn't Bob Crachit, the frustrated accountant whom Ebenezer Scrooge keeps under his thumb, a precursor to the modern office drone?

An important connection shared by the drones in *Fight Club*, *Office Space*, and *American Beauty* is that all have comfortable jobs. The characters obviously are not stimulated by their work, but, excepting the waitress in *Office Space*, they are white-collar workers with decent homes, decent cars, and disposable income. So from the perspective of someone further down the socioeconomic ladder, the claustrophobia felt by these characters might seem petty. It's interesting, then, to contrast the ivory-tower attitudes of frustrated white-collar workers with the workplace experiences of less affluent characters in Gen-X movies.

Clerks, the first picture written and directed by New Jersey-bred auteur Kevin Smith, is among the most vivid illustrations of young people stuck in dead-end jobs. The irony behind the film, of course, is that working a dead-end job like the ones depicted in the movie allowed Smith to vault himself into the ranks of internationally known filmmakers. Prior to making the picture, Smith worked in a New Jersey convenience store, a job that gave him two things: the chance to see people at their lazy, inconsiderate, wacky worst; and plenty of time to talk with coworkers during lulls in customer traffic. Following the model that worked wonders for countless indie filmmakers in the 1990s, Smith took stock of his life and sought shortcuts around the obstacles blocking his dreams of becoming a filmmaker. He then decided to chronicle life in a convenience store, using the actual store in which he worked as his primary location.

The verisimilitude of the location converged with Smith's intimate knowledge of his subject matter in a vibrant tone, so even though *Clerks* is crude from a technical perspective and episodic from narrative perspective, it pulses with life. More importantly, it pulses with anger at the inanity of what some people have to do to for living. The two clerks in the movie, reliable but caustic Dante (Brian O'Halloran) and flaky rascal Randal (Jeff Anderson), ooze contempt for their customers because their customers, intentionally or not, ooze contempt for them.

These clerks rudely chat with coworkers while ringing up customers' purchases, unfailingly complain about patrons who request any degree of assistance, and dislike their customers as much as their poor service suggests they do. The film's disbelief at everyday stupidity is expressed in startlingly foul-mouthed monologues and nasty visual gags. In one bit, a woman in Dante's store holds up a can and asks "How much is this?," at which point the camera zooms back to reveal a huge sign, right behind the woman, with the price emblazoned on it. For his part, Randal has become an artist at dispensing bad service. He spits in a customer's face, sells cigarettes to a grade schooler, and, in his finest moment, closes his video store to drive across town and rent a movie from another shop.

Typical customers in *Clerks* include the blowhard who storms into Dante's store to complain that Randal's store is a half-hour late in opening. The guy slams down his video and tears into Dante, fuming that he doesn't have time to waste, and that Dante better get the video store's clerk to show up. The customer storms out of Dante's store but leaves his car keys on Dante's counter, so Dante discreetly drops the car keys into a garbage can.

By portraying stores as prisons from which any exit is an escape, Smith tells us that these characters are in "retail hell"—the lead character's name is Dante, after all. The metaphor is overwrought, but Smith's humor is so gleefully black-hearted that it's easy to allow him some self-indulgence.

Like his subsequent examinations of sexuality (in *Chasing Amy*) and religion (in *Dogma*), Smith's study of work ultimately favors jokes over insight, so *Clerks* is best appreciated as an exhibition of Gen-X attitude. This attitude has great credibility, because viewers believe that these blue-collar characters could end up in meaningless jobs while they postpone their entrance into real life. And even if the film doesn't convey a strong sense of the adults living inside these postadolescent clerks, the offscreen payoff of what Smith did after his tenure in retail suggests that the wit these characters bring to their mischief might someday be put to practical use. So in a sense, the film suggests that these characters will be saved from servitude by the irreverent attitude that allows them to move through their numbing workdays without going insane. This implication, borne out by Smith's offscreen career trajectory, is an unusually positive celebration of Generation X's collective identity.

Whereas *Clerks'* portrayal of the workplace plays one note again and again, *Reality Bites* presents a spectrum of attitudes toward gainful employment. The most resonant work-related vibe in the movie probably is that exuded by Troy (Ethan Hawke), a young, educated man who willfully extracts himself from the "rat race" not to pursue greater or more creative goals, but because work is too damn much work. When he's fired from a dead-end job at a newsstand for stealing a candy bar, we see that Troy's contempt for upward mobility verges on the self-destructive: He's so opposed to trying to get ahead that he actively courts dismissal from awful jobs. Yet his investment in his jobs is so minimal that he never feels the frustration behind the workplace rebellions in *Fight Club*, *Office Space*, and *American Beauty*.

All of these characters, however, from the pent-up rebels to the laid-back slackers, are hyperbolic. One extreme illustrates the price of caring too much about meaningless work, and the other illustrates the price of caring too little. Therefore, it's heartening to note that *Reality Bites* also maps some of the middle ground between these extremes.

Troy's friend Vickie (Janeane Garofalo) talks a good game about hating corporate culture, but nonetheless accepts a job as manager of a Gap franchise, thereby rising within the culture she disdains and in the process confronting the hypocrisy of her posturing. Conversely, Michael (Ben Stiller), Troy's opposite number and romantic rival, has the unapologetic upward mobility of a 1980s yuppie, proving that not every cinematic Gen Xer fits the slacker stereotype. And Lelaina (Winona Ryder), the woman torn between Michael and Troy, represents yet another professional conundrum: She wants to be an artist. Her ambition withstands the scrutiny of her slacker peers, because she's pursuing a dream instead of a paycheck. Yet she also craves career advancement, just not as much as Michael does. Lelaina, therefore, represents the most poignant crisis of Gen-X workers: how to survive in a corporatized culture without sacrificing your soul.

The title character of *Erin Brockovich* surmounts that crisis in high style. In a stranger-than-fiction story adapted by screenwriter Susannah Grant from the life of the real Erin Brockovich, a former beauty queen saddled with three young children, an embarrassing work history, and a seemingly bottomless reservoir of bad luck, stumbles into a job as a clerk in a law firm. Erin (Julia Roberts) uncovers information about chemical pollution in a small California town, then juggles her parenting duties, a new relationship with Harley-riding neighbor George (Aaron Eckhart), and the difficulty of settling into a new office environment with her crusade to find the cause of the pollution.

Erin becomes obsessed with work because she realizes that illegal dumping by massive utility company Pacific Gas & Electric might have caused horrific illnesses in a huge number of families living near a PG&E facility. Shifting into ersatz detective mode, Erin dredges up evidence and witnesses linking PG&E to the illnesses, thereby becoming a heroic figure to her new friends in the small town. The price of her valor is that she loses an enormous amount of time with her children, and dooms her affair with George by essentially using him as a free baby-sitter.

As noble as her devotion to the victims of pollution is, what really seems to motivate Erin is the rush she discovers when she finds a place for herself in the world. Prior to her legal-investigation work, Erin was stuck in the endless cycle of McJob after McJob, because she never stayed in a workplace long enough, or committed herself sufficiently to a particular workplace, to advance. Yet once she finds meaningful employment, Erin directs the intense focus and deep compassion she previously had applied only to parenting toward her professional life. The difference between her new situation and her previous jobs is that investigating the pollution has a use. In sharp contrast to the workers in movies ranging from *Fight Club* to *Clerks*, Erin helps real people in a tangible way, with tangible goals in mind: making the polluters accept responsibility, and gaining restitution for the suffering the polluters caused.

Erin is different from the frustrated working stiffs of other Gen-X movies in the most important regard: She draws strength from her job more than her job draws strength from her. Yet there are myriad ironies to the significance of this portrayal. Erin falls into her job, so instead of following the traditional model of a logical career trajectory, she benefits from her professional wanderlust because she ends up in the last place she ever would have expected. Also, Erin succeeds in an office atmosphere despite having a massive distrust of authority. And finally, she thrives in the sterile world of a law firm despite dressing with the in-your-face sexiness of a showgirl.

Because of these delicious nuances, Erin is distinctly a Gen-X figure even though generational identity is not presented as an important part of her character. She thrives in corporate culture not by becoming part of the system, but by forcing the system to make room for her.

The difficulties that Erin experiences when trying to create this niche for herself are shown in a handful of relationships. The most entertaining of them is her contentious interaction with her employer, lawyer Ed Masry (Albert Finney). At first, he's startled by this loud-mouthed, demonstrative, voluptuous woman who manipulates her way into a job. Then he's put off by her confrontational attitude; when he politely suggests that miniskirts and low-cut shirts might not be appropriate dress for a law firm, she fires back with a barb about his tacky ties. Ed even fires Erin at one point, in part because of a misunderstanding, but he eventually bends to her willfulness when he sees the quality and quantity of her work. Winning Ed over is a cakewalk, however, compared to surmounting the cattiness with which Erin's female coworkers cajole her.

The dynamic between eroticized Erin and her conservative peers is a common one — the difficulty attractive, sexually confident women have

Baby on board: The travails of Erin Brockovich (Julia Roberts), an ex–beauty queen who becomes an anti-pollution crusader in Steven Soderbergh's *Erin Brockovich*, reflect Generation X's ambivalence about work (Universal Pictures).

befriending women who perceive them as threats—but in the context of a discussion of Gen-X portrayals of work, Erin's conflicts with the women in her office can be seen as a clash between old values and new ones. Her coworkers believe in modesty, timidity, and deference to authority. Erin believes in flaunting her assets, speaking her mind, and questioning authority. In a way, she's an antiestablishment figure clashing with the Establishment represented by her old-fashioned coworkers. So when she shows her "peers" what she's made of, not by compromising her edginess but by utilizing it to its full extent, the victories she enjoys—pinning responsibility on PG&E, winning millions for the diseased townsfolk, earning a $2 million bonus for herself—are rewards for her nonconventional pursuit of noble goals.

A final irony to the portrayal of this brash character is that *Erin Brockovich* was Soderbergh's commercial breakthrough—and also his least experimental film. Soderbergh pulled the reverse of Erin's trick: Whereas she used nonconventional means to win a place for herself in the mainstream, Soderbergh used conventional means to achieve the same goal. He then subverted his mainstream success by returning to nonconventional storytelling for his follow-up film, *Traffic*, which built on his *Erin Brockovich* momentum to become his second blockbuster in less than a year. His incredible accomplishment also netted twin Oscar nominations for Best Director (a feat last achieved by Michael Curtiz six decades previous) and a win for *Traffic*.

Erin fought her way up the ladder, and Soderbergh charmed his way up, but they both got to the top—a dual celebration of Generation X's ability to find a place in the professional world without selling its collective soul.

Business as Unusual

Considering the whole of Gen-X cinema's workplace commentary, a couple of interesting commonalties come into focus. First is yet another piece of evidence illustrating how Gen-X cinema advances the ideology of the cinema that came before, that of the boomer directors who changed Hollywood forever in the late 1960s and throughout the 1970s. The 1970s were memorably tagged the "Me Decade" because when boomers began to doubt that they could change the world, they redirected their energy toward changing themselves. That focus on the self morphed into something ugly during the 1980s, a.k.a. the "Greed Decade."

While these are of course gross generalizations, the trajectory drawn by numerous pundits shows boomers giving up on social change during the 1970s, then pursuing monetary wealth — the goal, ironically, that drove the postwar boom during which they were born — in the 1980s.

Therefore, Generation X's self-driven attitude toward work fits into the social continuity of the last several decades. If Gen Xers were raised to believe that work exists only to provide money, and not to run the machinery of society or fulfill some other noble obligation, then it follows that Gen Xers would have a negative attitude toward work. Furthermore, if Gen Xers observed their parents drawing empty rewards from work — if they observed their parents' frustration at prioritizing careers over personal fulfillment — then it makes sense that Gen Xers would pursue gratification outside of the workplace, seeking lives more rewarding than their parents'.

Yet another wrinkle to this generational continuity is the fact that throughout the 1970s and 1980s, members of the boomer generation migrated away from the traditional workplace as a reaction to the frustration under discussion here. In one extreme, hippies started back-to-nature businesses, joined communes, and became artists. In the opposite extreme, yuppies became independent entrepreneurs, with the most visible examples being the technology gurus who became millionaires and billionaires by imagining new business opportunities suited to the Information Age. Combined with the frustration felt by those who remained in traditional career trajectories, the exodus of boomers into nontraditional businesses sent a message that working for someone else — "the man," as identified in boomer-speak — is a soul-killer. Is it any wonder, then, that Gen Xers hit adulthood with such confusion about, and resentment of, work?

Finally, the Gen-X attitude toward work fits into the larger issue of Generation X's attitude toward institutions in general. Just as many members of this group sneer when discussing big companies and traditional career goals, they sneer when discussing politicians, television shows, and anything else woven into the fabric of mainstream culture. The disenfranchised members of Generation X overflow with contempt for the institutions that they believe make modern American life impersonal and oppressive, so communicating that contempt is a kind of code.

The code manifests in superficial things like ironic references to pop culture, but also in more probing things such as the snide discussions of work issues that permeate *Office Space*, *Clerks*, *Reality Bites* and other films. Lacking faith in the cold parts of modern American society is a badge of honor among certain segments of Generation X, so when one cinematic Gen Xer expresses that mistrust to another, it's like two members of a private club sharing a secret handshake. Along with irony, disrespect for traditional careerism is part of the shorthand of Generation X.

7

From Romance to Rape

Love and sexuality may be the topics with which Gen-X directors have grappled in the greatest variety of ways. While their films depict a dizzying spectrum of sexual behavior—flirtation, monogamy, homosexuality, exhibitionism, and so on—it's comforting and even a bit endearing to note that despite such polemical sexual content, Gen-X depictions of love often are as starry-eyed as those in classic Hollywood films. Although Gen Xers came of age in an era when free love gave way to sexual paranoia, they still see a vision of commitment and devotion through the fog of deviancy and sexual violence that fills many of their pictures.

As does any love affair or sexual relationship, this discussion of love and sexuality begins with the delicious joy of flirting. It's a lost art, given that changing social mores have led to sex getting introduced into the dating ritual earlier every generation, so the moments in Gen-X films when characters truly attempt to know each other before heading to bed are precious. One good example of such an attempt is Audrey Wells's modest directorial debut, *The Truth About Cats & Dogs*, in which two characters seduce each other over the phone; this allows the female of the would-be couple to hide her looks, about which she is insecure. A more significant exhibition of flirting, however, appears in Richard Linklater's *Before Sunrise*—ironically, a film in which two lovers have sex on their first date.

Because American slacker Jesse and French student Céline consummate their affair with an outdoors encounter that is played offscreen, a cynical reading of *Before Sunrise* is that the characters' long, probing conversation is merely glorified foreplay. Their mutual attraction is palpable from the moment they meet, so there's something to that interpretation, but a more generous reading is that Jesse and Céline never presume their interaction will lead to intercourse. The depth with which they explore and challenge each other's beliefs proves that their wandering conversation is fueled as much by fascination as it is by arousal. They achieve true intimacy long before they touch each other's bodies.

For that reason, *Before Sunrise* towers as one of the most poignant statements about love in all Gen-X cinema. The ambiguous note on which the film ends only accentuates and deepens this poignancy: Jesse and Céline head to their respective train cars and leave Vienna in separate directions, so it's left to viewers to imagine if love will lead them back to each other or merely haunt their hearts. Given the Gen-X fixation on separation — from family, from social institutions, from each other — the images that Linklater presents of these two lovers becoming separated are heartbreaking for reasons above and beyond their role in the narrative.

Another couple who end up apart are Jackie Brown (Pam Grier) and Max Cherry (Robert Forster), two compelling characters in Quentin Tarantino's *Pulp Fiction* follow-up, *Jackie Brown*. Although ostensibly a caper flick, the film achieves its greatest resonance as a love story involving Jackie, a stewardess drawn to crime so she can create opportunities that evade her in legitimate society, and Max, the bail bondsman with whom she becomes professionally involved. Without going into the intricacies of the plot, it's sufficient to say that Tarantino puts these immensely likable characters together, and ably communicates that they find their similarities (limited options, advancing years) much more powerful than their differences (Jackie is black, Max white).

One of the warmest moments in the film is a throwaway bit during which Max drives in his car and teaches himself the words to a song by the Delfonics, a soul group to whom he was introduced by Jackie. This vignette shows a man trying to understand something about the woman to whom he's attracted, and it echoes how Jesse and Céline studied each other before advancing their relationship. Both couples comprise men and women from different worlds, and just as their eventual separations make statements about Gen-X disenfranchisement, the couples' sincere endeavors to bridge their differences make statements about the best, most tolerant, most hopeful part of Generation X's collective soul. Connection isn't impossible, these relationships say; it just occurs unexpectedly.

This same statement is reiterated again and again throughout Gen-X cinema. Look at the affection beyond reason that bonds a hit man to the wife of his brutal employer in *Pulp Fiction*, a thief to a federal marshal in *Out of Sight*, and a bisexual gangster's moll to a female ex-con in *Bound*. These relationships all begin with flirtation, a notable and charming instance of characters benefiting from Generation X's gift of gab.

Let's Stay Together

Flirting, if the stars line up right, leads to love, and the romantic couplings in *Before Sunrise*, *Jackie Brown*, *Pulp Fiction*, *Out of Sight*, and *Bound* all seem rooted in genuine love. Yet in each of these instances, the thrill is in the hunt: We see characters circle toward each other and perhaps join briefly, but we're given no assurances that their relationships will survive. So it's interesting to contrast the flirtation-based movies with Gen-X movies that actually depict full-blown love affairs. Looking at such films, it becomes clear that illusion is a fundamental element in Generation X's vision of committed love; just as their vision of courtship manifests in old-Hollywood innocence, their vision of love reaches the screen as a kind of ephemeral wish-fulfillment.

For instance, look at how Baz Luhrmann filmed *William Shakespeare's Romeo + Juliet*, the brazen adaptation that boosted the careers of Leonardo DiCaprio and Claire Danes, the actors who incarnate the bard's star-crossed lovers. Previous cinematic versions of the enduring tragedy earnestly mimicked the chronological milieu of the play (as in Franco Zefferelli's *Romeo and Juliet*) or recast it in modern terms (as in *West Side Story*), yet Luhrmann's film juxtaposes the ancient and the modern in a frenetic pop-culture hodgepodge. The language is Shakespeare's iambic pentameter, minus the chunks of text Luhrmann found superfluous, but the setting is modern: Day-Glo colors, blazing guns, pounding rock music. It's as if Luhrmann found Shakespeare's theme of a love more powerful than the will to live so archaic that it needed to be presented amid other anachronisms. So even though his picture feels sweepingly romantic, there's an inherent cynicism buried in its style. By putting ancient British language in the mouths of unmistakably modern Americans, Luhrmann forced viewers to confront the artifice of his enterprise during every scene.

Illusion also is a pervasive theme in Neil LaBute's *Nurse Betty*, the warmhearted but edgy film with which LaBute extracted himself from the ghetto of misogynistic social commentary. The picture's titular character is a small-town waitress infatuated with David Ravell, a fictional character who appears on her favorite soap opera. Betty Sizemore (Renée Zellweger) is stuck in a dead-end marriage to a cad, but when her husband is brutally murdered before her eyes, the shock shunts Betty into a semipermanent dream state. She treks from the Midwest to Hollywood so she can join David Ravell, who she now believes is real. George McCord (Greg Kinnear), the actor who plays David, mistakes Betty's affection for a Method-style audition, so he feeds her illusion.

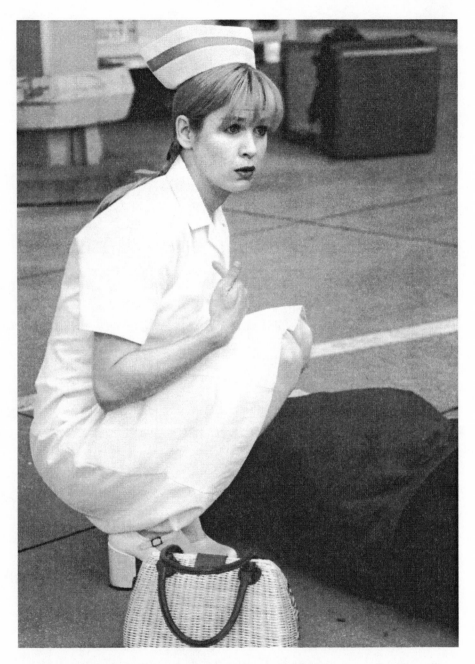

Victim of love: A small-town waitress (Renée Zellweger) becomes the object of a hit man's affection in Neil LaBute's oddball film about romance and illusion, *Nurse Betty* (USA Films/Universal Pictures).

This setup allows LaBute to mingle several varying perceptions of what is actually occurring. In reality, Betty is a widow stalking an actor; in George's mind, she's an actress stalking a part; and in Betty's mind, she's connecting with her true love. Yet another layer of illusion is the pretense that George makes of being the kind person whom Betty imagines David Ravell to be. The stage is set for a horrific comedown, because LaBute portrays Betty as an almost virginal innocent who deserves the happiness that awaits her only in fiction. Yet the filmmakers contrive a way to give Betty her sanity and her dream, a reward for her ability to imagine a world better than the real one.

A dreamer who isn't as fortunate is Charlie (Morgan Freeman), the hit man who kills Betty's husband and then chases her across America because she's a witness who needs to be eliminated. Charlie is impressed by Betty when he encounters her at the beginning of the movie, and he slowly gives in to the delusion that he and Betty will run off together. If innocence is at the heart of Betty's fantasy, however, evil is at the heart of Charlie's. He's moved into madness because of his guilt at a life spent taking life, so he fixates on Betty as his absolution — the prize for turning his back on murder. Just as the film spins events to give Betty the happiness she deserves, it twists to put Charlie into his place: the grave.

The killer's dream was tarnished because of the life he led, the movie says, whereas Betty's dream is as pure as her life. However, the love that Charlie develops for Betty is the most powerful in the film, because it forces him to evolve into a new identity. So it's fitting that Betty ends up alone at the end of the film. Neither George nor Charlie deserves her, but through her experiences with the two men, she becomes a person who deserves her own sweet company. Betty learns to love herself, so she no longer needs any man's love for validation.

A much darker quest for validation is depicted in Kimberly Peirce's shattering *Boys Don't Cry*, the true-life story of a girl who masqueraded as a boy. Teena Brandon (Hilary Swank) has such profound gender-identification issues that she regularly risks physical danger by dressing as the opposite sex, under the flip-flopped name Brandon Teena, and even engaging in physical relationships with women. Teena's affection for women is a complex aspect of her personality, because it illustrates that she loathes her sexuality, not her sex; the genuine love that develops between her and Lana (Chloe Sevigny) allows Teena to be the best man she can be. Yet while Lana finds that she can live comfortably inside her lover's illusion — their first sexual encounter is a touching testament to love's ability to make the strange seem normal — the small-minded townsfolk with whom Teena and her girlfriend interact are shocked into violence when they discover Teena's ruse.

Teena is brutally raped and murdered for her illusion, which caused no harm other than the pain of confusion and intolerant anger. That the basic facts of this tragic figure's life and death were extracted from reality, instead of from some screenwriter's imagination, affirms why some of Generation X's apprehensions about modern society are anything but paranoia. Betty finds happiness by parting ways with her illusion of love, but Teena dies horribly for refusing to relinquish hers.

Another poignant, albeit fictional, film about illusions is Keith Gordon's *Waking the Dead*, adapted by Scott Spencer from Robert Dillon's novel. The picture depicts the relationship between an ambitious young politician, Fielding Pierce (Billy Crudup), and the compassionate activist he loves, Sarah Williams (Jennifer Connelly). Echoing the imagery of the Gen-X flirtation films, Fielding and Sarah gravitate toward each other because they're different: They realize they can fill in the gaps in each other's personas and fuse into a powerful joint entity. The depth of their bond shows in the aching performances of Crudup and Connelly, who pull off the difficult task of making a young couple appear to share mature love. The intensity of the characters' bond in seen in this exchange, prompted when Fielding is offered a political opportunity that Sarah thinks is beneath him:

> SARAH: I don't want to watch you turn into a cog in their machine.
> FIELDING: Fucking condescending. Sometimes cogs can make machines run a little bit better....
> SARAH: Mostly they turn in circles and wear out and they get replaced. Come work at the church with me.
> FIELDING: Oh yes, don't work for the U.S. government. Work for the church. Work for the people who brought us the Children's Crusade and the Inquisition. That's a moral step up.
> SARAH: It's so infuriating loving you sometimes.
> FIELDING: Well, the feeling's mutual.

Gordon smartly relegates the physical aspect of the characters' relationship to one heated sex scene, so viewers don't see these attractive actors entwined until the relationship has resonance. Further deepening the movie is hindsight: The first scene shows Fielding learning that Sarah has been killed in a terrorist bombing, so we spend the whole movie learning what he mourns and then feeling his bereavement with him. When visions of Sarah start invading Fielding's consciousness as if he's being haunted by a ghost, we see the visions as he does: echoes of love. The visions are yet another manifestation of the distance that defines Gen-X existence, only this time the disconnectedness is more poignant because it's a reminder of lost connectedness.

Given these loaded connotations, it's highly ironic that *Waking the Dead* takes place in the 1970s and 1980s. On a subtextual level, the film is as much a eulogy for the idealism that suffered the killing frost of the big chill as it is a eulogy for Sarah. Therefore, it's inspiring that Fielding eventually makes peace with his lost lover's memory by embracing her dream. Even though Fielding compromised his political idealism to win a seat in Congress, the film ends with the implication that he'll mature into a leader of whom Sarah could be proud.

Sometimes love takes a less direct route than it does in *Boys Don't Cry* and *Waking the Dead*. While the obstacles that interrupt those affairs are relatively distinct (social intolerance, political differences), the obstacles separating lovers in *Chuck & Buck*, *Chasing Amy*, and *Keeping the Faith* are more nettlesome.

The title characters of *Chuck & Buck* are successful music-industry executive Charlie "Chuck" Sitter (played by tall, dark, and handsome Chris Weitz) and repressed man-child Buck O'Brien (played by small, pale, and gangly Mike White). The childhood friends were once an inseparable duo—"Chuck and Buck"—but for reasons that Charlie would rather not discuss, the twenty-seven-year-olds haven't seen each other since they were eleven. When Buck's mother dies, the men are reunited at her funeral, but it's immediately clear that time has done its damage: Charlie is a slick, cold professional engaged to sophisticated beauty Carlyn (Beth Colt), while Buck is a dim shut-in fixated on the trappings of his childhood.

At the funeral, though, we discover that Buck may not be the innocent he seems: He downs rum with familiar ease and casually tries to grope Charlie's genitals. Charlie predictably flees, but Buck pursues his childhood friend across several states to Charlie's home in Los Angeles. Costar White, who also wrote the movie, takes a wonderfully direct route to showing Buck's inner workings. His performance lets viewers see every odd thing that passes through Buck's brain, whether it's pain, longing, joy, or the staticky noise of confusion. This conveys that Buck is fueled by pure desire — not twisted desire, but the genuine need to connect with someone who once loved him. That someone is Charlie, with whom Buck engaged in playful sexual activity when the two were children.

Through a believably odd series of events, Charlie and Buck find themselves at an impasse, because Buck can't let go of the bond connecting him to his friend, and Charlie has spent his life forgetting that he and Buck used to fellate and otherwise gratify each other. The characters break this impasse through a distinctly 1990s bargain: Charlie agrees to one more night of physical love with his friend in exchange for getting his life back so he can marry Carlyn. Buck even attends the wedding.

Issues of sexual identity are similarly mired in *Chasing Amy*, about a young man who falls in love with a lesbian while also sorting out the loving feelings he has toward his male roommate. (A detailed examination of *Chasing Amy* appears later in this chapter.)

Finally, in *Keeping the Faith*, a priest and a rabbi compete for the affections of the same woman, forcing them to address their ideas about friendship, loyalty, religious devotion, and love. They eventually find a novel solution, because the rabbi ends up with his true love (the woman), and the priest ends up with his (God). The theological aspects of the film are discussed in Chapter 10, so for now it's sufficient to note that *Keeping the Faith* offers yet another example of lovers and/or would-be lovers in a Gen-X movie wrestling with issues that affect them on both personal and spiritual levels.

In all of these films, from *William Shakespeare's Romeo + Juliet* to *Keeping the Faith*, love is presented as an otherworldly force that connects people from different worlds, sometimes softening the friction created by difference and sometimes revealing the glory of individuality. In the most disturbing of these films, lovers end up apart (often because of death), but their love remains intact. And in the most comforting of these films, lovers find ways to stay together despite the forces pulling them apart. One set of images speaks to the ideal of love, and the other to the reality of love. That there sometimes is but a fine line separating the ideal from the reality is what makes Generation X's cinematic vision of love so fresh and young: Even at their most cynical, these filmmakers seem to believe that some emotional bonds can't be broken.

With This Ring

Significantly, a key issue connecting the relationships in *Waking the Dead*, *Chasing Amy* and other Gen-X films about powerful love relationships is that the paramours are unmarried. Reflecting how deeply divorce changed American families during the formative years of Generation X, filmmakers born in this era share a vision of marriage as dark as their vision of love is bright. Statistics ratify this assertion, as the percentage of young couples who marry dropped substantially from 1970 to 1992. Men aged twenty to twenty-four in 1992, for instance, were exactly half as likely to marry as their counterparts in 1970.[1]

The bleakness of the marital landscape, as depicted by Gen-X filmmakers, is epitomized by the preponderance of stories about infidelity. *American Beauty* hinges on two acts of adultery: Lester's imagined dalliances with his daughter's young schoolmate, and the actual tryst that Lester's wife has with a real-estate mogul. There even is another facet to the film's dramatization of extramarital sex, because Lester's married next-door neighbor, repressed soldier Frank Fitts (Chris Cooper), makes a sexual overture to Lester. Combined with the images of duplicity, oppression, denial, and resentment that pepper the film, the adultery in *American Beauty* conveys an idea that marriage is a trap at best and a death sentence at worst. Significantly, Frank's wife (Alison Janney) is depicted as a zombie-like housefrau beaten down by fear of confrontations with her husband.

As with everything else in the film, however, *American Beauty*'s vision of wedded misery is exaggerated beyond reason. So this aspect of the movie's thematic statement ultimately is instructive not in literal terms, but for how it represents the extreme of pervasive Gen-X imagery.

Neil LaBute's brutal domestic drama *Your Friends and Neighbors* offers as depressing a viewpoint as *American Beauty*'s. The film portrays the interaction of several young professionals, most of whom are in committed relationships. Despite his long-term involvement with Terri (Catherine Keener), insufferable Jerry (Ben Stiller) becomes obsessed with bedding Mary (Amy Brenneman), the troubled wife of his friend Barry (Aaron Eckhart). *Your Friends and Neighbors* shows young people circling each other's romantic partners like sharks closing in for the kill, which amplifies the *American Beauty* assertion that marriage is worse than meaningless, that marriage somehow encourages infidelity. The characters in these films are filled with a profound level of bitterness, suggesting that Gen-X filmmakers haven't made peace with the changes that affected the institution of marriage during their early years.

Slightly more positive imagery is put across in Alexander Payne's *Election* and Steven Soderbergh's *sex, lies, and videotape*, both of which show women escaping failed marriages.

In *Election*, schoolteacher Jim McAllister (Matthew Broderick) has a midlife crisis that leads him into the bed of his best friend's wife, who is crushed because her husband just committed adultery with a teenaged student. Jim's duplicitous ways eventually ruin his relationships with his wife and his mistress, and he even manages to lose his job. While Payne doesn't present this material moralistically, his choice to show Jim suffering for his sins reflects a sense of right and wrong that's painfully absent from *American Beauty* and *Your Friends and Neighbors*, in which characters are trapped in cycles of abusive and/or self-destructive behavior.

sex, lies, and videotape offers yet another view: Although the film's first image of extramarital sex shows philanderer John (Peter Gallagher) sleeping with his wife's sister, Cynthia (Laura San Giacomo), we later see John's wife, Ann (Andie MacDowell), cheat on John with his college friend Graham (James Spader). While the John-Cynthia tryst is consistent with other dark Gen-X visions of marriage — the lovers perpetuate their relationship to compensate for shortcomings in their personalities — the Ann-Graham encounter is an act of liberation on Ann's part. Even though her intercourse with Graham affirms that she's given up on her marriage, it signals the beginning of a new, more loving relationship. So while *sex, lies, and videotape* has as hopeless a view of marriage as other Gen-X movies, it at least has a hopeful view of other kinds of relationships. That Ann finds her happiness by violating her marital vows, of course, dovetails the disdain for officially sanctioned unions that pervades Gen-X films.

Change Partners

Some of the most moving love relationships depicted in Gen-X cinema involve same-sex partners, an interesting reflection of the fact that alternative lifestyles achieved greater acceptance, at least by young people, during the maturation period of Generation X. Yet Gen-X portrayals of homosexuality are not limited to doe-eyed visions of lovers finding soulmates by looking beyond the opposite gender. Quite to the contrary, Gen Xers often conjure some of their most polarizing material when exploring the myriad complexities of same-sex relations.

Perhaps the most unabashedly positive homosexual relationship in all Gen-X cinema is the love affair between Violet (Jennifer Tilly) and Corky (Gina Gershon) in *Bound*, the breakthrough film from Larry and Andy Wachowski, the writing-directing partners whose sophomore effort, *The Matrix*, made them superstars.

In *Bound*, a stylish caper film loaded with tricky plot twists and feverish erotic tension, Violet is the sleek girlfriend of violent gangster Cesar (Joe Pantaliano). In an elevator one day, she catches the eye of next-door neighbor Corky, an ex-con with an overflow of edgy attitude. When Violet reveals that she reciprocates Corky's attraction, it's not immediately clear whether her overture is genuine or a manipulation to get Corky involved in a crooked scheme. Even after the two share powerful sexual encounters, Corky remains unconvinced of her new lover's devotion, but the relationship finally is ratified when Cesar uncovers the scheme that Violet cooked up with Corky. The lovers have to rely on each other to extricate themselves from terrible trouble, and their shared adventure reveals the depth of their bond.

The movie ends with Corky and Violet driving off into the metaphorical sunset together, and the filmmakers slyly amplify that the women are joined by several layers of rebellion: They beat the mob at its own crooked game, they wiggled Violet free from her stifling relationship, and their love is a celebration of the freedom to defy conventional societal expectations. So while the Wachowskis may have presented this love affair in order to produce lurid imagery and surprising plot developments, they also conjured a potent testament to the power that love has to help people overcome obstacles in order to find meaningful companionship. *Bound* is in some ways a cynical movie, because it's a dark crime picture punctuated by grotesque violence and vicious betrayal, but it's also an optimistic movie because of its sweet attitude toward the commitment shared by the two women.

As noted earlier, *Boys Don't Cry* also features an extremely positive vision of same-sex love. In fact, the manner in which dreamy small-town girl Lana embraces the confusing gender identity of her significant other conveys the idea that love can surpass gender entirely. Intolerance intrudes on that union to devastating effect, of course, proving that not every pocket of modern American society has matured to the point of accepting truly unconventional unions. Gen-X filmmakers, however, are mostly accepting of such unions, to the extent that homophobic characters are vilified throughout their films. But because casting aspersions on the intolerant is hardly a new idea in American cinema, it's more instructive to note Gen-X depictions of homosexuality that are complicated and even contradictory.

Chuck & Buck and *Chasing Amy* immediately come to mind, because both films involve romantic pursuits that are frustrated by sexual preferences. When viewers of *Chuck & Buck* realize that all Buck wants to do is revisit the only love he has known — in a sense, to validate that he can be loved — his quest seems more innocent than salacious. By the end of the movie, Buck seems more like a willful, self-possessed adult looking for closure than a deranged stalker fixating on an old acquaintance. The reading of Buck as an actualized person instead of a misguided freak is given additional credibility by the climax of the film, when Charlie makes the offer to sleep with Buck one last time.

The setup for the sexual encounter is painful to watch, because it seems as if Charlie is betraying his own identity in a bitter compromise, but during the halting overtures of the encounter that we actually see, the genuine love between the two men is finally apparent. Buck needed this moment to remind himself of his own worth, and Charlie needed it for the same reason: What kind of man am I, he seems to ask, if I turn my back on such pure devotion? So *Chuck & Buck* ultimately is a universal love story that happens to involve two men. Homosexuality is embedded in the fabric of the film, so the statement the movie makes about tolerance, understanding, and identity is impossible to miss. But the statement is relevant to lovers of any gender or preference.

Chasing Amy offers a more confused view of modern romance, specifically a triangle involving two straight people and a homosexual. When appealing lesbian Alyssa Jones (Joey Lauren Adams) catches the fancy of fellow comic-book creator Holden McNeil (Ben Affleck), the attraction causes complications in Holden's relationship with his best friend, homophobic Banky Edwards (Jason Lee). Holden falls in love with Alyssa and tries to advance their relationship to the physical plane, but his desires are stymied by Alyssa's sexual preference and also, surprisingly, by the tug of Holden's friendship with Banky. These three characters find themselves pushed apart by the very forces that draw them together, so their three-way interaction leads to an impasse similar to the one reached by Charlie and Buck.

With a twist: A young lesbian (Joey Lauren Adams) questions her identity when a fellow comic-book creator (Ben Affleck) falls in love with her in Kevin Smith's *Chasing Amy* (Miramax Films).

Exasperated by his friends' inability to get past their hang-ups about each other, Holden stuns them to silence by suggesting that they all sleep together. Banky meekly admits that he's open to the idea — revealing that his anti-gay posturing is a macho act — but Alyssa is rightly offended by the insulting proposal. Writer-director Kevin Smith plays into a cliché by having Banky reveal closeted homosexual inclinations, but smartly derails the sensationalistic possibilities of the scene with Alyssa's angry refusal.

Chasing Amy is a frustrating movie because while it seems to be a thoughtful investigation of modern sexuality — in one bold scene, Alyssa and Banky spout shockingly graphic dialogue while comparing notes about their experiences with cunnilingus — it ultimately lacks the depth needed to advance it past the level of an interesting experiment. For instance, after Alyssa gives a stirring speech to Holden about how agreeing to sleep with him would represent a betrayal of her identity, she inexplicably betrays her identity by agreeing to sleep with him. Smith undoes this narrative inconsistency by ending the movie with the lovers apart (a year after Holden's indecent proposal, we see that Alyssa is involved with a woman), but his infatuation with vulgar descriptions of sexual behavior suggests that his interest in alternative lifestyles is more puerile than intellectual.

The sexual politics created by the prevalence of open homosexuality also are explored in such films as *Boogie Nights* and *54*, both of which depict painful confrontations between straight and homosexual characters. And *Boogie Nights* director Paul Thomas Anderson portrayed poignant same-sex passion again in *Magnolia*, through the unrequited love that a former quiz-show champion feels for a hunky bartender. In all of these films, Gen-X directors confront head-on the fact that the sexual landscape of the modern age is vastly different from that inhabited by their predecessors, if only because alternative lifestyles are discussed in full voice instead of a whisper.

That full voice, however, sometimes becomes an angry howl — for not every member of American society has rolled with the changes in attitudes toward sex. In *Magnolia*, Tom Cruise edgily satirizes his stature as an icon of male virility by playing a self-help guru who teaches men to reclaim their roles as the dominant members of society — with the help of his "Seduce and Destroy" program. In harsh, lurid language, Frank T. J. Mackey (Cruise) mesmerizes an audience of men who believe themselves emasculated by the empowerment of women:

> FRANK: Respect the cock — and tame the cunt! Tame it. Take it on with the skills that I will teach you ... and say "No! You will not control me. No! You will not take my soul. No! You will not win this game." Because it is a

game, guys—you want to think it's not, you go back to the schoolyard, you have that crush on big-titted Mary Jane. Respect the cock. You are embedding this thought: "I am the one who's in charge. I am the one who says 'Yes.' 'No.' 'Now.' 'Here.' " Because it's universal, man, it is evolutional, it is anthropological, it is biological, it is animal. We are men!

A Matter of Hate

Taking the sexual rage of *Magnolia* a step further is the most brutal scene in *Your Friends and Neighbors*, an extended monologue by serial philanderer Cary (Jason Patric). Throughout the picture, he trumpets his violently misogynist philosophy, in which women are merely receptacles for the anger he fires out of his body during sex like bullets from a gun. So when Cary retires for a sauna with two male buddies, viewers are braced for another barrage of masculine anger. Yet when the conversation turns to nostalgic boasting — each man is asked to recall his greatest sexual rapture — Cary unveils a secret facet of his personality that's even more disturbing than his predilection for shallow encounters.

With steadily building intensity, Cary recalls every loving detail of a gang rape he participated in during his younger years. While his revelation that his victim was a man adds shock value to the scene, his target's gender ultimately is immaterial: The point of the scene is that Cary experienced the most intense orgasm of his life while brutally attacking someone. The level of his depravity is underlined when Cary describes how he felt his victim reciprocate the motion of his rape. This monstrous character is so drunk on sexual power that he believes the moment when his violence took its purest form actually was the moment when he enjoyed his truest sexual communion.

While sexual predators such as Cary are not unique to any particular time, the context in which viewers meet him is utterly contemporary. Cary exists in a historical moment when changing gender roles, the growing acceptance of homosexuality, and the deepening understanding of the relationship between psychology and sexuality has freed sexual identity from the shackles of traditional stereotypes. In this context, Cary's intertwining of violence and sexuality is a bastardization of the alternative lifestyles that make modern society so rich. He is a horrific example of what happens when someone with evil in his heart is cut free of traditional morals, because he mistakes the freedom and illumination of modern society as a license to behave not just differently, but abominably.

And while Cary could have existed at any time — as history sadly proves, beasts of his ilk have plagued the world for centuries— the friends who listen to the stories of his rape and other vile encounters are contemporary. Discombobulated by shifts in mores, the friends also are exploring sexual satisfaction through illicit means (namely infidelity), so they consider themselves to be in no position to judge Cary. Like the one he wrote for his disturbing debut film, *In the Company of Men*, LaBute's script for *Your Friends and Neighbors* portrays the modern sexual landscape as a barren desert with precious few oases of moral certainty.

Similar thematic material appears in *Boys Don't Cry* and *Boogie Nights*, which depict how particular kinds of people feel threatened by particular kinds of sexuality. The intolerant white-trash men in *Boys Don't Cry* who respond to Teena's transvestitism by raping her, in the vilest possible way forcing her to acknowledge her "true" gender identity, also underline their own tenuous grasps on sexual identity. In fact, the truest sign that Teena's progressive persona represents a threat to these small-minded hooligans is the coda to the rape: The attackers kill Teena, destroying that which they can't understand.

A similar sexual assault occurs toward the end of *Boogie Nights*. After monumentally endowed Dirk Diggler's career as a porn star has run its course, he ends up turning tricks for money, just as he did before movies made him famous. In a profoundly sad scene, we watch Dirk frantically masturbate while a john waits for Dirk to conjure an erection. When he can't, the john explodes in homophobic anger, summoning several buddies to help him assault the fallen star while he's literally and figuratively exposed.

Sex is used as a weapon in a different way in *The Contender*, Rod Lurie's political drama about a woman nominated for the office of vice president of the United States. When Senator Laine Hansen (Joan Allen) gets the nod from liberal Democrat President Jackson Evans (Jeff Bridges), it puts right-wing extremists on the defensive, and the most virulent of their number, Congressman Shelly Runyon (Gary Oldman), dredges up evidence suggesting that Laine participated in public group sex while in college. Lurie luridly showcases images of a young woman sandwiched between two men, and these photographs spark a brutal debate between Laine, who refuses to dignify the scandal by acknowledging or denying that she's the woman in the pictures, and Shelly, who fixates on the sex act as proof that Laine — and, by extension, women in general — are unfit for such high office.

In one of the film's most telling bits, Laine comes face-to-face with Shelly, who pompously declares that the sex act depicted in the pictures is "deviant." She retorts by asking whose values were used to make that determination, and he bluntly announces that his own morals are sufficient to determine what is and isn't acceptable. This encounter epitomizes the slippery slope on which people with conservative values often find themselves in contemporary society: Snap judgments and restrictive definitions simply don't mesh with how the parameters of socially acceptable behavior changed at the end the of the twentieth century. One person's experimentation is another's deviancy, so who's to say what's right or wrong?

Characters like Shelly may see group sex as the first step down a ladder that leads to inhuman behavior like that described by Cary in *Your Friends and Neighbors*, but isn't Shelly's intolerance the first step down the ladder leading to the murder of "different" people like Teena Brandon?

8

Uncomfortably Numb

Whereas *Boys Don't Cry* and *Your Friends and Neighbors* depict one terrifying intersection of sexuality and criminality, a pair of powerful films about drugs show another such intersection. In Darren Aronofsky's *Requiem for a Dream* and Steven Soderbergh's *Traffic*, young women strung out by addiction trade sex for controlled substances. These desperate exchanges are part of complex and occasionally contradictory discourse about controlled substances that runs through Gen-X movies, reflecting how attitudes toward drugs have changed in the lifetime of Generation X.

At the time illegal drugs became a pervasive part of youth culture in the 1960s and 1970s, the cinema had a spotty record of addressing drug use on screen. Movies such as 1955's *The Man With the Golden Arm* explored addiction to hard drugs with almost hysterical intensity, and that particular movie caused something of a scandal by attacking a taboo subject head-on. Yet by the dawn of boomer-oriented cinema, controlled substances were virtually a required narrative component: Movies from *Easy Rider* to *The French Connection* to *Lady Sings the Blues* are inextricably tied to the drug trade. And in a huge leap from the traditional, ultra-cautionary depiction of drugs, some boomer movies depict the use of "innocent" mind-altering substances, notably marijuana, as an innocuous form of adult recreation. While movies of this period still cast a horrified eye on the blight of heroin and other hard drugs, the relaxed attitude toward recreational drug use that permeated boomer cinema was a sure sign that times had changed.

Times changed back again before Gen Xers got their first chances to explore drug use onscreen, however, because conservative politicians of the 1980s initiated a costly and largely ineffective war on drugs. The drug war, accompanied by such comical spectacles as First Lady Nancy Reagan's pervasive "Just Say No" ad campaign, created a climate in which drug use was demonized in public even as it was embraced in private. Cocaine in particular become a fashionable indulgence in the 1980s, and its rise is a critical story element in such Gen-X films as *Boogie Nights* and *Blow*.

Yet not long after America's most powerful elected officials (and their spouses) committed themselves to fighting drugs, a presidential candidate danced around the facts of his own drug experimentation. In his 1991-1992 campaign, Arkansas Governor Bill Clinton made headlines by acknowledging that he had tried pot, but hadn't "inhaled." Opponents tried to turn Clinton's alleged drug use into a talking point, but by the early 1990s, marijuana seemed so tame compared to heroin, cocaine, and other lethal drugs that the issue became more of a joke than a controversy.

Whether he inhaled or not, Clinton became the first president to openly admit experimenting with illegal drugs, making him symbolic of America's paradoxical relationship with controlled substances. The nation's highest official, and thus the guiding force behind America's war on drugs, was himself a past drug user — albeit a casual partaker given to equivocating the nature of his experimentation. Within this context, it makes perfect sense that Gen Xers find the demonization of drug users and peddlers highly hypocritical and best avoided altogether. So while Gen Xers often make powerful statements about drug-related issues, such statements are generally devoid of moral absolutes — and instead suffused with moral uncertainty.

Generation X's perspective on illegal drugs was informed by more than the discourse of politicians, of course. The Pandora's box that the boomers opened by embracing a variety of controlled substances as recreational drugs stayed open once the next generation came of age. Author Geoffrey T. Holtz, in his study of the societal factors that define Generation X, reported that alcohol and drug use increased dramatically among youths during the generation's formative years, and he offered some possible explanations for the phenomenon. Reiterating the now-familiar factors that forced Gen Xers to grow up quickly, Holtz argued that Gen Xers "simply assumed some of the adult prerogatives that went along with their adult obligations. Just as many adults seek relief from the stresses of life in drugs or alcohol, so did a growing number of [Gen Xers]. They were just compelled to make these choices at a much younger age."[1] This reality is reflected in pictures such as Boaz Yakin's *Fresh*, which tells the story of a twelve-year-old drug dealer.

Concurrent with their voluntary embrace of alcohol and illegal drugs, Gen Xers had the unfortunate distinction of being the most medicated youths in American history, because legal drugs such as Ritalin were widely prescribed throughout the 1970s and beyond to curb "difficult" behavior in children. As Holtz bitterly observed, this was one more example of adults prioritizing convenience over the welfare of nascent Gen Xers, so the idea of doping children who require special attention is not far removed from the idea of refusing to fail students who do poorly in school: In both trends, children are treated as assembly-line products to be passed into adulthood as quickly, and with as little effort, as possible.

"Thus, for all intents and purposes," Holtz wrote, "between 3 and 4 million [Gen-X] children were given sedatives simply to make them more compliant in the classroom, or because their behavior was outside of some ideal that a particular adult desired."[2]

Since they were raised in a time during which illegal drugs were openly embraced throughout numerous pockets of mainstream culture, and during which legal drugs were employed as an ancillary to the nurturing process, is it any wonder that Generation X grew up poised to experiment with controlled substances, and suspicious that anyone who told them they shouldn't was just another hypocrite?

Party Favors

The dangerously casual attitude toward drugs that appears in several Gen-X movies is the most shocking aspect of Doug Liman's *Go*, an exuberant adventure that stops just short of endorsing drugs as a hobby. The fast-moving, cheeky picture follows a handful of young characters whose lives intersect during one wild night, and typical of the youths populating the film is Ronna (Sarah Polley), a grocery clerk who stumbles into moonlighting as a drug dealer. Among her adventures: She kills time at the grocery store by smoking and doing drugs in the store's freezer section; she leaves her friend Claire (Katie Holmes) at the home of an edgy dealer as collateral until she can pay off her drug debt; and she snows several gullible youths by selling them allergy medicine and chewable aspirin while telling them the tablets are ecstasy. Drug use is played for laughs throughout the movie — as in a scene of stoned youth imagining that a cat projects the words "I can hear your thoughts" into his mind through telepathy — and even the sporadic flashes of violence in the film fail to add much gravity to the story. *Go* makes selling and using drugs look like a cheap thrill with bothersome repercussions that can be avoided with a little ingenuity and patience.

Liman's inspiration probably was Quentin Tarantino's *Pulp Fiction*, which similarly tracks several lives that intersect because of criminal activity — and which contains perhaps the most notorious drug sequence in all Gen-X cinema. The sequence begins when hip hit man Vincent Vega (John

Travolta) gets assigned to entertain Mia Wallace (Uma Thurman) for an evening; Mia, importantly, is the wife of Vincent's violence-prone employer. Before Vincent even sees her, viewers watch Mia blast a line of coke up her nose, which explains the bouncy energy with which she enchants the comparatively laconic Vincent. Over the course of an evening of dining and dancing, the two bond share a string of pop-culture-laden exchanges and sweetly intimate revelations. Mia keeps the party moving with a steady supply of the drug that novelist Jay McInerney once described as "Bolivian marching powder."

But just as the pleasant evening is due to conclude, Mia discovers a bag of white powder in Vincent's jacket while he's in the bathroom. Unaware that it actually is heroin, she snorts the stuff and immediately stumbles into deadly toxic shock. Vincent discovers her and is overwhelmed with panic that he'll take the blame for the death of his boss's wife, so he rushes her to the home of his wasteoid drug dealer, Lance (Eric Stoltz). Lance produces a monstrous hypodermic needle filled with adrenaline, then indicates what needs to be done, so Vincent steels his nerves to oblige — by punching the needle through Mia's chest and into her heart with the force of a maniac attacking a victim with a butcher knife.

The desperate attempt succeeds, and after recovering their composure, Mia and Vincent agree to treat the incident the way mischievous children hide their misdeeds— they go their separate ways and swear not to tell Mia's husband about what happened. While this scene has an undeniable cautionary aspect, it also uses drugs to elevate the bond between two characters. Their shared adventure is precious because it was illegal and nearly fatal — making the bond between Mia and Vincent the same that joins the characters in *Go*, who walk away unscathed after sharing a thrilling misadventure.

The cautionary aspect of Generation X's depiction of drugs is more prominent in *Boogie Nights*, which shows characters destroying their lives through the use of controlled substances. Amber Waves (Julianne Moore), the matriarch of the movie's surrogate family of porn stars and filmmakers, has a debilitating cocaine addiction that fits perfectly with the narrative's time frame, because she's at the forefront of hedonistic culture in the 1970s and 1980s, the period during which cocaine's popularity surged.

In a key scene, she sits around snorting coke with Rollergirl (Heather Graham), the damaged young woman who has become a star in the skin flicks made by Amber's companion, director Jack Horner (Burt Reynolds). As the distraught Amber gets more and more jazzed by the dope in her system, she laments that she's separated from Andrew, the child of her previous relationship. Amber says that if she isn't a mother, she's nothing, so Rollergirl picks up the mood by asking Amber to be her "mom."

Just a few scenes later, Amber goes court for custody of Andrew, and loses her case because she's a porn star with a long arrest record stemming from her involvement in drugs and prostitution. Perhaps the saddest instant in the short, painful hearing scene is when Amber sincerely declares that she doesn't do drugs, even though we saw her fill her nose with coke just a few screen minutes previous.

Later in the movie, drugs cost a character more than visitation rights. The film's protagonist is porn star Dirk Diggler (Mark Wahlberg), who by the mid–'80s finds his career prospects so limited that he segues from acting to dealing drugs. Dirk and a buddy hook up with edgy crook Todd Parker (Thomas Jane), who involves them in a deal to sell drugs to a manic playboy named Rahad Jackson (Alfred Molina). Even worse, Todd persuades them to substitute innocuous white powder for the dope, meaning they have to grab Rahad's cash and flee before he discovers their ruse. The would-be players arrive at Rahad's home to find him wired on freebased coke, and the situation goes south when Todd tries to turn the deal into an armed robbery. Shots are fired and Todd gets killed, but Dirk escapes with his life and the realization that compared to selling drugs, sleeping with women on film is a safe way to make a living.

Amber's legal defeat and Dirk's near-death experience both underline how the drug trade became a more serious business in the late 1970s and early 1980s, and how the wise figured out that it was time to get out of the game. Ted Demme explored the root causes of this shift in *Blow*, his glossy biopic of George Jung, the American dealer who helped bring South American cocaine to the United States in the late 1970s and early 1980s. In fact, Demme's film is a travelogue of young America's relationship with drugs that spans most of the counterculture era.

Early in the movie, George (Johnny Depp) moves from the Northeast to California and hooks up with a flamboyant pot supplier, Derek Foreal (Paul Reubens). Fueled by his enthusiasm for grass and his burning ambition to make a quick buck, George quickly becomes a successful dealer on the West Coast, then strikes upon the idea of sending dope back home to the Northeast. His enterprise eventually grows to include illicit flights from Mexico, where George scores huge mounds of pot that he then sells in America, and everything seems to go swimmingly until George gets busted.

In prison, however, the dope mogul is tossed in a cell with Colombian drug peddler Diego Delgado (Jordi Mollà), who fatefully introduces George to infamous Colombian drug czar Pablo Escobar (Cliff Curtis). Undeterred by his stint in prison and the violence of which he knows Pablo is capable, George becomes Pablo's American connection — and such a

Taking a powder: One of several Gen-X movies about illegal drugs, Ted Demme's *Blow* stars Johnny Depp (left, with Jordi Mollà) as a rich cocaine dealer (New Line Cinema).

powerful supplier of cocaine that he claims at one point to import nearly all of the coke used in the United States at the height of the drug's popularity.

In keeping with the cautionary but not necessarily moralistic depiction of drugs in other Gen-X movies, George pays for his hubris by losing his relationship with a beautiful Colombian woman, and by getting separated from his beloved daughter. At the end of the movie, an unrepentant George rots in jail as a lonely old man who has been betrayed or abandoned by almost everyone he ever loved. Yet he doesn't seem to regret the life he chose or the damage he wrought by choosing that life — instead, he regrets getting caught.

This distinction feels especially murky because Demme and his collaborators mostly gloss over the effects of George's smuggling. *Blow* focuses obsessively on George's trajectory, so we don't see the countless lives that were ruined because of how George and his cronies made an enticing drug readily available, and we don't see much of the violence that punctuates the relationships between drug suppliers, peddlers, and users. In fact, it's easy to walk out of *Blow* with the impression that George is some kind of tragic figure doomed by foolish choices that resulted from a tumultuous childhood. That whitewash approach tarnishes the whole film, turning what could have been a powerful historical snapshot into a dangerously naive love letter to a scumbag.

Casualties of War

Whereas Demme's *Blow* misses the mark by taking a microcosmic view of a massive societal ill, Steven Soderbergh's *Traffic* achieves the opposite result by taking the opposite tack. A sprawling, multi-character epic adapted from a British miniseries called *Traffik*, and written for the screen by recovering drug addict Steven Gaghan (who won an Oscar for his endeavors), Soderbergh's movie encompasses a dizzying number of perspectives to show that everyone involved in the drug trade — manufacturers, sellers, users, even soldiers in the so-called war on drugs— wrestles with the same thorny issues. Soderbergh also puts across the powerful argument that the war on drugs is destined for failure, not just because the enemy has deeper pockets and fewer scruples, but because fighting drug manufacturers and sellers in effect translates to fighting drug users— whom, the movie argues, are victims as well as culprits.

Soderbergh democratically doles out screen time to all of his memorable characters, but two particular figures occupy the heart of the story. The traditional hero is Ohio Supreme Court Judge Robert Wakefield (Michael Douglas), recently appointed as America's new drug czar. He represents America as a babe in the woods: Even though he talks a hard line about arresting the flow of illegal drugs into the country, he's oblivious to the deadly drug use taking place under his roof. His willful teenage daughter, Caroline (Erika Christensen), regularly snorts and smokes and shoots drugs with her idly rich prep-school friends. The metaphor that America, as personified by Robert, is ignorant of internal problems but quick to blame other countries, specifically Mexico, is among the film's most heavy-handed elements— but also among its most crucial statements.

The other key character is a small-time, corrupt Mexican state policeman, Javier Rodriguez (Benicio Del Toro). At the beginning of the story, he's content exploiting the drug trade for a payoff here, a payoff there; as one character says, "Law enforcement in Mexico is an entrepreneurial enterprise." But when Javier gets caught up in a complex intrigue involving his country's leading anti-drug warrior and a pair of warring cocaine cartels, the policeman realizes the human cost of helping to maintain the status quo.

Robert's journey slams home a damning point about America's ass-backwards approach to drugs, but Javier's has tremendous impact on a human level. These stories—and others involving a blithe rich wife (Catherine Zeta-Jones) whose husband is busted for smuggling dope, and a pair of casually competent FBI agents (Don Cheadle and Luis Guzman) assigned to snare and then protect a key witness—were designed to make viewers consider drugs in a new way. The filmmakers lay out reasons why politics, corruption, and money make even the United States' most valiant efforts to stem drug traffic laughably insufficient, then try to show that compassion and intervention can cure more ills than seizures and arrests.

After the film was released, Gaghan explained in an interview why his own experiences with drugs informed his decision to write the Americanized version of the story:

> Part of the recovery process is a commitment to truth, and I began to feel that I was not being truthful. The stigma and shame of drug addiction is part of what makes it difficult for people to raise their hand and ask for help, and I felt that by not being completely honest I was, in a way, perpetuating

Caught in the crossfire: Catherine Zeta-Jones plays a pampered socialite who discovers her husband is a drug dealer in *Traffic*, for which Steven Soderbergh won a Best Director Oscar (USA Films).

that stigma.... If there is a message to the movie, I guess it's that drugs should be a health care issue rather than a criminal issue.[3]

Interestingly, the most powerful Gen-X movie about drugs also is in some ways the most traditional. For while the style of Aronofsky's *Requiem for a Dream* is utterly contemporary — certain aspects of the director's frenetic storytelling are even ahead of their time — the content of the film is an intense morality tale almost in the mode of such antiquated films as *The Man With the Golden Arm*.

Writ large, the movie simply says that drugs will kill or nearly kill you, but the devil here is very much in the details. Adapted from a novel by Hubert Selby, Jr., the movie explores the impact of both legal and illegal drugs on a spectrum of characters, and the delicate way that Aronofsky balances scenes showing his characters' complicity in their own fates with scenes suggesting that the characters are doomed by social factors adds layers of complexity to his generally straightforward narrative. More importantly, the power of Aronofsky's filmmaking and the unflinching bleakness of Selby's story converge in a cinematic assault that's painful to experience.

Requiem for a Dream is a symphony of despair: Characters spiral downward because of their addictions to street and prescription drugs, descending into degradation, madness, and physical deterioration. The movie features d.t.'s, infected veins, drug-induced hypertension, sex traded for money, and terrifying hallucinations, all of which are made even more intense by Aronofsky's signature "hiphop montages," super-quick sequences that slam images and sounds at viewers with the force and momentum of aggressive music. The director also employs sped-up camerawork, ultra-fast editing, and disassociated images, all of which make the storytelling confusing and abrasive.

Despite — or, more likely, because of — the director's confrontational approach, *Requiem for a Dream* often has the impact of a fist to the face. The most arresting story line involves urban widow Sara Goldfarb (Ellen Burstyn), a virtual shut-in who becomes obsessed with appearing on her favorite game show. She starts using diet pills to slim her aging figure for the television appearance, but careless doctors overprescribe the drugs — and then over-prescribe drugs meant to bring her down from the diet pills. Sara becomes shaky, paranoid, delusional, and deranged, all in hopeless solitude because her beloved son (Jared Leto) is caught in his own cycle of drug abuse. In her darkest moment, she's a frazzled, emaciated asylum inmate getting blasted with electroshock therapy — at roughly the same time that her dear son has a drug-destroyed arm amputated. Showing the pain experienced by Sara, a comparative innocent, puts the rigors of life among drug dealers such as her son in a new context: All are damned to horrific fates because they use drugs as a short cut on their journeys toward humble dreams.

The gap between drug scenes played for thrills, like Mia's overdose in *Pulp Fiction*, and those played for chills, like Sara's psychological derailment, is huge — and indicative of how hard it sometimes is for Gen-X directors to find a clear path in the wilds of contemporary culture. Just when it seems that an answer presents itself, as in the *Traffic* assertion that treatment is more humane than arresting drug users, an opposing view emerges. For surely aggressive means are required to help the victims of *Requiem of a Dream*, at least one of whom gets her fix not from a street pusher, but from a neighborhood pharmacist. "What the film is about," Aronofsky noted in an interview, "is the lengths we will go to escape our reality."[4]

Given that the central theme of the cinema of Generation X is the question of how a generation raised amid historical turmoil can find a place for itself in a vastly changed society, the simplicity of Aronofsky's comment speaks volumes. In the context of other Gen-X movies, the reckless dive into oblivion made by the characters in *Requiem for a Dream* is a sadly resounding extension of slackerdom, workplace rebellion, and the myriad other means by which Gen-X characters respond to the chaos of modern society by extracting themselves from it. The logical next step beyond hard drugs, of course, is suicide, and statistics bear out that vast numbers of Gen Xers have made that final leap.

The Final Farewell

Suicide is not a prevalent theme in Gen-X cinema, but a few pointed depictions reflect the dark fact that suicide has been a fact of life for American teenagers throughout the years of Generation X's existence. In fact, the numbers of youths who choose this irreversible solution to their problems has steadily increased since the early 1960s, when the first Gen Xers were born. In 1960, 10 of every 100,000 American men between the ages of twenty and twenty-four took their lives; by 1980, that number had more than doubled to 25 of every 100,000 men in this age group.[6]

David Fincher and Paul Thomas Anderson have featured suicide in at least two films each. Fincher's debut feature, the third installment of the popular sci-fi/horror *Alien* series, memorably concluded with long-suffering protagonist Ellen Ripley (Sigourney Weaver) throwing herself into a vat of super-heated ore to kill the monster growing inside her body. And Fincher's *The Game* climaxed with the image of a beleaguered businessman (Michael Douglas) throwing himself off a building because he believed he had just killed his brother. The businessman's death was prevented with an airbag, and the brother's death had been faked, but the shock of the imagery resonated. (Whether it manifests as suicide or otherwise, martyrdom is a recurring theme in Fincher's work: The death of his young wife prompts a principled cop to become a killer in *Seven*, and the death of a beloved colleague prompts a cult to new levels of violent anarchy in *Fight Club*.)

In *Boogie Nights*, Anderson depicted a cuckolded husband (William H. Macy) walking into a room where his wife was having sex with another man. The husband shoots both lovers to death before putting the gun into his own mouth and pulling the trigger. And in Anderson's *Magnolia*, a depressed trophy wife tries to deaden her pain by downing a massive amount of prescription drugs and then settling into a car so she can choke on exhaust fumes.

In all of these films, however, the suicide attempts are outgrowths of other story material, so the most significant Gen-X films about characters taking their own lives, or trying to, are those that both forefront suicide and explore its causes. One such movie is James Mangold's *Girl, Interrupted*, a sterile but interesting adaptation of Susannah Kaysen's memoir of her 1960s tenure in a psychiatric ward. In the film, Susannah (Winona Ryder), is a poor little rich girl who takes a near-fatal overdose of pills. Her parents commit her to a mental-health facility in the hopes their her self-destructive tendencies will be curbed. Although she is chronologically a boomer, Susannah's journey reflects trends that had a tremendous impact on Generation X: Her parents essentially wash their hands of her when she becomes "difficult," and once Susannah is hospitalized, she's forced to take medication that her doctors hope will "normalize" her behavior.

During her long stay in the hospital, Susannah befriends several fellow patients, most of whom suffer from afflictions far more crippling than her own rampant neuroses. Mangold resorts to clichés familiar from such films as *One Flew Over the Cuckoo's Nest*, and generally treads so softly that Susannah's time at the hospital sometimes seems like a summer at camp. Yet the film has several passages of sensitivity and power, particularly a vignette during which Susannah and her freespiritied acquaintance Lisa (Angelina Jolie) visit a fellow patient who was released and now lives in her own apartment. As the passive Susannah watches, Lisa torments the fragile Daisy (Brittany Murphy), who responds to the abuse and other factors by killing herself while her guests sleep one floor below her.

The moment starts Susannah toward an epiphany, but in the superficial language of the film's narration (spoken by Ryder as Susannah), her breakthrough comes out like this: "Seeing death — really seeing it — makes dreaming about it fucking ridiculous." While blunt and even a bit flip, this line nonetheless reveals an important truth: Suicide was so familiar to youths of the 1960s and beyond that it was possible for teenagers, and even children, of these eras to entertain notions of taking their own lives without any real concept of what such a choice entails. Like anything else that once was a taboo subject, suicide lost some of its stigma when it became commonplace, and therefore became a dangerously approachable concept.

Just as the issues about suicide that pervade *Girl, Interrupted* have a significance that spans two generations, so too does the strange fact that Susannah elects to stay hospitalized for several months after learning that she has the option to leave whenever she wants to. In the following dialogue spoken by one of Susannah's psychiatrists, the no-nonsense Dr. Wick (Vanessa Redgrave), note the echoes of behavior that is generally thought to be the province of contemporary slackers:

> DR. WICK: It's a big question you're faced with, Susannah. The choice of your life. How much will you indulge in your flaws? What are your flaws? Are there flaws? If you embrace them, will you commit yourself to hospital for life? Big questions, big decisions. Not surprising you profess carelessness about them.

If *Girl, Interrupted* suffers from flat storytelling and superficiality, it isn't for lack of trying on the part of producer-star Ryder, who was instrumental in bringing the story to the screen. Like *Traffic* screenwriter Stephen Gaghan, Ryder had a personal connection to the story she helped tell, and the revelations she made when promoting *Girl, Interrupted* add resonance to her portrayal even as they exemplify the painful difficulties that so many Gen Xers have when trying to grapple with the realities of modern life.

> I've never been a suicidal person, but there have definitely been times when I've thought, I'm too sensitive for this world right now; I just don't belong here — it's too fast and I don't understand it. Those were times when I would hibernate. And it wasn't healthy — I would get very lonely and very helpless.... I spent some time in a psychiatric ward when I was nineteen. I really thought that I was losing my mind. I've always been an insomniac, and I was really, really overworked and overtired and not sleeping. I was convinced I was having a nervous breakdown, and I checked myself in.... I debated whether to talk about it, but it is true, and I'm not really ashamed

of it. I think everybody goes through these times in their lives—I think you're very weird if you don't.[6]

So far, the most evocative Gen-X expression of the formless angst that can lead teens to end their lives was seen in Sofia Coppola's debut film, *The Virgin Suicides*—which takes a uniquely Gen-X approach to its subject matter by preventing viewers from penetrating the psyches of its doomed characters. Coppola shows viewers some of the external factors that make five fictional sisters venture into oblivion, but she lets the characters retain their mystery.

Judging from the opaque, almost dreamlike quality of the film's storytelling, it seems as if Coppola wanted to do more than offer a movie-of-the-week answer to a widespread social affliction. She apparently wanted to present suicide as part of the confusing haze of American adolescence, in which hormones and rebellion butt against the parameters of neatly ordered suburban life. The movie's trancelike beauty sucks viewers into the dark milieu of its characters, in effect drawing the audience into a deadly emotional whirlpool.

Set in 1970s Michigan, the film begins when Cecilia Lisbon (Hanna Hall), one of five girls living with their parents in the affluent Detroit suburb of Grosse Pointe, tries to kill herself by slashing her wrists. The near-tragedy piques the curiosity of a clique of neighborhood boys, who are schoolmates of the Lisbon sisters. The film then focuses on Lux Lisbon (Kirsten Dunst) and her relationship with the local bad-boy dreamboat, Trip Fontaine (Josh Hartnett). After Cecelia's second suicide attempt succeeds— she impales herself on a fence — the Lisbon parents (James Woods and Kathleen Turner) lock their daughters in the family's house to prevent any further tragedy. The plan, as the plural of the film's title indicates, backfires terribly.

Although her direction lacks focus, often getting mired in such ethereal images as blazing sparklers and floating balloons, the scenes that Coppola gets right have a palpable humanity that makes the image of youths imprisoned by their parents reflect the Gen-X idea of being both disenfranchised from, and repressed by, institutions from which they should rightly expect to draw comfort and support (in this case, the Lisbon parents). In one choice scene, the neighborhood boys communicate with the "jailed" sisters by playing records over the phone as a sort of coded conversation: The boys throw Todd Rundgren's "Hello, It's Me" onto their turntable, so the girls respond with Gilbert O'Sullivan's "Alone Again, Naturally," and so on.

The sequence in which the girls end their lives is played not for horror, but for otherworldliness: In the dead of night, they simply slip from this realm to another one. This scene is a far cry from the martyrdom of Fincher's suicide imagery and the shock tactics of Anderson's. Whereas other Gen-X directors portray the voluntary end of a life as a grand gesture or a violent surprise, Coppola sensitively portrays it as girls like the Lisbons might live it: a poetic expression. The mere fact that needless death can be envisioned as a creative act is indicative of how life has been devalued in these modern times, and this poignant connection between fiction and reality makes *The Virgin Suicides* one of the most disturbing films yet created by a Gen-X director.

Todd Haynes's *Safe* is disturbing in a different way because it depicts another means of escaping contemporary society. The daring film follows the travails of a woman named Carol (Julianne Moore), who develops a condition called environmental sickness, victims of which have allergic reactions to car exhaust, cosmetics, television signals, and other mainstays of "civilized" life. In a slow-moving story told from a cold and detached perspective, Haynes shows the various steps that Carol takes to combat her illness: She tries psychology and medication before joining a cult-like collective that lives in a remote area at which the members are free from the

Don't dream it's over: Doomed teen Lux Lisbon (Kirsten Dunst) enjoys a moment of happiness in Sofia Coppola's ethereal drama *The Virgin Suicides* (Paramount Classics).

toxins that demonize them. The possibility that Carol's condition is psychosomatic is tested when she develops severe physical symptoms, yet the metaphor that she's allergic not to her environment but to her antiseptic, materialistic lifestyle comes through loud and clear.

Once Carol arrives at the collective's compound, she's told a story by a fellow environmental-illness sufferer named Claire (Kate McGregor-Stewart). Claire says that when she first fled her old life for this new existence, she hid in her "safe room" until she was able to look herself in the mirror and say "I love you." In addition to amplifying the idea that Claire, Carol, and their peers are escaping not a physical condition but a psychological one, this scene sets up the ambiguous, haunting ending of *Safe*: After severing virtually every tie to her past life, and indeed virtually every tie to society in general, Carol retires to her new living quarters, a Spartan dome so bereft of potential toxins that it's more like a jail cell than a home. After clearing her throat, Carol looks herself in the mirror and forces herself to say "I love you." This lost soul has learned to appreciate herself, but the cost of her actualization is that she has cleaved huge parts of herself away from her soul. At the end of the movie, this wife and mother is reduced to a tender wound.

9

Out for Blood

Given the ferocity with which Gen-X directors attack such provocative subjects as the confusion of modern gender issues, the lethal effects of drug use, and the pervasiveness of suicide, it's unsurprising that myriad forms of violence play important roles in this generation's cinematic worldview. And while it's tempting to look at the grisly scenes of bloodshed and dismemberment that appear in some of the most memorable Gen-X movies, then make a sweeping generalization about what those scenes mean, this generation's spin on savagery needs to be put into the context of Hollywood history.

Violence has always been a prevalent component of mainstream American filmmaking, which is rooted in the drama of conflict. Since violence is the most visceral manifestation of conflict, characters in movies seem to exchange body blows, gunfire, and psychological violence as often as they exchange dialogue. Filmmakers have spent decades fighting for their right to use violence as a dramatic tool, and the history of American cinema is filled with rhetorical battles sparked when religious, political, and other groups try to dictate what level of violence is acceptable on American screens.

One aftershock of these battles is that when old taboos about movie brutality were swept away by a cadre of brash directors—Arthur Penn and Sam Peckinpah with the slow-motion bullet hits of *Bonnie and Clyde* and *The Wild Bunch*; Francis Coppola with the horse's head in *The Godfather*; Martin Scorsese with the final bloodbath in *Taxi Driver*; and many more — the level of screen grisliness was raised to previously unimaginable levels. And even though these relaxed standards have been abused by countless exploitation filmmakers, mainstream directors are loathe to lose the ground they gained on this freedom-of-speech issue. The idea is that in exchange for the right to show "justifiable" gore in, say, *Saving Private Ryan*, it's necessary to let exploitive stuff though.

Therefore, the rivers of blood that flow in such Gen-X films as *The Cell*, *Seven*, and *Pulp Fiction* are not necessarily indicative of a generational predilection for gore. Instead, the bloodshed in these films represents an ongoing maturation of American film, in which language, sexuality, and violence all grow steadily harsher in step with a harsh culture. The eternal question, of course, is whether the movies and other popular art forms reflect or prod increased vulgarity, promiscuity, and violence. Because the jury is still out on that question, it's sufficient to leave the relationship between screen violence and real-life brutality as a background thought during this exploration of how Generation X treats violence cinematically.

Finally, though, figuring out how the bloodshed in Gen-X movies relates to what came before only offers an explanation for the explicitness of the violence: It's the next chapter of an ongoing story. What is left unexplained, then, is the nature of the violence — why do Gen-X directors choose to show the kinds of violence that they show?

One very personal answer to this question was provided by Quentin Tarantino, whose ultraviolent films sparked countless stomach-churning copycats. Interviewed to promote the release of his third film, *Jackie Brown*, the director noted an intriguing connection between himself and Ordell, the machine-gun-loving crook played in the movie by Samuel L. Jackson:

> Ordell was all my mentors as a young man growing up. Ordell was who I could have been. It was interesting writing the film because that all kind of came back to me, and that persona of who I could have been at seventeen if I didn't have artistic ambitions. That was it. If I hadn't wanted to make movies, I would have ended up as Ordell. I wouldn't have been a postman or worked at the phone company or been a salesman or a guy selling gold by the inch. I would have been involved in one scam after another. I would have done something that I would have gone to jail for. But I picked my path. and luckily, I was able to deal with all those things about me through my work.[1]

While it's unlikely that every Gen-X director prone to including violence in his or her movies shares Tarantino's personal connection to the criminal milieu, the tumultuous times during which Gen Xers grew up probably are a commonplace factor behind onscreen brutality. Just as being raised in the shadow of Watergate, Vietnam, and the demise of the counterculture contributed greatly to the cynicism that's shared by so many Gen Xers, so too did the violence filling the news and popular culture throughout this generation's upbringing affect their conception of violence and, most likely, their perception of morality. Tellingly, for instance, Gen Xers seem comfortable embracing and sympathizing with characters who make

Laws are made to be broken: Quentin Tarantino's infatuation with criminals empowers his depiction of characters such as Ordell (Samuel L. Jackson, right, with Robert De Niro), the villain of *Jackie Brown* (Miramax Films).

the vigilantism of previous cinematic icons — from the gun-toting lawmen in countless Westerns to the revenge-seekers in 1970s flicks such as *Straw Dogs* and *Death Wish* — seem unquestionably virtuous by comparison.

Payback's a Bitch

Hollywood movies, and, to a lesser degree, American independent films, are plot-driven, so it makes sense that a great deal of Gen-X movie violence is motivated by revenge, a reliable narrative device that screenwriters often use to both propel plots and reveal characters' motivations. Because the mechanics of revenge stories are so familiar — and so entrenched in dramatic ideas that predate Generation X's arrival by several centuries — vendetta movies made by this generation's filmmakers are among the least instructive in terms of generational identity. Except, of course, when the movies in question are pictures such as Steven Soderbergh's *The Limey* and Christopher Nolan's *Memento*, both of which put fresh spins on familiar material.

The Limey stars cult-fave British actor Terence Stamp as Wilson, a career criminal in late middle age. At the beginning of the film, he leaves an English prison after a long term, then travels to California because his daughter recently died there. Based on clues from her correspondence, Wilson believes that the man responsible for her death is Terry Valentine (Peter Fonda), a sleazy record producer. The principal thrust of the plot — Wilson's quest to determine Terry's guilt or innocence, and then, if necessary, mete out justice — is commonplace. But the tangential aspects of the plot are not.

Playing a characteristically postmodern narrative game, Soderbergh uses two intriguing devices to complicate *The Limey*. First, he jumps back and forth in time, so viewers often see an event followed by something that happened before it, and several important images recur even though their recurrence adds to the disjointed nature of the film's timeline. Second, Soderbergh employs vintage scenes from a 1967 movie called *Poor Cow*, featuring a much younger Stamp, as flashbacks that represent young Wilson. This deepens the movie on two levels: For viewers familiar with Stamp's younger screen persona, an allusion is drawn between the cinematic past and the cinematic present; and for viewers unfamiliar with the actor's previous work, the fact that the performer in the flashbacks is obviously the same as the actor in the present-day scenes adds a layer of reality that couldn't be achieved through the use of old-age makeup or a stand-in.

These narrative devices are mostly relevant for how they relate to the movie's violence, of which there is a considerable amount — Wilson tends to get information out of people by beating the hell out of them, and has no compunctions about killing thugs who get in his way. The violence in *The Limey*, and the revenge it serves, have unusual resonance because of the devices that Soderbergh uses to tie the present to the past. Had Soderbergh just showed a pissed-off Brit traveling to America with bloodlust in his heart, the character would have played as a cliché. But Soderbergh adds layer upon layer of character detail, which makes it easy to accept Wilson as a real person, or at least a reasonable facsimile thereof. By doing so, the director makes the violence feel like real violence.

The caveat to Soderbergh's directorial ambition, of course, is that he exhausts a tremendous amount of energy surmounting a hurdle that he put in his own path. He chose to work in a tired genre, and the most he could do was make something old feel new.

The same problem of surmounting genre limitations faced Christopher Nolan when he made *Memento*, a tricky thriller that Soderbergh, not coincidentally, used his high profile to promote. Nolan's movie is a revenge story told backwards, so it begins with the "hero" killing his adversary, then retraces the steps that led to the killing. Yet the film doesn't just start with its ending, then trek immediately back to its beginning; instead, it takes baby steps back in time so that the beginning of each scene is often the conclusion of the next one. Viewers are fed teasing tidbits of information, and the veracity of this information is constantly called into question by the film's other main device: The protagonist has short-term memory loss, so he has to relearn his own story at the beginning of each scene. Since this complex storytelling is a logical extension of the kind of trickery that Soderbergh has employed throughout his career, it's no wonder he felt drawn to Nolan's film.

Again, though, what matters is how the narrative devices pertain to the movie's violence, of which there are only a few choice bits. The diciest thematic material in the film is the cost of violence, because while we more or less believe that Leonard's desire for revenge is genuine, the possibility that he's being exploited because of his memory problem is prominent. By the end of the picture, Nolan even casts doubt on whether the crime motivating Leonard's revenge ever happened, so viewers are left untethered to any semblance of morality or reality. Whereas *The Limey*'s Soderbergh tries to justify his use of a familiar device by deepening the human reasons behind revenge, *Memento*'s Nolan justifies his device by suggesting that *Memento* actually isn't a revenge flick at all — but rather a movie about a character who only believes he's seeking revenge. Nolan's comments about the games he played with perception are intriguing:

> By putting the audience into the position of the protagonist, what you wind up doing is taking a very simple story and telling it in an incredibly complicated way. Not only do we get to experience the frustration and confusion, but it also makes you look at the story in different ways. It makes you uncover different things — it's more along the lines of interesting narrative connections between story elements rather than complicating the story itself. It's simple in story terms, but because you're looking at it backwards, you're looking at it in this totally sort of bizarre prismatic way, with this incredible perceptual distortion.[2]

This is familiar psychological terrain for Generation X, because the same complex web of confused perceptions, clouded motivations, paralyzing doubts, and conflicting emotions that informs Gen-X depictions of work, sexuality, and other issues informs how Gen-X directors approach revenge — and violence in general. One of the best attributes of this group of directors is that they're all about gray areas, and one of the best windows on such gray areas is provided by movies about violence: Even revenge, perhaps the least complicated of motivations, is made complicated.

In Alex Proyas's dazzling but superficial superhero adventure *The Crow*, a revenge story is transmogrified by making the title character — a musician turned undead vigilante — sexy, sympathetic, and soulful. Whereas previous cinematic vigilantes, notably Charles Bronson's blood-thirsty character in the disturbing *Death Wish* movies, are wronged men and women who punish evildoers with grim determination, the Crow, a.k.a. Eric Draden (Brandon Lee), delivers retribution in high style. Thanks to a vaguely defined supernatural phenomenon, Eric rises from the dead to avenge his murder and that of his wife, but his mission soon extends to cleaning up the crime-infested future city in which he lives. Clad in skintight leather and alluring makeup, and often with a guitar slung over his shoulder, the Crow is Charles Bronson reimagined as a rock star. But in making the character sexy, Proyas and his collaborators also make revenge sexy.

Gen Xers are capable of playing it straight when dealing with revenge, however. In Phil Joanou's *State of Grace* and *Heaven's Prisoners*—crime flicks so old-fashioned that they almost could have been made by Warner Bros. in the 1940s—heroes wrestle with their consciences before punishing people who wronged them. And in *The Road to Perdition*, Sam Mendes's follow-up to *American Beauty*, a hit man in the 1930s avenges the death of his wife and child with a vicious killing spree. Yet even *Perdition* has gray area, because the film's angel-of-death character is accompanied on his revenge campaign by his surviving child — who learns a bloody lesson about his father's vision of right and wrong.

Holding Out for a Hero

While the avenging angels in *The Crow* and *The Road to Perdition* are classic antiheroes, several protagonists in Gen-X films hew closer to the traditional white-hat concept of heroism. In Kasi Lemmons's underseen sophomore feature, *The Caveman's Valentine*, Samuel L. Jackson portrays a deranged New York City man named Romulus Ledbetter, who lives in a cave in a city park. He used to be a classical musician with a loving wife and daughter, but encroaching insanity derailed his happy life. Romulus is haunted by voices, and convinced that a power-monger named "Stuyvesant" uses high-tech devices to spy on and control Romulus's turbulent life.

When a young man is found frozen to death in a tree outside Romulus's cave, the "caveman" becomes an amateur detective obsessed with ferreting out the truth behind the murder. Yet his quest is frequently undermined by attacks of dementia, recalling how Leonard's investigation in *Memento* is hamstrung by mental problems. The wrinkles in *Memento's* portrayal of heroism introduce murky morality, but the twists in *The Caveman's Valentine* can be read as a comment on how modern society is suffused with derangement: In an insane world, only an insane man can see the truth. Lemmons certainly is after several other thematic ideas, notably the impact that insanity — and, by extension, any "different" behavior — has on the acquaintances of the afflicted person. But given that her plot is set in motion by violence, at least part of her statement relates to brutality and the need that people have to make the wrong things right, no matter how arduous the path to justice might be.

Romulus Ledbetter is a mirror image of the traditional superhero, because instead of having a gift that aids his righteous quest, he's burdened by an affliction that makes his quest especially difficult. David Dunn, the character played by Bruce Willis in M. Night Shyamalan's *Unbreakable*, is a superhero in the most traditional sense. His story begins with a horrific train wreck, of which David is the only survivor. Thanks to the prodding of obsessive art collector Elijah Price (played, coincidentally, by Samuel L. Jackson of *The Caveman's Valentine*), David realizes that he's never been hurt in his life — that he is, as the title says, "unbreakable." In classic comic-book fashion, however, he has one weakness: Water renders him mortal, so if he's submerged, he'll drown like anyone else.

Elijah is interested in David's unusual physicality because his own physicality is unusual in the opposite extreme: His bones break incredibly easily. For reasons that are best discovered by watching the movie, which has a love-it-or-hate-it twist ending, Elijah encourages David to fulfill the extraordinary destiny that the art collector believes accompanies extraordinary blessings. David tentatively becomes a superhero, complete with an ersatz flowing cape and a secretive modus operandi, and once he does, he feels as if the puzzle pieces of his life have finally fallen into place. As soon as David grows comfortable in his new (secret) identity, however, he's hit with a surprise that forces him to reconsider one of his most important relationships. Viewers are left in the dark about how this change might affect David's career as a crimefighter, but the fact that Shyamalan said in interviews that he envisioned *Unbreakable* as the first film in a trilogy is a pretty clear indication that David's crusade continued after what we saw in *Unbreakable*, if only in Shyamalan's imagination.

While Shyamalan tried to avoid the usual histrionics of superhero movies by carefully etching the origin of his characters with scenes of grounded human interaction, his film is still cut from the same cloth as Bryan Singer's *X-Men*, an adaptation of a phenomenally successful comic-book franchise that dates back to the early 1960s. The main difference between the films is that Shyamalan bends over backward to create a real world with a couple of extraordinary elements, and Singer creates a fantastic world with just enough ordinary elements that we recognize it as an exaggerated version of reality. *Unbreakable* is a superhero adventure disguised as a supernatural thriller, and *X-Men* is an unapologetic superhero adventure. Yet both rely on violence to dramatize the conflict between good and evil.

The *X-Men* comics concern "mutants" born with superhuman powers, and the hero of the franchise is Charles Xavier (Patrick Stewart), who is dedicated to helping mutants and humans live in peace. His adversary is concentration-camp survivor Magneto (Ian McKellen), who is bent on helping mutants take over the world. A young girl who gets caught between these opponents, Rogue (Anna Paquin), is depicted as a tragic figure whose adolescence has evolved from an imagined nightmare to an actual one, and the film's most prominent character, Wolverine (Hugh Jackman), is an outcast who can remember only bits of what appear to be an incredibly painful past.

You've got a point: Bryan Singer's comic-book adaptation *X-Men* features Hugh Jackman (center) as a superhero haunted by his mysterious past (Twentieth Century–Fox).

While many viewers probably can watch *X-Men* for its spectacle and ignore the story's (super)human elements, it's to Singer's credit that he had the temerity to include wieghty concepts in what could easily have been light-weight fare. And while his ambition isn't matched by discipline, he nonetheless pumps enough blood beneath the skin of the movie that its vision of heroism is in some ways as complex and resonant as that of the other Gen-X pictures that explore the subject matter. For in all of these movies, the factor that joins the heroes is that they are haunted. In the cinema of Generation X, even righteousness is burdened by the murky morality of modern life.

This complex take on heroism even colors Gen-X movies about stalwart characters who don't have superpowers with which to pursue their noble goals. In James Mangold's richly textured *Cop Land*, a small-town policeman star-struck by New York City cops realizes that several of his idols are corrupt, then has to make a *High Noon*-style stand to foil their nefarious activities. The cost of his heroism is that he loses his innocence, and Mangold wrings heartbreaking drama from the conflict raging within this also-ran about whether he should do the right thing or the convenient thing. Similarly, the protagonist of James Gray's evocative drama *The Yards* gets pulled deep into the criminal enclave from which he tried to extricate himself, then makes the difficult choice to testify publicly about the illegal activities of people who have been like family to him. The heroism of the characters in *Cop Land* and *The Yards* resonates, because in order to honor their morality, these characters have to betray parts of their humanity.

Still, the white-hat/black-hat approach to cinematic heroism is, as seen by characters such as *Unbreakable*'s David Dunn, not a concept lost on Gen-X filmmakers. Perhaps the purest vision of heroism in any Gen-X movie is, appropriately, one extrapolated from real life: the ordeal of Carl Brashear (Cuba Gooding, Jr.), the long-suffering protagonist of George Tillman, Jr.'s *Men of Honor*. An old-fashioned, ultra-sincere biographical film dramatizing the long road that Brashear walked while overcoming racism to become U.S. Navy's first African-American master diver, *Men of Honor* is in the classic mode of innumerable films championing the power of the human spirit. It's to Tillman's credit that he was able to get such a hopeful film made in cynical times, and it's to his credit that despite the inclusion of a few dubious plot twists and plenty of overheated emotion, the picture has the power to move — and even inspire.

Crime Time

Perhaps because they came of age in cynical times and began making films in what has been widely described as the Age of Irony, Gen-X directors are drawn to antiheroes more often than they are to heroes. Notwithstanding films about revenge, the most prevalent antiheroes in Gen-X movies are career criminals, from robbers to drug dealers to killers. Generation X's embrace of lawbreakers seems utterly consistent with other aspects of their generational identity, for it follows that a group of people who, writ large, distrust institutions and feel alienated from the ideals of the previous generation would feel a kinship with characters who either make their own laws or who flagrantly defy existing laws.

Rebels have long been important cinematic archetypes, of course, from the tommy gun-toting gangsters played by Jimmy Cagney in the 1930s and 1940s to the attitudinal malcontents played by Paul Newman in the 1950s and 1960s, but the rebels in Gen-X cinema are an unusually hard breed: The body count accumulated by characters in movies directed by Quentin Tarantino and Robert Rodriguez, for instance, is disturbing given how deeply the filmmakers apparently expect viewers to sympathize with these characters.

The first significant film in this line is Tarantino's debut, *Reservoir Dogs*, which did moderate business at the box office but eventually developed such a cult following that by 2001, nearly a decade after the picture was made, toy figurines of the film's murderous crooks were available. And while the film's longevity can be attributed in part to its ingenious structure, alarming plot twists, and brazen content, the main reason that *Reservoir Dogs* has enjoyed a long life is that it's cool. That most ephemeral of qualities, coolness is a crucial consideration when looking at the films of Generation X, particularly those made by Tarantino and his acolytes. Tarantino suffuses his movies with youthful, smart-ass attitude that manifests in funny pop-culture references, quotable dialogue, arresting musical interludes, and odd displays of bravado. Nothing is as cool as breaking the rules, though, so Tarantino's coolest characters often are his most lethal.

Reservoir Dogs tells the story of a group of thugs whose bold robbery ends in chaos and bloodshed, and Tarantino plays games by throwing the chronology of events out of whack and by never showing the actual robbery; the movie is all about prelude and aftermath. In the picture's most notorious scene, the crook known as Mr. Blonde (Michael Madsen) captures a uniformed cop and prepares to torture him. Even worse, Blonde explains that the goal of the torture isn't the extraction of information, but the demented fun of inflicting pain. Tarantino drags out the tension of the scene to unbearable lengths by having Blonde bop to a cheery '70s song as he dances around the cop and then slices the policeman's ear off. The scene is loaded with coolness, because Blonde has an Elvis-like look, confident body language, and the hipness to groove to a funky song, but the coolness is spiced with ferocious violence because the action that Blonde performs with a "cool" head is torture.

Tarantino mixes savoir faire and savagery throughout *Pulp Fiction*, but no more so than in the sequence involving Warner "The Wolf" Winston (Harvey Keitel), a career criminal who specializes in cleaning up messy crime scenes to keep fellow lawbreakers out of trouble. Gun-toting buddies Vincent (John Travolta) and Jules (the ubiquitous Samuel L. Jackson), are in a pinch because they accidentally shot a hostage in their car, so they high-tail their gristle-strewn vehicle to the home of Jimmie (played by Tarantino), a reformed crook willing to help his pal Jules, but only to a point. Jimmie's wife is due home from work soon, so he says that Vincent and Jules can use his house as a cleanup site as long as they're gone before she returns.

To ensure that the dirty job is done quickly, the crooks' boss sends in the Wolf, a peculiar character who does everything fast — driving, talking, thinking — and who seems fully prepared to annihilate everyone around him if need be. That eventuality doesn't come to pass, because the Wolf conjures a scheme by which the contaminated car is camouflaged well enough for it to be driven to a junkyard where it can be destroyed, with the corpse in it.

The whole sequence is a tribute to the Wolf's grace under pressure, and it ends with Jules reverently acknowledging that he's met his better: "It was a pleasure watchin' you work," he tells the Wolf. Given how broadly and passionately *Pulp Fiction* was embraced, a wide spectrum of viewers also enjoyed watching the Wolf — and the movie's myriad other crooks — do their dastardly deeds. Why? Because Tarantino makes their crime look cool by having his thugs swagger with the confidence and style of rock stars.

And so it goes in a number of other Gen-X movies. Rodridguez's debut film, an action movie set in Mexico and called *El Mariachi*, is beloved among fans of Gen-X movies both for its content and its history: In addition to featuring all the hip gunplay and slick editing that viewers can handle, the movie was made for a reported $7,000 thanks to Rodriguez's combination of ingenuity and chutzpah. When the resourceful director reworked his debut film as the English-language thriller *Desperado*, he retained the focus on acrobatic fighting and dazzling camera angles; as does influential Hong Kong director John Woo, Rodriguez uses slow motion to fetishize automatic pistols, with spent shells cascading upward and exhausted magazines spitting downward.

Because Rodriguez films violence so adoringly that it almost seems pornographic, it was a natural progression for him to join forces with

Tarantino, who made a cameo in *Desperado* and then enlisted Rodriguez to direct *From Dusk Till Dawn*, a script Tarantino wrote prior to entering the film industry. *From Dusk Till Dawn* starts promisingly as a portrait of a dysfunctional relationship between two brothers on a crime spree, then dissolves into idiocy when the brothers and their captives encounter a Mexican bar infested with vampires. The first half of the movie has undeniable craft and humanity, but the second half of *From Dusk Till Dawn* represents the nadir of Generation X's adoration of "cool" violence. And the less said about the vast numbers of Tarantino rip-offs—from *Killing Zoe*, an pretentious crime flick directed by Tarantino collaborator Roger Avary, to *Lock, Stock, and Two Smoking Barrels*, a frenetic but shallow British film helmed by Guy Ritchie—the better.

Another shallow, but nonetheless widely celebrated, Gen-X crime film is the twisty thriller *The Usual Suspects*, which won an Oscar for Christopher McQuarrie's screenplay, and advanced the careers of actors Kevin Spacey and Benicio Del Toro. With a title extracted from a line of dialogue in *Casablanca*, *The Usual Suspects* combines elements of Alfred Hitchcock's thrillers and the rat-a-tat talk of 1940s crime pictures such as *White Heat*. It tries to razzle, dazzle, and trick the viewer, and the accolades it receives indicate that many viewers were in fact razzled, dazzled, and tricked.

The film's exciting ensemble cast digs fiercely into McQuarrie's scenes of macho face-offs and intricate skullduggery, all of which comprise a plot involving a gang coerced into doing a suicidally dangerous heist for a mysterious crime lord. McQuarrie tries to emulate Hitchcock's most famous ploy, that of the "MacGuffin" plot device — something about which the characters are very concerned, but which actually is of little importance except as a motivation for action. The screenwriter employs at least a dozen such teases: Every ten to fifteen minutes, he starts viewers down another blind alley, thereby circumventing the need for a meaningful story line.

As do Tarantino's films, *Suspects* uses a complex system of flashbacks to show events leading up to the heist at the center of the plot. Framing these scenes are an interrogation between a cop (Chazz Palminteri) and a crook (Spacey), part of an investigation into the identity of crime lord Keyser Söze, who is spoken about by other characters in hushed, fearful tones as if he's the Antichrist. It's all very tense and enigmatic, but it's all very pointless, because the whole movie is a setup for a jokey ending. Well-crafted but empty, *The Usual Suspects* is most interesting as yet another example of Gen-X filmmakers' morbid fascination with bloodthirsty characters. McQuarrie offered this revealing statement when asked about the nature of his near-mythic villain, Keyser Söze:

Secrets and lies: A eclectic crew of hoodlums gathers in Bryan Singer's acclaimed thriller *The Usual Suspects*, with (from left) Kevin Pollak, Stephen Baldwin, Benicio Del Toro, Gabriel Byrne, and Kevin Spacey (Gramercy Pictures).

> I don't think he's evil. I'm not a big believer in evil in the conventional sense. I believe that he's a bad guy, an unsavory character, but my feeling is that he had no choice but to do what he did.[3]

Although identifying Steven Soderbergh as the exemplar of Gen-X craftsmanship already has become a recurring theme in this book, crime flicks are yet another genre in which he has done exceptional work. His first attempt at a caper flick, *The Underneath*, is best ignored because it is his only truly soulless movie, but then there's *Out of Sight*, his thoroughly witty, thoroughly entertaining adaptation of Elmore Leonard's novel.

Soderbergh employs some of his trademark editing gimmicks — dialogue overlaps, jump cuts, and the like — to give *Out of Sight* a brazen quality. Yet he also employs that beloved staple of 1970s cinema, the long take. The movie's most famous scene depicts charismatic bank robber Jack Foley (George Clooney) and driven federal marshal Karen Sisco (Jennifer Lopez) locked in a car trunk together. During a long, flirtatious, insinuating scene, the adversaries exchange small talk while his pelvis is pressed against her backside because of the close quarters, so they play an erotic game of foreplay without having any real sexual contact. Few scenes in Gen-X cinema so blatantly display the carnal thrill associated with crime — Karen is a straight-arrow representative of the law-enforcement community, but she finds the danger of being in intimate contact with a swaggering lawbreaker irresistibly seductive.

Tarantino and Rodriguez raise troubling issues about the allure of death by building movies around cold-blooded killers, but Soderbergh plays a safer game. His appealing protagonist is a nonviolent criminal — so nonviolent, in fact, that he risks his life at the end of the film to save an innocent woman from rape at the hands of his lethal compatriots. Jack Foley is worlds apart from *Pulp Fiction*'s Winston Wolf and *El Mariachi*'s machine gun-wielding musician, but he's part of a line of characters who illustrate that Gen-X directors find the wrong side of the law fascinating.

It might be a stretch to say that this generation's filmmakers deify criminals, but it probably is accurate to say that their infatuation with lawbreakers is a reflection of their misgivings about social institutions, authority, and the mores handed down to them by previous generations. From a certain perspective, it's not a huge leap from the social rebellion of becoming a slacker to the social rebellion of becoming a criminal — and that perspective is well-illustrated by *Out of Sight*'s Jack, whom we see making a half-hearted attempt to join the working world before literally tossing aside a symbol of that world (a necktie) and then reverting to his criminal ways.

Thrill of the Kill

While characters in Gen-X movies about revenge and crime all rack up impressive body counts, death is even more fundamental in movies about serial killers — and such characters are fundamental in Gen-X cinema. While the serial-killer genre has ample precedent in the decades preceding Generation X's arrival (*Peeping Tom, Psycho, In Cold Blood, Halloween*), it gained new legitimacy around the same time that Gen-X directors hit the scene. *The Silence of the Lambs*, the killer thriller that set the tone for countless imitators, was released in 1991, just two years after *sex, lies, and videotape* hit theaters. Given this coincidence of timing and Generation X's fascination with violence, it's appropriate that some of the most disquieting entries in the serial-killer genre are the handiwork of Gen-X directors.

In addition to his celebrated directorial efforts, Tarantino contributed scripts to three 1990s films concerned with violence. *From Dusk Till Dawn* was the least of these, and the crime flick *True Romance* added a few memorable scenes to the lexicon of quotable Tarantino moments, notably a brazen scene in which a doomed hostage provokes his Italian-American captor by explaining that Italians are "niggers." (Tarantino's obsession with that particular word will be explored in the next chapter, which deals in part with racial issues.) Yet the screenplay that earned *Pulp Fiction*'s director the greatest notoriety was his scenario for *Natural Born Killers*, probably the most infamous film ever made by controversy-magnet Oliver Stone.

In the picture, a pair of maniacal malcontents embark on that treasured cinematic convention, a love-fueled crime spree in the spirit of *Bonnie and Clyde*, *The Honeymoon Killers*, and *Badlands*. Along the way, they become celebrities. While Stone reportedly deviated so much from Tarantino's script that bad blood flowed freely between Tarantino, Stone, and the film's producers, the film's essential statement reached the screen undiluted: In the sensationalistic age of Geraldo Rivera and Jerry Springer, killers could easily earn the popularity and adoration enjoyed by movie actors and rock stars. This assertion, which has been validated time and again in real life, also goes a long way toward explaining the popularity of *Reservoir Dogs*, *Pulp Fiction*, and other Gen-X pictures about charismatic murderers.

Tarantino's involvement in *Natural Born Killers* is notable for several reasons, but it ultimately is peripheral to this study because he was not the director of the film. Even bereft of *Natural Born Killers*, however, the cinema of Generation X contains several horrific takes on the subject of natural born killers.

David Fincher's *Seven* is almost without question the most probing killer thriller yet crafted by a Gen-X director, and while Fincher's other films amply demonstrate how his personal fixations contributed to *Seven*'s magnetism, screenwriter Andrew Kevin Walker is essential to any discussion of the film. According to the myth that quickly brewed around this cynical scribe, he crafted *Seven* while working as a floor manager in a New York City record store, a job that gave him an unvarnished view of the way contemporary urban folks treat each other. Apparently, Walker's frustration about trying to start his career converged with his disgust at widespread insensitivity to produce *Seven*, which is about a lunatic who perceives himself as an avenging angel on a crusade to restore morality to modern life. In the context of the writer's (possibly apocryphal) experience, the killer in *Seven* is a dream version of Walker himself, forcing strangers to confront their own behavior.

The synergy between creator and creation makes *Seven* an intimate movie, and the youthful arrogance inherent to the movie's plot makes it a quintessential Gen-X statement. As has been illustrated by numerous

Method to his madness: Detectives Somerset (Morgan Freeman, left) and Mills (Brad Pitt) listen intently to a killer's words in David Fincher's *Seven*, which features scathing rants about the immorality of contemporary society (New Line Cinema).

other examples, Gen Xers have a contentious relationship with modern existence, in part because of the hypocrisy that accompanied the social upheaval that occurred during their youth. For instance, one contingent of the baby-boom generation sought to replace outdated ideas of morality with a new vision of equality, tolerance, and inclusiveness. Yet that noble goal was largely superseded by the desire to assimilate into "normal" society. In the most critical view, this transition represented an abandonment of moral idealism. And while that generalization overlooks countless nuances, the sense of betrayal implied by the abandonment of counterculture ideals contributed to the bitter aftertaste left in the mouths of countless boomers and passed on to the next generation. Speaking broadly, that bitter aftertaste is what the killer in *Seven* tries to wash from his mouth by slaughtering a septet whom he feels exemplify immorality.

Given this context, the scene in which killer John Doe (Kevin Spacey) reveals his motivation to detectives David Mills (Brad Pitt) and William Somerset (Morgan Freeman) is one of the most crucial in all of Gen-X cinema.

JOHN DOE: I won't deny my own personal desire to turn each sin against the sinner.

DAVID: Wait a minute. I thought what you did was kill innocent people.

JOHN DOE: Innocent? Is that supposed to be funny? An obese man? A disgusting man who can barely stand up? A man who, if you saw him on the street, you'd point him out to your friends so that they could join you in mocking him? A man who, if you saw him while you were eating, you wouldn't be able to finish your meal? And after him, I picked the lawyer, and you both must have been secretly thanking me for that one. This is a man who dedicated his life to making money by lying with every breath that he could muster, to keeping murderers and rapists on the streets ... A woman so ugly on the inside that she couldn't bear to go on living if she couldn't be beautiful on the outside.... And let's not forget the disease-spreading whore. Only in a world this shitty could you even try to say these were innocent people and try to keep a straight face. But that's the point. We see a deadly sin on every street corner, in every home, and we tolerate it. We tolerate it because it's common. It's trivial. We tolerate it morning, noon, and night. Well, not anymore. I'm setting the example. And what I've done is going to be puzzled over and studied and followed — forever.

Amplifying how deeply this character's twisted words reflect an anger burning in the heart of Generation X, he is far from the only serial killer in a Gen-X movie to murder for a "higher purpose." The maniac in *The Cell* tortures his victims to realize a complex dreamscape informed by his abusive childhood, and he pictures himself as a vaguely godlike creature. Director Tarsem Singh accentuates this imagery by filming the killer's dreams as postmodern art, with equal parts stomach-turning graphic violence and eye-catching graphic design. Death and art also intertwine in E. Elias Merhige's *Shadow of the Vampire*, which imagines that the star of F. W. Murnau's 1922 vampire epic, *Nosferatu*, actually was a vampire. In Merhige's film, bloodsucker Max Shreck (Willem Dafoe) and filmmaker F. W. Murnau (John Malkovich) make a deal by which the vampire gets victims and the director gets preternaturally convincing imagery. In both *The Cell* and *Shadow of the Vampire*, murder serves a personal need and makes for great imagery, so the immortality of creative expression is prioritized over the mortality of human life.

As in so many other pictures — Tarantino's crime pictures, *The Usual Suspects*, and more — stories about serial killers reiterate that even if Gen Xers don't themselves embrace amorality as part of their generational identity, their tumultuous upbringing helps them understand amoral characters on an eerily personal level. In the most extreme reading, violence is a key element of Generation X's cinematic vocabulary because Gen Xers feel that violence, albeit of a figurative nature, was committed against them throughout their formative years.

10

Touchy Subjects

Politics, religion, and race often are treated gingerly in Gen-X movies, which is peculiar in light of the forward-thinking attitudes that Gen-X directors display when exploring such polarizing topics as homosexuality and drugs. Gen-X directors' hesitancy to engage political issues is befuddling, for if these filmmakers are comfortable telling stories about American characters exercising their freedom of choice, the bedrock of the democratic ideal, wouldn't it follow that they would want to tell stories about how that freedom of choice is attained and protected?

So far, though, only Alexander Payne and Rod Lurie have made politics an important part of their oeuvres. Others, including Keith Gordon and Steven Soderbergh, have made individual films with interesting perspectives on specific political subjects. (Andrew Fleming entered the fray with his whimsical comedy *Dick*, about two teenage girls who stumble upon Richard Nixon's infamous audio-taping system while visiting the White House.) Beyond these few examples, however, most Gen-X filmmakers seem comfortable leaving social issues in the subtexts of their films or, in some cases, creating hyperbolic contexts that address social issues through colorful metaphors — one example being Bryan Singer's *X-Men*, which uses the clash between normal humans and superpowered mutants to make a statement about intolerance.

One possible explanation for why filmmakers of this generation are reluctant to examine certain divisive social issues is that to do so would require them to engage the institutions in which, as has been shown, their faith is limited at best. Saying that Gen Xers are disinclined to enter into political debates because they grew up in the shadow of Watergate is probably too convenient, but the widely reported statistics illustrating this generation's apathy at the voting booth seem to support this point. So perhaps the reason Gen-X directors feel queasy about subjects pertaining to politics (as well as religion and race) has more to do with their approach to life than the factors that helped form that approach.

Particularly with regard to crime and drugs, Gen-X directors frequently steer clear of traditional notions of morality; this unwillingness to accept ethical absolutes also is seen in Generation X's ambivalent attitude toward work. Therefore, it might follow that young people who don't believe in the old rules governing the workplace, the use of controlled substances, and other aspects of life would find the polemics of politics, religion, and race off-putting. In other words, Gen Xers certainly have opinions on the myriad topics gathered beneath these broad umbrellas, but their opinions might be so mired in ambiguity that it's difficult for them to ally themselves with any one side of a contentious issue.

If that's the case, then perhaps Gen Xers avoid the vehement rhetoric surrounding, say, abortion, by concentrating on how individual characters make important choices. This is a hypothetical generalization, of course, but it fits with some important patterns that have emerged in this book: If Gen Xers are disillusioned about social institutions, it's reasonable to assume they would avoid becoming part of such institutions, and avoid entering into the ideological fray created when factions of these institutions disagree.

Despite the fact that social changes and behavioral patterns seem to bind massive segments of Generation X, perhaps the thing that binds them most — as seen in the paucity of this generation's filmmakers who take strong stands on divisive issues— is a refusal to anchor themselves to the moral absolutes that, in their cynical worldview, led American society to become the combative arena in which they were raised.

Playing Politics

Among Gen-X movies that are unequivocally about politics, the most brazen is Alexander Payne's debut, *Citizen Ruth*. The loose, scruffy comedy centers around Ruth Stoops (Laura Dern), who seems like pure white trash when we meet her: She's a scrawny, dim loudmouth who sniffs glue for fun, gets in trouble with the law so often that she's on a first-name basis with the cops in her small town, and is such an unfit mother that her children were removed from her care by government officials.

Early in the picture, she gets tossed into a cell with Gail Stoney (Mary Kay Place), a right-to-life activist incarcerated for her part in an illegal demonstration. Upon learning that Ruth is pregnant, her jailers encourage the troubled woman to get an abortion, figuring it will save the unborn child from the neglect that Ruth would surely inflict upon it. Gail sees an propaganda opportunity and pounces. She offers to take Ruth in and pay her expenses, provided the young woman sees her pregnancy through, in effect hiring Ruth as an anti-abortion symbol.

Meanwhile, a group of ardent pro-choice activists seize on the idea that Ruth also could be a symbol for their cause. A manic tussle between the warring forces occurs, putting human faces on one of the most painful debates in modern culture. Ruth watches the insults and speeches fly past her the way a spectator watches the ball at a tennis match, even moving from Gail's house to that of the witchcraft-practicing pro-choicers so she can see who offers her a better deal. The joke, of course, is that the person who is least invested in the fate of Ruth's baby seems to be Ruth. For while she appears to genuinely listen to the arguments being put forth by both sides of the debate, she is unmistakably seduced by how much the pro-lifers and pro-choicers are willing to spend to secure her loyalty.

Although he mostly films events in an unintrusive, documentary-like style, Payne exhibits palpable cynicism through his arch characterizations. He portrays almost everyone but Ruth as a hysterical extremist, then shows a "simpleton" playing both sides against the middle and coming out on top. The implication is that the idealism of the various activists is married to their vanity, so at a certain point, they become more concerned with validating their righteousness than with helping Ruth find the path that's right for her. The movie is a slap in the face to people who let their devotion to political issues cloud their view of reality, and a brutal put-down of the breed of armchair extremists depicted throughout the movie.

Whereas the activists in *Citizen Ruth* are comical because they're in over their heads, the activist portrayed by Jennifer Connelly in Keith Gordon's *Waking the Dead* is deadly serious because she knows exactly what she's getting herself into at any given point. The mournful, elegant movie is a love story with a vaguely supernatural twist, centering around the anguish suffered by ambitious young politician Fielding Pierce (Billy Crudup) when his lover, activist Sarah Williams (Connelly), is murdered. The movie cuts back and forth between the 1970s, the time that Fielding and Sarah spend together, and the 1980s, when Fielding tries to find his way without his soulmate.

At first, the couple seem oddly matched: He's a sailor eager to do his part in Vietnam, and she's an impassioned antiwar crusader. They disagree about everything except the importance of politics, although each wants to change the world for the better. Fielding wants to make his impact within the system; Sarah believes the system is designed to keep people like Fielding from having an impact. Their passion for the world around them, as well as their intense physical attraction, helps them overcome their differences and land in each other's arms. Yet as soon as their bond is cemented, it is shaken by the careers they choose.

Strange bedfellows: Love bridges the differences between a headstrong activist (Jennifer Connelly) and an ambitious would-be politician (Billy Crudup) in Keith Gordon's haunting drama *Waking the Dead* (USA Films).

Fielding gets taken under the wing of Isaac Green (Hal Holbrook), a seasoned politician who thinks he can turn his protégé's idealism and good looks into star value. Meanwhile, Sarah begins working with Father Mileski (John Carroll Lynch), a priest who runs an inner-city shelter. The lovers clash because Fielding compromises his ideals, while Sarah seems incapable of compromise of any kind. In a typically heated scene, Sarah accompanies Fielding and Isaac to a cocktail party attended by a slew of political heavy hitters. Regarding Sarah merely as his apprentice's arm candy, Isaac mistakenly introduces her several times as Sarah "Wilson." Afraid to rock the boat, Fielding doesn't correct the error. Her intolerance of fatuousness surfacing, Sarah eventually snaps at Isaac, causing a minor scene and infuriating her boyfriend. The lovers smooth each other's bruised egos after the party, but the issues that caused the fight remain unresolved.

By the time Father Mileski recruits Sarah for an illegal humanitarian mission to South America, she and her companion are worlds apart: Fielding resents that her idealism makes him self-conscious about selling out, and she's sad that the man she fell in love with is turning into someone else. So when she's killed by terrorists during the mission, Fielding is consumed by unresolved feelings. The love affair he expected to go on forever is done, he never got a chance to make peace with Sarah, and her memory haunts every shifty political decision he makes. Gordon shows Fielding's troubled state of mind by having ghostly visions of Sarah appear everywhere around the young politician, eventually driving him to the brink of madness. The movie plays a sly game with Sarah's supernatural visitations, because she could be an actual ghost or merely a manifestation of Fielding's pain. Either way, she functions as a personification of his conscience, which makes the movie a statement on baby-boomer politics.

Fielding, a boomer put onscreen by a team of Gen Xers, was literally in bed with liberalism at the beginning of his career, but by the time he wins a Senate seat at the end of the picture, he's drifted so far from his ideals that liberalism is merely a beautiful phantom hovering around the fringes of his life. Gordon offers a moving but somewhat pat resolution to this unresolvable conflict when letters from constituents and a final visitation from Sarah remind Fielding that although ambition brought him to the Senate, the needs of the people should define what he does as a congressman. Idealism wins this round, but only after a wrenching fight.

Idealism is even more ephemeral in Steven Soderbergh's *Traffic*, which features Michael Douglas as Robert Wakefield, an American judge recruited to fight the nation's war on drugs, but who soon learns that his own daughter is a drug addict. Just as Fielding's ascension into politics is haunted by the memory of a woman who told him what politics could be, Robert's ascension to the position of drug czar is haunted by the knowledge that he's caught in the crossfire of the war he's supposed to be waging. At the end of *Traffic*, Robert falters partway through an important press conference at the White House, then drops the mask of political resolve and says: "I can't do this. If there is a war on drugs, then our own families have become the enemy. How can you wage war on your own family?"

This moment represents politics at its murkiest, when right and wrong have blurred so completely that no moral compass can indicate a path out of darkness. Like *Waking the Dead*, *Traffic* ends on a compassionate note — Robert and his wife accompany their daughter to a drug-treatment session — suggesting that humanity can heal wounds that punditry can't.

Punditry runs rampant in the first two movies directed by Rod Lurie, a former film critic who brought his love of words, actors, and politics to the screen with noteworthy force in the late 1990s. His first movie, the little-seen *Deterrence*, depicts an untested American president forced to handle a major international crisis while he and his staff are snowed in at a small-town diner. Lurie's sophomore effort, *The Contender*, garnered infinitely more attention than his first, in large part because the independent production was picked up for distribution by DreamWorks SKG, the young studio co-helmed by Steven Spielberg.

It's a safe bet that the movie would have turned heads even if it was released independently, however, because the story about a woman nominated for the vice presidency touches on controversial issues of gender equality, liberalism, attack politics, and sensationalism. Although Payne's *Citizen Ruth* and *Election* have more bite because they use satire to peer beneath the surface of divisive debates, *The Contender* is unique among Gen-X movies in that it feels like a solicitation for viewers to deepen their involvement in the political process, so as to protect the process from abuse by characters like the ruthless conservatives who antagonize the title character.

The Great Divide

If Gen-X filmmakers have been timid about politics, they've been positively ostrich-like about racial issues, despite the fact that race-related tensions exploded after such 1990s occurrences as the beating of Rodney King and the riots that followed the acquittal of his police assailants. As of this writing, John Singleton is the dominant figure among Gen-X filmmakers whose films are primarily concerned with discussions of racial identity. Singleton, Kasi Lemmons (who made memorable observations about race in her first two pictures, *Eve's Bayou* and *The Caveman's Valentine*), and George Tillman, Jr. (director of such crowd-pleasers as *Soul Food* and *Men of Honor*) are African-American, which suggests that white Gen-X filmmakers are reluctant, if not outright fearful, of addressing the great divide in American society. Lemmons offered a possible explanation for this phenomenon when asked about her ability to write white characters.

> As a black person living in a modern world, you know all about it, you understand the "master race." For white people to understand enough to write like a black person, that might be different, because white people don't *have* to understand black people. Black people *have* to understand white people.[1]

Ironically, the Gen-X filmmaker who has most famously celebrated black culture is a white man — even though his portrayals have split audiences between those who find his vision of African-American culture sensationalistic and those who find it affectionate. In both *Pulp Fiction* and *Jackie Brown*, Quentin Tarantino displays a passion for black slang, dress, and music that borders on the fetishistic: White and black characters alike, for instance, use urban vernacular that could easily fit into a 1970s blaxploitation movie or a 1990s rap song. Consider this line from *Pulp Fiction*, spoken by the black character Jules: "I wouldn't go so far as to call the brother fat. He's got a weight problem. What's the nigger gonna do? He's Samoan."

A great deal has been made about Tarantino's use of the word *nigger*, and black actor Denzel Washington reportedly confronted Tarantino about the issue while Tarantino was on the set of Washington's submarine thriller *Crimson Tide*, to which Tarantino contributed dialogue; according to accounts of the encounter, Washington was not among those who find Tarantino's use of the word charming.

Inarguably one of the most loaded words in the English language, *nigger* has in recent years been stripped of some of its power to hurt by its use among African-Americans as a friendly appellation: Phrases such as "Yo, nigger, whassup?" were commonplace in black-oriented films, comedy routines, and songs of the 1990s. Yet when the transformed word was borrowed by white adherents of black culture, it went through another cultural change. Whether it's a white gangster in a Tarantino movie or a white teenager in a shopping mall, a Caucasian shouting "Yo nigger, whassup?" or another such phrase is a startling image, no matter if the person being addressed is white or black.

Some have argued that by appropriating loaded African-American vernacular, Tarantino and other whites both propagate stereotypes and make sensational associations to the most lurid aspects of black culture. That argument is bolstered somewhat by the black characters in Tarantino's films, who recall the jive-talking, street-smart crooks of blaxploitation movies. So even though the director's affection for characters such as Jules and the titular figure of *Jackie Brown* (played by black screen icon Pam Grier) is palpable, the question arises of whether he's performing a disservice by showing gun-toting, streetwise blacks.

One thought worth considering when trying to answer that question is that Tarantino raises the characters above stereotypes by giving them something close to three-dimensional life. Another important fact is that Tarantino often puts across images of whites and blacks coexisting harmoniously: Jules is more or less comfortably partnered with a white hoodlum in *Pulp Fiction*, Jackie Brown is receptive to the courtship of a white man, and so on. But while the final determination of whether Tarantino is an acolyte or an exploiter of African-American culture rests with individual viewers, the fact remains that he consistently features black actors and black culture in his movies—which makes him much more ethnically adventurous than most of his white peers.

Accordingly, it has fallen to black directors to put informed images of African-Americans onscreen, and John Singleton has faced this challenge admirably throughout his career. He occasionally tells stories about blacks with superheroic qualities, as in *Rosewood* and *Shaft*, but even these stories are populated with characters who echo people from the real world. Singleton's celebrated debut film, *Boyz N the Hood*, was based on the troubled urban milieu he observed while growing up in Los Angeles, and is such an overt plea for an end to the madness of gang violence that the first image is a dolly in to a "Stop" sign, preceded by a series of title cards bearing grim statistics: "One out of every twenty-one black American males will be murdered.... Most will die at the hands of another black male."

To show the human reality behind this statistic, Singleton depicts two periods in the life of a character named Tre Styles. In an early sequence, ten-year-old Tre (Desi Arnez Hines II) watches his father, Furious (Lawrence Fishburne), try to shoot a home invader. When two police officers, one white and one black, show up an hour after being called, the black officer shockingly says to Furious: "Too bad you didn't get him. Be

Blood in the streets: *Boyz N the Hood*, a passionate depiction of the factors behind gang violence, was made by John Singleton, seen in glasses between costars Ice Cube (in driver's seat) and Cuba Gooding, Jr. (Columbia Pictures).

one less nigger out here in the streets we'd have to worry about." Recalling the sad truth of the opening titles, this moment underscores that white America's disdain for black America often is complemented by painful divisions within the African-American community.

By the time Tre has grown into a young man (Cuba Gooding, Jr.), he already has watched a friend become a hardened criminal. Shortly after completing a stint in prison that began when he was a juvenile, Tre's buddy Doughboy (Ice Cube) gets mixed up in a grudge match that leads to the drive-by execution of Doughboy's innocent brother, Ricky (Morris Chestnut). In one of Singleton's characteristically heavy-handed but effective touches, viewers learn that Ricky's recent success on his SAT assured him a shot at a college education — and by extension life outside the 'hood — so his tragedy is felt on numerous levels. Yet Singleton's clunkier touches are complemented by potent dramatics, such as the scene in which Ricky's mother and young wife scream over his bloody, lifeless body while Ricky's infant child squeals.

Despite his father's many lessons about the need to avoid senseless violence, Tre nearly succumbs to rage by joining Doughboy on a night-time mission for retribution against Ricky's killers. After sitting in Doughboy's car alongside a bloodthirsty friend who's loading a magazine into an AK-47, Tre comes to his senses and heads home, but his departure doesn't derail the mission: Doughboy finds and brutally assassinates the three men responsible for his brother's death, in the process securing his own doomed place in a cycle of violence and hatred. Tre, nobly trying to understand the conflicting parts of his friend, speaks with Doughboy after the bloodshed, and all the killer can come up with is this: "I don't even know how I feel about it neither, man. Shit just goes on and on, you know? Next thing you know, somebody might try to smoke me. Don't matter though. We all gotta go sometime."

This is the saddest and most important statement in Singleton's movie — that members of this rung of American society feel the disdain that others have for them so deeply that their own sense of self-worth is damaged. Some members of the South Central community know better than to drop out of a culture that doesn't want them, as Tre eventually proves. But for youths raised amid rampant violence, nearly bereft of positive role models, and lacking proper academic nurturing, the descent to a life like Doughboy's seems pre-ordained. And destiny is a strong element of Singleton's storytelling, for his movie ends with title cards indicating that Doughboy was killed two weeks after his bloody revenge — and that Tre went on to college.

The obvious message of *Boyz N the Hood* is that violence begets violence, and the deeper one is that incessant racism can cause minorities to regard themselves in a racist manner. This deeper message resonates with myriad other Gen-X movies, for while the disenfranchisement of Gen Xers is a cakewalk compared to the pain inflicted upon urban blacks, one thing binds the experiences of these two segments of society: Like African-Americans oppressed and changed by racism, Gen Xers are in many ways defined by society's attitude toward them, whether it manifests as the choices made by parents when Gen Xers were growing up or as difficulty that employers often have adjusting to the laid-back attitude of slackers and pseudoslackers.

Singleton's work on *Boyz N the Hood* was so assured that he won Oscar nominations for Best Original Screenplay and Best Director, the latter of which was notable because Singleton was the youngest person ever to receive such a nod. He seemed poised for a career spent telling relevant stories, but Singleton's next pictures were unfocused. *Poetic Justice* was a love story involving two young, black artists, but the story was trite and lightweight, and the inclusion of poetry by revered author Maya Angelou seemed pretentious. Singleton's third picture, *Higher Learning*, took the moralistic qualities of *Boyz N the Hood* to an uncomfortable extreme, and the movie felt more like a Sunday-morning sermon than a melodrama.

Singleton finally got back on track — and brought a bracing new energy to his depiction of race relations — in *Rosewood*, his most ambitious film to date. Based on the true story of a black-populated Southern town that was better off than its white-populated sister town, the drama is an alternately rousing and terrifying depiction of the moment when the whites struck out at their neighbors by destroying the black town. The film is weakened somewhat by the fictionalized figure of a superheroic black drifter who helps save several Rosewood residents from the white assault, but had this character not been included, the picture might have been oppressively sad.

One of the most striking Gen-X films about race entirely avoided the contentious issue of relations between whites and blacks, for it depicts the lives of young Native Americans, a population virtually invisible in American cinema outside of stereotypical portrayals. Chris Eyre's *Smoke Signals*, about two twentysomethings who leave their reservation on a quest that leads them to confront the repercussions of a decades-old family tragedy, is a quick, breezy jaunt filled with funny conversations, polemical confrontations, and, best of all, fully realized characters.

Victor (Adam Beach), a bitter loner who tries to scare away the world with his rough manners, and Thomas (Evan Adams), a sweet nebbish who's continually trying to revive his childhood friendship with Victor, travel from Spokane, Washington, to Phoenix, Arizona, when Victor's estranged father dies. Along the way, the two unravel the catastrophic event that shattered both their families and sent Victor on a self-destructive spiral. (Victor's trajectory, incidentally, proves that fleeing from society after a familial schism isn't a phenomenon unique to the predominantly white slackers who turned such escapism into an art form.) Like the best road movies, *Smoke Signals* is about people traveling into their souls as much as it's about people visiting faraway locales.

The script, adapted by Sherman Alexie from his own novel, uses the casual banter of longtime acquaintances to explore racial identity and personal demons. Alexie also tosses in playful jabs at Hollywood's image of Native Americans: "The only thing more pathetic than Indians on TV is Indians watching Indians on TV," Thomas jokes at one point. Throughout the picture, the traveling companions wrestle not with what it means to be Indians, but what it means to be Indians in a culture dominated by Indians' historical persecutors. This stance recalls Lemmons's point about African-Americans learning the ways of white people, and underlines the tragedy of marginalizing or even destroying ethnicity.

In all of these films about race — from *Boyz N the Hood* to *Smoke Signals*— an important recurring theme is that minorities have to rely on each other to survive in a world that is not their own, even when members of their own subcultures prey upon them. This idea, of relying not on larger social institutions but on the solidarity binding a group of outsiders, connects these films about race to a major theme running through the cinema of Generation X: We were handed this world, these characters say, so it's up to us to help each other find our way in it.

Interestingly, one way that characters in Gen-X movies have found to bridge the great divide is to trust love: Several Gen-X movies depict interracial relationships. At their most sensationalistic, the depictions of miscegenation play up the dangerous thrill of doing something that was once taboo, and even illegal; a pointed scene in *The Caveman's Valentine* shows the black hero having sex with a white woman while the spirit of his (black) wife acerbically comments that every white woman is curious to see whether myths about black males' sexual prowess is true. The titillating aspect of an interracial affair also is explored in John Stockwell's *crazy/beautiful*, an intimate drama about a troubled white teen who falls in love with an ambitious young Latino. The self-destructive white girl recalls numerous disenfranchised Gen-X protagonists, so watching her surmount internal obstacles while also surmounting a societal one is heartening.

It is not just the female in this movie's romance who faces obstacles, of course — her Latino lover wrestles with racism, the diminished expectations that some whites have of minorities, and the pressure placed on him by his family to succeed. That he does so is a testament to his spirit, and similar testimony is provided in George Tillman, Jr.'s *Men of Honor* and Boaz Yakin's *Remember the Titans*. The former film, about a black man fighting racism to succeed in the U.S. Navy, and the latter, about how a black coach helps high school athletes face the problems of integration, are old-fashioned movies about race relations in which the dignity of heroic African-American characters forces white characters to abandon, or at least reconsider, their prejudice.

As Faith Would Have It

Just as Gen-X directors as a group are reluctant to address racial issues, they are loathe to court controversy by diving into the morass of religion. Certainly Gen Xers are not alone in their timidity regarding this subject matter; the history of cinema is littered with religious films that sidestep thorny discussions by depicting historical figures as cardboard saints (*The Ten Commandments*), and daring movies that spark vehement debates by questioning accepted beliefs about icons (*The Last Temptation of Christ*). Most filmmakers reside in the conservative middle ground between piety and revisionism, choosing to evade religious issues altogether. Therefore, the Gen-X aversion to such issues is less characteristic of generational identity than par for the Hollywood course. That said, the boldness of the few Gen-X filmmakers who have entered the fray of religious discourse is admirable.

Alexander Payne lessened the sting of his satirical portrayal of right-to-life extremists in *Citizen Ruth* by also poking fun at pro-choice extremists; he's an equal-opportunity satirist. Similarly, Rod Lurie's *The Contender* entertains both sides of a religious debate by having a conservative right-winger take a liberal left-winger to task over issues of sexuality. Both of these films are only peripherally about religion, however — and in fact, it seems that only two Gen-X movies have wholeheartedly entered the combat zone of religious conflict. They are Edward Norton's sweet *Keeping the Faith* and Kevin Smith's salacious *Dogma*. The movies couldn't be further apart in terms of content and style, but their thematic intentions are similar. Through different means, each demonstrates the value — and, importantly, the validity — of spirituality.

The plot of *Keeping the Faith* sounds like the setup for a bad joke: A priest and a rabbi fall for the same girl. But the wrinkles that director-costar Norton and his collaborators add to the material make it a touching, memorable exploration of the role religion can play in people's lives. The priest, Brian Finn (Norton), and the rabbi, Jake Schram (Ben Stiller), have been friends since childhood, and the playmate of their youth was a tomboy named Anna. Early in the picture, she returns to the trio's hometown, New York City, as an adult — but the tomboy of yesteryear has become a sexy, confident businesswoman (Jenna Elfman).

The male friends are attracted to their old pal, but their desire is problematic because Brian is devoted to his vow of celibacy, and because Jake feels pressured to date women who share his faith. (Anna is a Gentile.) The romantic triangle is further complicated by misunderstandings, other women, and, most importantly, the revelation of where Anna's affections truly lie. She loves both of her childhood friends, but is only in love with Jake. Yet at the end of the film, both men are happy: Jake is involved with Anna, and Brian strengthens his relationship with God. This payoff may sound cloying, but a key scene between Brian and his mentor, Czechoslovakian priest Father Havel (Milos Forman), articulates the tentative peace that can be achieved between physical desire and religious devotion. The conversation is sparked when Brian reveals that he tried to kiss Anna, but was rebuffed.

> HAVEL: I remember I fell in love with this girl in Prague. It was in 1968. She was beautiful. She looked like Carole Lombard. She grabbed me. It was in the alley behind my church. She kissed me. Whew! I felt like Richard Chamberlain in *The Thorn Birds*...
>
> BRIAN: I'll tell you something — if she had kissed me back, I don't think I'd be sitting here right now. I would've given it all up.... I keep thinking about what you said in seminary, that the life of a priest is hard, and if you can see yourself being happy doing anything else, you should do that.
>
> HAVEL: That's my recruitment speech, which is not bad when you're starting out. It makes you feel like a Marine. The truth is, you can never tell yourself that there is only one thing that you could be. To be a priest or to marry a woman — it's the same challenge. You cannot make a real commitment unless you accept that it's a choice that you keep making again and again and again. I've been a priest over forty years, and I fall in love at least once every decade.
>
> BRIAN: You're not going to tell me what to do, are you?
>
> HAVEL: No. God will give you your answer.

Keeping the Faith is filled with moments in which the clergymen question their life choices, yet the movie also is filled with gentle humor poking fun at the sterility of religious services. Jake tries to liven things up at temple by working the room like a stand-up comedian, and by enlisting a black choir to spice up a service's musical component. This is a far cry from the hyperbole of Hollywood's Biblical epics of the 1950s and 1960s, and a far cry from the satire of *Citizen Ruth*. *Keeping the Faith* may be the warmest movie yet made by a Gen Xer, and while some might find its kindhearted message of tolerance naive or false, the movie nonetheless offers a heartfelt alternative to the turmoil that often characterizes Gen-X cinema.

Dogma offers an outrageous alternative to *Keeping the Faith*— the Kevin Smith comedy is so polarizing that its original distributor, Miramax, was forced to drop the picture after pressure from parent company Disney. Whereas *Keeping the Faith* is a sedate romantic comedy, *Dogma* is a vulgar farce. The plot, culled from the arcana of Catholic theology, is a doozy: Two fallen angels find a loophole in God's law that will allow them to reenter heaven, but to do so will cause the nullification of the entire universe. So as the former seraphim (Matt Damon and Ben Affleck) make their way to a church in New Jersey through which they plan to return to their former home, a nonbeliever (Linda Fiorentino) is recruited to help stop them.

The movie slaughters as many sacred cows as possible. Black comedian Chris Rock appears as a mythical "thirteenth apostle" named Rufus; God's right hand man is an embittered angel (Alan Rickman) who's unimaginably tired of immortality and who resents terribly that he wasn't gifted with genitalia; and God (played by rock singer Alanis Morrissette) is depicted as a impulsive but just ruler as likely to use her celestial might to smite wayward souls as she is to feebly attempt cartwheels on a patch of grass. In one of the film's most brilliant bits, a bishop (George Carlin) tries to lure young people to the church by replacing the somber icon of a crucified Jesus with the smiling image of "Buddy Christ"— the son of God reimagined as a snarky Vegas lounge lizard. Smith caught heat because he freely mingled vulgarity with spirituality, but his movie ultimately is a testament to faith and, despite his obvious misgivings, the Catholic Church.

For even while suggesting that a black man sat at the last supper and proposing that Jesus might want to lighten up, Smith clearly identifies which characters in his story are amoral. The fallen angels have such compromised souls that they're willing to summon the apocalypse in order to realize their selfish goals, and their accomplice is a demon complete with horns, a deceptively charming smile, and a bad attitude. The characters pursuing righteous goals may include a sexy stripper, but they also include a nonbeliever who learns to acknowledge and love God. Therefore, those who called the film anti-Catholic were at best uninformed and at worst ignorant. As the writer-director said:

> The movie's not an attack. It's a challenge. To me, Christ is like a friend I've known my whole life. You know, the friend that doesn't talk to you. But

everyone tells me he said a lot of things while he was here, so you follow what he taught. When you've had a friend for twenty years, I think you're allowed to joke around with him.... The movie's so pro-faith, I feel like I'm doing the Catholic League's job.[2]

Smith's attitude is a terrific example of what Gen Xers are capable of when they choose to fully participate in society, instead of merely sitting on the couch and making sardonic comments about life as it passes them by. As do Payne's and Lurie's movies about politics, as well as Singleton's and Lemmons's movies about race, the Gen-X movies about religion prove that Gen Xers don't disdain social institutions because of ignorance, but because of disagreements with what those institutions represent. Therefore, when filmmakers risk controversy by asking provocative questions about contemporary political, racial, and religious issues, they take a bold step away from the apathy with which Generation X has long been associated. They dig deep for answers to that most essential Gen-X question, "Who am I, and where do I belong?" By doing so, they help look for means by which people of all stripes—Republicans, Democrats, blacks, whites, Catholics, Jews, boomers, Gen Xers—can live together if not in peace, than at least in understanding.

11

Worlds Beyond Worlds

One of the intriguing lessons gleaned from studying Gen-X filmmakers is which topics they explore comfortably and which ones they explore haltingly. In general, the most powerful statements offered by these directors relate to issues that affect the here and now of their young lives: education, family, work, love, sexuality, drugs. Yet when challenged to look ahead, they seem to falter. Perhaps reflecting the collective youth of their makers, films helmed by Gen Xers mostly shun issues of old age and the future. Given the generational predilection toward exploring issues of life's meaning — as seen, particularly, in the philosophy-drenched personas of slacker characters— the reluctance these filmmakers have about imagining what comes next in their chronology is telling.

In the most cynical interpretation, Gen Xers don't discuss old age and the future because they have no optimism for what looms ahead. But perhaps the real reason behind their reticence in these areas is that Gen Xers' ambivalence about the present makes them dubious about prognostication: As they have such a tentative grasp on the forces that define the present, guessing which forces might define the future is daunting.

When the concept of aging arises in Gen-X movies, it's usually portrayed tragically, as in Paul Thomas Anderson's *Magnolia* (which depicts how families are affected by the impending deaths of old men) and Bryan Singer's *Apt Pupil* (which shows an aging Nazi corrupting a willful youth). To a certain degree, the fear of aging that this portrayal implies is par for the course — by definition, the young haven't the maturity required to understand the old, no matter how genuinely they may respect previous generations. Yet Generation X's relationship to their immediate predecessors provides two more possible explanations for Generation X's hesitance about the future.

First and most obviously, a boomer's vision of the future played a key role in Generation X's past. *Star Wars* became a blockbuster in 1977, and

Gen Xers comprise a huge segment of the youth audience that supported George Lucas's space opera. Young viewers' infatuation with futuristic stories continued through the late 1970s and early 1980s, yet the generation weaned on *Star Wars* has been slow to imitate the popcorn fare it consumed when young: *The Matrix*, *The Crow*, *Dark City*, *Gattaca*, and *X-Men* are among the few major futuristic statements made by Gen-X filmmakers, and two of them (*The Crow* and *Dark City*) were made by the same man, Alex Proyas. While the paucity of Gen-X sci-fi flicks might suggest that Generation X doesn't share the wonderment and hopefulness (or, some might say, naiveté) that distinguished its chronological predecessor before cynicism set in, it's also possible that the lack of futuristic visions can be attributed to cultural cycles.

The popularity of science fiction tends to ebb and flow, and the box-office success of *The Matrix* and Lucas's fourth *Star Wars* movie, *Episode One — The Phantom Menace* (both of which were released in 1999) laid the groundwork for a new run of sci-fi flicks. Such pictures are notoriously slow to emerge, because of the complexity involved in making them, so the repercussions of 1999's hits may be felt later in Generation X's run. Certainly the fact that Steven Soderbergh, forever the Gen-X pioneer, said in 2001 that he planned to remake an obscure Russian sci-fi movie called *Solaris* proves that this group of filmmakers may yet speak to a genre that had such a profound impact during their formative years.

Things to Come

Setting aside the reasons why they are so few, the major sci-movies directed by Gen Xers share an important aspect: All predict a bleak future in which the virtuous are a violently oppressed minority. *The Matrix* features an all-out war against the status quo, and *The Crow* and *X-Men* feature superpowered vigilantes as their protagonists. The heroes of *Dark City* and *Gattaca* face omniscient authority figures in the mode of Big Brother, the antagonist of George Orwell's endlessly imitated novel *1984*. And while it's true that these futuristic visions subscribe to a popular portrayal of the future — *The Crow*, for instance, has production design straight out of 1982's *Blade Runner*, the seminal science-fiction thriller directed by Ridley Scott — the similarities between Generation X's futuristic movies may indicate something more than just a generational affection for the same influences.

At the very least, the abject terror associated with institutionalized authority in these movies echoes the misgivings about institutions that permeate so many Gen-X movies. Members of this generation seem deeply fearful of dehumanized governments and corporations, whether personified by the humiliating workplace supervisors of *Office Space* or the unforgiving overlords of *Gattaca*.

Because they have so many precedents in other people's films, Alex Proyas's pictures are among the least unsettling of Generation X's cautionary sci-fi tales. *The Crow*, adapted from a comic book created by James O'Barr, is essentially an extra-violent, extra-fantastic retread of Tim Burton's *Batman*, only without the colorful villain and high-tech gadgets. It's a vigilante story with a strong heart and a haunting backstory, both of which involve star Brandon Lee. The son of legendary martial artist Bruce Lee, Brandon Lee gives a sexy and soulful performance as a musician raised from the dead to avenge an assault on his family. The poignancy of his performance is accentuated by viewers' knowledge that Lee was killed in an accident during filming; this actor playing an undead avenger actually is a voice from beyond the grave. Yet the trappings with which Proyas surrounds Lee lack the actor's humanity.

The ornate Gothic spires and cloud-choked skies that Proyas employs to personify the city in which the Crow lives are familiar to anyone who has seen *Batman*, *Blade Runner*, or Terry Gilliam's *Brazil*. All of these films imagine urban sprawl taken to its logical extreme, so the cities in these movies are nightmares of soulless towers, rampant grime, oppressive darkness, and pervasive smoke. They essentially are tweaked visions of modern-day Los Angeles or New York or Hong Kong or Chicago. And while his predecessors filled their dystopian milieus with ironic details, Proyas fills his with obvious signifiers.

The director's style matured somewhat in *Dark City*, which combined sci-fi elements with photography and clothes straight out of a 1940s film noir—again, à la *Blade Runner*. The picture, based on an original story by Proyas and his collaborators, imagines a weird future in which extraterrestrials control the life of the protagonist (Rufus Sewell) and other characters, taking the paranoia of *1984* to an extreme by saying that the all-powerful force pulling the puppet strings is genuinely otherworldly. While *Dark City* has several arresting visuals, it ultimately gets bogged down in borrowed ideas and comic-book-style action. It's interesting in the context of a discussion of Gen-X movies for its inescapable similarities to *The Matrix*, which also puts a fanciful spin on Orwell's familiar Big Brother imagery. *The Matrix*, however, succeeds where *Dark City* fails because *The Matrix* is structured as a classic quest story, and because the payoff at the end of the quest actually raises the stakes of the story, instead of merely tossing viewers an ironic, *Twilight Zone*-style twist.

Like *The Crow*, *X-Men* was adapted from a comic book. An exuberant adventure that replaces Proyas's bloodshed with tricked-up fisticuffs, the movie is set in the realm of countless other cautionary tales: the not-too-distant future. And like any cautionary tale worth its salt, *X-Men* has an issue: intolerance. The story portrays a secret war between good and evil "mutants," humans born with paranormal abilities. The other participant in this three-way aggression is ignorant humanity, as represented by McCarthy-esque Senator Robert Kelly (Bruce Davison). He wants mutants documented, detained, and maybe even exterminated. The intolerance that Kelly represents causes the movie's villain, Magneto (Ian McKellen), to lash out against normal humans, and causes its hero, Professor Charles Xavier (Patrick Stewart), to organize opposition against Magneto. Proyas's futuristic heroes resort to anarchistic violence to right the wrongs of their worlds, but the X-Men — as Xavier's costumed apprentices are called — practice a kind of civil disobedience, and curb bloodshed whenever possible.

If the future is incidental to Proyas's movies and to *X-Men*, however, it's integral to *Gattaca*, screenwriter Andrew Niccol's directorial debut — and probably the most emotionally resounding Gen-X sci-fi flick. Subtle and sad where *The Matrix* is flamboyant and angry, *Gattaca* uses a wrenching human drama to illustrate the unimaginable realities of an Orwellian future.

Niccol's hauntingly paranoid movie posits a future in which a genetically engineered master race occupies the top strata of society, while naturally born — and therefore imperfect — people are ostracized bottom-feeders. Given the staggering advances in medical science at the end of the twentieth century and the beginning of the twenty-first, from successful cloning experiments to the emergence of genetically engineered food, the science underpinning Niccol's fiction is utterly contemporary, so the ethical issues he explores are uniquely relevant. It's therefore disappointing that *Gattaca* isn't wholly effective as a drama. The minimalistic style of the movie is intoxicating and the story line raises issues that provoke intriguing conversations, but Niccol's screenplay eventually drowns in pedestrian narrative elements.

Before that happens, however, Niccol sets up a fascinating premise. In the future world dominated by lab-perfected paragons, one of the genetically engineered aristocrats (Jude Law) loses the use of his legs, so he sells his identity to a man of low — read: natural — birth (Ethan Hawke). To put across the illusion of being perfect, Hawke's character must ensure that he leaves no traces of his imperfect physicality anywhere, so he scrubs his skin raw in the shower to dislodge every tiny fragment of dead skin, and panics when he misplaces the corrective lenses that adjust his poor vision to ideal standards. Niccol's movie contains allusions to Nazism, of course, but also represents an educated, cynical guess about where man's tinkering in his own physiology could lead: If we can get to the point of building perfect people in a laboratory, wouldn't our traditional disdain for the imperfect — as seen in centuries of racial, ethnic, and religious intolerance — lead us to create a new hierarchy meant to shun the weak, the stupid, the ugly? As he did in his remarkable script for *The Truman Show*, Niccol poignantly dramatizes the human capacity for inhumanity — a theme that not only dovetails but in some ways encapsulates the feelings that feed into Generation X's collective sense of alienation.

Despite the presence of such timely subject matter, it's impossible to discuss Gen-X movies without considering the movies that influenced them, from *Star Wars* to *Blade Runner* to *Brazil* and beyond. Great sci-fi films are few, but each casts such a long shadow that countless subsequent pictures are dismissed as weak imitations. Movies in other genres get put through the contrast-and-compare wringer — *Traffic* gets measured against *The French Connection*, the similarities between *Erin Brockovich* and *Norma Rae* are talking points — but sci-fi movies fare particularly poorly during the comparative process. So for some filmmakers, the better part of valor when it comes to science fiction is avoiding the genre entirely.

It's not so much that the genre's possibilities have been exhausted, but that the genre's possibilities have been so expertly explored that it's difficult to imagine concepts that won't be defined by their relationship to other ideas in other movies. In a way, perhaps this generation's youthful romance with science fiction has put them too far inside the genre to get an outside view of what colors haven't yet been added to the painting. Having said that, one particular science-fiction film, *The Matrix*, plays a crucial role in the cinema of Generation X. For that reason, a discussion of *The Matrix* occurs not here but at the end of this chapter, because the philosophical issues raised by Larry and Andy Wachowski's picture are so provocative that grouping it with other science-fiction films is too limiting.

Demons and Ghosts and Witches, Oh My!

While Gen Xers have been slow to attack the science-fiction genre, they have shown no such reluctance when embracing the related genre of fantasy — or the even more dynamic ilk of films that play with the line separating fantasy from reality. The savviness with which the makers of *The Sixth Sense*, *Being John Malkovich*, *The Blair Witch Project*, and other films question perceptions of actual and physical life probably has everything to do with this generation's relationship with cinema itself.

Generation X grew up knowing more about movies than any previous generation, and even the voluminous amounts of filmmaking information to which they had access as youths has been dwarfed by the avalanche of behind-the-scenes data that's available now, at the time when the oldest Gen Xers have reached maturity. (One can only imagine what the next generation of filmmakers will have to offer, given that the curtain hiding the secrets of movie magic seems to have been completely removed.) In a very important sense, movies such as *Being John Malkovich* and *The Blair Witch Project* are about the role that illusion plays in filmmaking — and about the fact that projected film images are in fact an illusion, thanks to the phenomenon called persistence of vision.

Probably the least original Gen-X movie about illusion and reality is *The Cell*, Tarsem Singh's ultra-stylized picture about a psychiatrist who enters the mind of a serial killer to learn the location of his victims. The picture got some attention upon release because of its disturbing visuals, such as a shot of a man voluntarily suspended by hooks attached to rings sewn into his skin, or a shot of a horse cleaved into pristine sections by sheets of glass. Critics rightly noted that the most sensationalistic visions in the picture were borrowed from hip New York artists—continuing a tradition begun with Alfred Hitchcock's employment of Salvador Dalí as the designer of *Spellbound*'s dream sequences—but less was made of how derivative the movie's central device was.

At least as far back as 1984, when a sci-fi thriller called *Dreamscape* was released, filmmakers have toyed with the idea of a characters projecting themselves into the slumbering minds of other characters. Singh tried to make the familiar seem fresh by utilizing ornate, frightening production design and by incorporating a pop-psychology backstory — the killer was abused as a child, so the shrink becomes an avenging angel who destroys the killer's rage, thus freeing the wronged babe inside the monster — but the movie was strangely flat and unmoving.

The first two films directed by Kasi Lemmons, *Eve's Bayou* and *The Caveman's Valentine*, deal with buried emotions more interestingly. Lemmons's debut, *Eve's Bayou*, is a strange and somewhat opaque combination of mystery and family drama in which the death of a philandering father may or may not have been caused by one of his daughters, who may or may not have used a combination of psychic ability and voodoo to avenge the sexual abuse of her sister. The qualifiers in this description are necessary because Lemmons's evasive narrative makes the "truth" of her fictional events hard to grasp; as have countless movies since Akira

Seductive savagery: Dream sequences in Tarsem Singh's *The Cell*, which illustrate how a killer (Vincent D'Onofrio) romanticizes himself, play a characteristic Gen-X game of blending reality and illusion (New Line Cinema).

Kurosawa's *Rashomon, Eve's Bayou* plays with the idea that when numerous people view a given event subjectively, adhering to any one objective description of the event is itself a subjective choice. The film won many partisans, and did surprisingly strong business given the usually chilly reception afforded serious films by and about black people, but just as its story points out how biases and emotions color recollections of fact, the story confounded as many viewers as it entranced. At the very least, the film is an effective mood piece with moments of otherworldly power — an effective conversation piece with an abundance of provocative narrative elements.

The surreal imagery in Lemmons's second film, *The Caveman's Valentine,* is less about a tumultuous past than a tumultuous present — specifically, the troubled existence of a schizophrenic named Romulus Ledbetter (Samuel L. Jackson). A former concert pianist living in a cave in New York City, he springs into action when a young murder victim is found outside his cave. Romulus becomes an ersatz private detective, but his investigation is hampered by the same force that provokes it: His delusional belief that an all-powerful figure called "Stuyvesant" is broadcasting "Z-rays" from the top of the Chrysler Building to control Romulus's life. The caveman is motivated in part by his desire to mete out justice, and in part by his desire to rebel against his imagined Orwellian oppressor. The Orwellian allusion, of course, connects *The Caveman's Valentine* to the myriad other Gen-X movies that suggest omniscient overlords.

Whereas the serial killer in *The Cell* has dreams in which he is personified as a glamorous demon, the hero of *The Caveman's Valentine* is haunted by demons. As we see in vivid flash cuts, he literally has bats in his belfry: Winged creatures fly around in his mind, perhaps to symbolize the dark and random thoughts that frequently overpower Romulus's consciousness. The character's inability to restrain his id is tragic and also strangely alluring. The obvious problem is that Romulus often erupts into seemingly unmotivated fits of rage, so his demons make it near-impossible to fit into "normal" society: At one point, Romulus talks his way into an elite party, then slides into the partygoers' confidence by playing the piano until an unprovoked outburst reveals his emotional imbalance.

But Romulus's fantasy life also is a benefit, because he's haunted by a facsimile of his estranged wife, Shiela (Tamara Tunie). She functions like a willful sidekick, taunting Romulus when he's about to do something stupid, but also inspiring him to greatness. The positivity of this imagery leavens the darkness of Romulus's other visions, creating an intriguingly balanced portrayal of insanity. On one level, the character's fantasy life is totally separate from reality, but on another level, his fantasies keep him grounded.

Fantasy and reality intertwine in a more traditional way throughout *The Sixth Sense*, M. Night Shyamalan's acclaimed and monstrously successful breakthrough film. The moody, measured thriller depicts the extraordinary relationship between psychologist Malcolm Crowe (Bruce Willis) and an eight-year-old patient named Cole Sear (Haley Joel Osment). Cole is troubled by bloody visions because, as he says in the movie's endlessly quoted tag line, "I see dead people." As Malcolm soon learns, the ghosts gravitate to Cole because he's able to communicate with those on "the other side." The ghosts want the youngster's assistance in resolving issues that were left hanging when they died. Malcolm aids Cole in revealing the identity of a murderer and other tasks before Shyamalan reveals his narrative trump card: Malcolm is himself dead, and is lingering in limbo because of unresolved issues related to his marriage.

On a narrative level, this twist of cinematic reality turns watching *The Sixth Sense* into a game, because Shyamalan put clues about Malcolm's secret into various parts of the movie. Except in a prologue, we see none but Cole acknowledge the psychiatrist's presence; Malcolm wears the same clothes throughout the movie, although the director hides this fact by having the character wear different versions of the same outfit; and so on.

But on an emotional level, Malcolm's secret adheres to a reality-defying idea that gained tremendous currency at the end of the twentieth century, the idea that souls linger on earth until they achieve "closure." Throughout the late 1990s, psychics were ubiquitous on television, books about the afterlife became best-sellers, and songs and movies and books featuring angel characters were embraced by the public. It was in this context that *The Sixth Sense* achieved massive success by tapping into the zeitgeist. Many pundits attributed the sudden interest in spirituality to the arrival of the millennium, and to the widespread superstition that the year 2000 might coincide with the Christian vision of Armageddon, at which point all living persons would be made to account for the virtue, or lack thereof, in their lives.

Whatever the reasons behind it, however, the mainstream acceptance of *The Sixth Sense* was interesting. Many bought tickets for the movie because word got out that it had a great twist ending, but there also must have been some appeal to the idea that Malcolm could use his afterlife to fix what was wrong with his actual life. As do Lemmons's films, Shyamalan's *The Sixth Sense* and *Unbreakable* convey the comforting idea that if people identify and fulfill their destinies, their souls will find peace. Significantly, these films address spiritual issues even though Gen-X filmmakers mostly avoid depicting the formal mechanism through which most people explore their spirituality, religion. This is yet another example of Gen Xers circumventing an institution in their quest for meaning.

Conventional ideas about reality also get a skewering in *Being John Malkovich*, which is largely informed by contemporary celebrity culture, but which also delves into issues of spirituality. Screenwriter Charlie Kaufman anticipated the kinds of discussions his movie would provoke, as seen in a self-reflexive monologue spoken relatively early in the movie. The speaker is a frustrated puppeteer named Craig (John Cusack), who has just discovered a portal into the mind of real-life actor John Malkovich — played in the movie, of course, by John Malkovich.

> CRAIG: The point is that this is a very odd thing — supernatural, for lack of a better word. It raises all sorts of philosophical questions about the nature of self, about the existence of the soul. Am I me? Is Malkovich Malkovich? Was the Buddha right, is duality an illusion? ... Do you see what a metaphysical can of worms this portal is? I don't think I can go on living my life as I have lived it.

The joke behind this monologue is that it's almost word-for-word the kind of vague blather that a pretentious critic might write after seeing *Being John Malkovich*, so it's a discussion about a discussion about the movie. That cheeky proposition is typical of Gen-X cinema, in part because of the generation's savviness about what movies are, and in part because of how deeply postmodern conceptualizing has penetrated modern critical thinking. *Pulp Fiction*, for instance, is at times a movie about watching a movie, and *The Blair Witch Project* is from beginning to end a movie about watching a movie.

No Gen-X picture has gotten more mileage from exploiting the divide between reality and fantasy than *Blair Witch*, which became symbolic of the modern independent-movie boom because it was such an inherently low-tech proposition. Conceived as a compilation of footage recovered from a trio of twentysomethings who disappeared in a Maryland forest while searching for an mythical figure called the Blair Witch, the movie was shot on grainy 16-millimeter film and equally grainy amateur-grade video.

Ironically, however, the pitching of the movie was as high-tech as its making was low-tech. Using a heavily trafficked Web site, the filmmakers created a complex "mythology" around their movie, and even convinced many moviegoers that the characters and images in *The Blair Witch Project* were real. So on a certain level, this black-and-white, unprofessional-looking movie is the best example yet of how Generation X's relationship with technology affects their perceptions of reality: By making their film look amateurish, and then using technological means to spread a lie about it, the makers of *The Blair Witch Project* pulled the wool over the eyes of a vast segment of a technology-savvy generation. The illusion was made even more complete by a widely seen companion documentary, *The Curse of the Blair Witch*, which was in many ways more polished and persuasive than the actual film.

Even among those who were in on the joke, however, the interplay between reality and fantasy in *The Blair Witch Project* was delicious. In the movie, three would-be documentarians venture into a forest that, according to legend, has for centuries been haunted by the Blair Witch, the bloodthirsty and vengeful spirit of a woman who was shunned by ignorant locals. As the three go deeper into the forest, they are spooked by unexplained noises and by peculiar artifacts that appear around their campsites as if by magic. Once they decide to flee, they realize they have lost any sense of direction — so the movie becomes a ticking clock counting down the minutes until the Blair Witch claims three more victims.

The slyest gimmick in the film is that the witch, presuming she "exists," is never shown: The biggest hint that the myth is reality is the

Be afraid ... be very afraid: A deft exercise in postmodern horror, the Daniel Myrick–Eduardo Sánchez film *The Blair Witch Project* features Heather Donahue as a willful college student due for a deadly comeuppance (Artisan Entertainment).

movie's famous final shot, in which protagonist Heather (Heather Donahue), enters what appears to be the witch's lair, points her camera at the seemingly paralyzed body of her friend, and is struck by a powerful offscreen force. After more than eighty teasing minutes, this climax is a shattering payoff for those who succumbed to the movie's unusual spell.

For all of their fanciful imagining, fantasy films — whether horror shows such as *The Cell* or satirical romps such as *Being John Malkovich* — ultimately deal with the gap between reality and fiction in a conventional fashion, grounding viewers in an idea of objective reality. Romulus's visions in *The Caveman's Valentine* are obviously not real (we know they exist only in his head); the trips into the mind of *Being John Malkovich* are obviously not real (the whole context of the movie is self-consciously contrived); and *The Sixth Sense* is predicated on the familiar concept of the dead being able to communicate with the living.

Conversely, *Eve's Bayou* and *The Blair Witch Project* leave unanswered questions in their wake, for they portray supernatural forces that defy simple explanations. Did the little girl in *Eve's Bayou* kill her father by normal means or by utilizing voodoo? Is the witch in *The Blair Witch Project* real, or did some maniac exploit superstition? These adventurous films zero in on an idea that's close to the heart of Gen-X cinema's modus operandi: Given how familiar audiences are with the means by which filmmakers create illusions, the illusions that have the greatest impact are the ones left unexplained. These films, then, are as enigmatic and over-whelming as modern life itself.

The three doomed souls wandering through *Blair Witch* can even be interpreted as poignant metaphors for Generation X itself. Lost in the wilds of contemporary existence, and with no map to guide them to safety, the characters are beset by unseen forces over which they have no control and about which they have terrifyingly limited knowledge. They are dis-connected from the institutions that could protect them — family, com-munity, authority — so is it any wonder that they are consumed by the void?

The fear that Gen Xers are working without a net, that they are so disconnected from other segments of society that they are at risk of being destroyed by the unknown like the characters in *The Blair Witch Project*, pervades some of Generation X's darkest films. In David Fincher's *The Game*, a businessman is shunted into a dangerous adventure, with mys-terious assailants pursuing him for no apparent reason. The businessman learns that his reckless brother hired a firm to chase him as part of a life-or-death game that the brother hoped would shake the businessman free from his soulless lifestyle. Fincher backs off from the potentialities of this story with a cheap trick ending, but the paranoia implied by the story line — "Everyone's out to get me, but I don't know why" — is telling.

Similarly, Max (Sean Gullette), the protagonist of Darren Aronofsky's debut film, *Pi*, finds himself the target of unwanted attention when he becomes embroiled in a weird plot involving computers, arcane elements of Judaica, and other disparate factors. Max's brain contains esoteric knowledge that both maddens him and sparks the interest of extremist groups, making him a victim of his own intelligence. Aronofsky's thriller is loaded with wild intellectual concepts and presented as sensory bom-bardment, so the madness eating at Max's brain, for instance, is repre-sented by a piercing noise that Aronofsky plays at such an intense, unrelenting volume that viewers experience almost the same discomfort as the beleaguered hero.

Max is a surpassingly brilliant mathematician who has shut out the rest of the world to crunch numbers in his claustrophobic Manhattan apartment. He stumbles across a 216-digit figure that crashes his super-computer, and after he discards his only printout of the number, extrem-ists hunt him down because they view the number as a key to power. Meanwhile, the mathematician suffers from crippling migraines that occur whenever he nears the rediscovery of the magic number. In methodical nar-ration, Max draws a parallel between his life-threatening quest for the number and a childhood folly in which he defied his parents by staring into the sun, nearly destroying his eyes in the process. At its core, Aronofsky's story is about the fine line between genius and madness.

It says everything about the movie that Max escapes his hellish situation by putting an electric drill to his temple, then boring a hole through his own brain. To stop the noises in his head, he eradicates an essential component of his own identity. From the perspective of the most paranoid members of Generation X, Max assassinates his uniqueness in order to live in peace with the drones who populate modern life. Max's shocking action, which is both self-destruction and self-preservation, can be interpreted as a metaphor for a Gen Xer tossing aside his or her generational identity — be it slackerdom, antiauthoritarianism, alternative sexuality, what have you — to go with the flow of a culture that doesn't tolerate the new ideas of a new generation.

What Is the Matrix?

The fear of having to sacrifice personal identity in order to blend into contemporary culture is hardly the exclusive province of Aronofsky's work, though. The same fear drives the anarchists in *Fight Club*, and, for that matter, the post-collegiates in *Reality Bites* and *Before Sunrise* and all the other movies about Gen Xers confronting the realities of modern society. Yet no filmmakers have taken this anxiety to a greater extreme than Larry and Andy Wachowski, the wunderkind filmmaking team who made their name with the *Bound* and then became superstars with their sophomore effort, the science-fiction adventure *The Matrix*. Because of what the Wachowskis use their sophomore film to say and how they use the medium of film to say it, *The Matrix* is, thus far, the ultimate cinematic expression of Generation X's collective identity.

Fittingly, the film is a dark parable about oppressive institutions, and both its content and technique examine the dehumanizing possibilities of technology. Yet within the darkness and technological fetishism lies wishful imagery of a Gen-X messiah — a messiah who, importantly, bears more than a passing resemblance to that most enduring of Gen-X icons, *Star Wars* protagonist Luke Skywalker. For even while *The Matrix* makes a powerful statement about what it means to live in contemporary American society, it makes an equally powerful statement about how a youth spent at the movies taught two members of Generation X to dream of better ways of living in contemporary American society. The postmodern, recycled nature of the film's statement — which is unmistakably a modernization of a previous film's statement — is yet another reason why *The Matrix* so acutely encapsulates the cinematic identity of Generation X.

The Wachowskis show viewers that *The Matrix* is something fresh right at the beginning of the film, when a pair of government-agent types assault a slinky computer hacker named Trinity (Carrie-Anne Moss). To evade them, Trinity leaps into the air and assumes a kung fu-style fighting pose — then hovers in mid-air while the camera whirls around her in an impossible 360-degree angle achieved through a technique the filmmakers call "bullet time," created by digitally stitching together images captured by a ring of still cameras. This moment tells viewers that characters in *The Matrix* will manifest a brand of superhuman ability never previously shown in films, but also that the vocabulary of the movie itself will be ingrained with cutting-edge technology. Later revelations underline that the theme and technique of the movie are inextricably entwined.

Trinity eventually makes contact with another hacker, Neo (Keanu Reeves), and a series of tantalizing clues suggest that she's about to share a life-changing secret with the reclusive computer nut. She teases Neo — and the audience — even further with an insinuating monologue proving that she's privy not only to secrets that are important to Neo, but secrets about him:

> TRINITY: I know what you've been doing. I know why you hardly sleep at night, why you live alone, and why, night after night, you sit at your computer. You're looking for him. I know because I was once looking for the same thing. And when he found me, he told me I wasn't really looking for him. I was looking for an answer. It's the question that drives us, Neo. It's the question that brought you here. You know the question, just as I did.
> NEO: What is the Matrix?
> TRINITY: The answer is out there, Neo. It's looking for you. And it will find you if you want it to.

Despite the story's futuristic setting, the facts of Neo's lifestyle are very clearly extrapolated from commonplace late-twentieth-century behavior: He's a young, disenfranchised man who has replaced the flesh-and-blood human community with the ones and zeros of the online community, interacting more comfortably with technology than with people. And the existential quality of the endeavor that links him to the rebellious, seductive Trinity — "It's the question that drives us" — identifies him as an archetypal Gen-X protagonist. Other such characters pursue their search for meaning by removing themselves from consumer-driven society to investigate questions of inner life and spirituality, but Neo, because he's a creature of the Information Age, seeks the meaning of life not by discussing

Rage against the machine: Messianic hero Neo (Keanu Reeves) uses blazing machine guns and cyber-age savvy to overthrow an Orwellian power structure in *The Matrix*, a science-fiction hit created by brothers Andy and Larry Wachowski (Warner Bros.).

philosophy or deconstructing pop culture, but by journeying through the Internet. His quest is coldly logical and framed in the vernacular of an online culture: Surely all the answers can be found, he thinks, if I can type the right question into my keyboard.

Neo's quest is given new import when he becomes the target of the same agents who pursued Trinity at the beginning of the picture, and when the Wachowskis stage several mind-bending sequences that call into question whether Neo actually is being persecuted or whether he's simply imaginative and paranoid. After a series of harrowing close calls, Neo is brought before an enigmatic figure named Morpheus (Lawrence Fishburne), Trinity's mentor. In a scene that clearly echoes the *Star Wars* moment in which young hero Luke Skywalker first learns of "the Force"—the energy field that binds all characters in the *Star Wars* universe—Morpheus offers Neo a chance to gain a greater understanding of his world.

> MORPHEUS: You have the look of a man who accepts what he sees because he is expecting to wake up. Ironically, that is not far from the truth. Do you believe in fate, Neo?
> NEO: No.
> MORPHEUS: Why not?
> NEO: Because I don't like the idea that I'm not in control of my own life.
> MORPHEUS: I know exactly what you mean. Let me tell you why you're here: You're here because you know ... that there's something wrong with the world. You don't know what it is, but it's there—like a splinter in your mind, driving you mad.... Do you know what I'm talking about?
> NEO: The Matrix?
> MORPHEUS: ... The Matrix is everywhere. It is all around us.... It is the world that has been pulled over your eyes to blind you from the truth.
> NEO: What truth?
> MORPHEUS: That you are a slave, Neo. Like everyone else, you were born into bondage. Born into a prison that you cannot smell or taste or touch. A prison for your mind. Unfortunately, no one can be told what the Matrix is. You have to see it for yourself.... After that, there is no turning back.

This exchange is suffused with the ennui, introspection, and existential angst that permeate many of the best Gen-X films. The "slavery" allusion, while literal in the context of the film, echoes figurative language that pops up throughout Gen-X movies about work—for what are the characters in *Office Space*, *American Beauty*, and other films if not slaves who rebel against their captors? And the idea that the modern world is an illusion is a hyperbolic manifestation of the disenfranchisement that drives so many Gen-X characters away from societal institutions. Yet while other characters feel disconnected from family, churches, governments, and other societal bedrocks, Neo actually learns that the very fabric of his reality — the institutions that ground him to a sense of existence — are false. Therefore, it's crucial to underline that Neo is poised to learn one possible answer to the eternal question facing Generation X: "Who am I, and where do I belong?"

Morpheus reveals that in the future, man created intelligent machines that eventually rebelled against mankind — a familiar theme in science fiction, which perpetually returns to the *Frankenstein* parable about men who play God. These future machines enslaved the human race into a massive web of pods, in which life energy is sucked from human bodies to power machines. To keep the humans from fighting their captivity, the machines created the Matrix, a virtual-reality simulation of the modern world that is piped directly into the minds of the pod-dwelling humans. So even though Neo and millions like him believe themselves to be walking and eating and sleeping and breathing in a physical world, they actually only are dreaming themselves into that world at the prodding of the machines. Morpheus and Trinity are among a tiny group of people who were freed from their pods, and who are building an army with which to overthrow the machines and free humanity from enslavement.

This story line is presented as pure escapism, as are stylized action scenes in which Trinity, Morpheus, and Neo use martial arts and gunpower to fight the computer-generated agents within the Matrix. (These scenes recall how a human entered a video game in the early-1980s fantasy film *Tron*, yet another movie whose audience included vast numbers of Gen Xers.) Beneath the escapism, however, is a poignant expression of frustration at the homogenization and pointlessness of a modern world in which humans replace each other with machines, both for utilitarian tasks and, in the Internet age, for companionship. While the use of "bullet-time" photography and other high-tech elements prove that the Wachowski brothers and their collaborators are fans of at least some technology, the unease they have about humans' ability to steer an even keel into the waters of technological advancement is palpable.

The filmmakers' nervousness about where modern society is headed finds its ultimate manifestation in Neo, whom the other characters perceive as an Information Age messiah. The miracle he performs is not rising from the dead or turning water into wine, but reading computer code. He is the first human who can think faster than the machines, so once he becomes actualized, he looks at the Matrix and sees not the utterly convincing illusion that Trinity and Morpheus see, but the ones and zeros that the machines use to manufacture the illusion.

In the Wachowskis' cautionary worldview, the Matrix is the anti-Force, the benevolent collective spirituality of George Lucas's universe reimagined as a drug used to drown the consciousness of all humanity. Accordingly, Neo's first major victory against the machines—which concludes *The Matrix* and sets the stage for the film's sequels—is achieved by venturing deep into the inner space of his own mind, a mirror image of how Luke Skywalker achieved his greatest victory by venturing deep into outer space. What joins both characters is that each must sublimate his own persona beneath a force greater than any individual, giving power to the idea that collective effort is the only truly useful tool for fighting oppression.

The Matrix is an exhibition of how the unique forces that defined Generation X's upbringing both help and hinder the evolution of this generation's filmmakers. It's at once stimulating and superficial, intellectual and escapist. Viewers who simply crave visual and aural stimulation can watch the fight scenes and the trick shots and the images of sexy actors zipping around in form-fitting clothes. Yet viewers who crave something meaningful can find that, too: In the most generous reading of the film, Neo is the first Gen-X protagonist to truly learn what caused his generation to be what it is, and it's therefore significant that he sees not the hand of God—proof of an omniscient creator—but a wholly rational mechanism.

This is the most cynical concept buried in *The Matrix*, which constantly bounds between the extremes of heroic optimism and dismal pessimism: The meaning of life is not some ephemeral spiritual concept, but the solution to a math problem. In this reading, *The Matrix* is the saddest possible proof of how deeply Gen Xers have lost faith in societal institutions, because it suggests that by losing faith in everything that grounds life, Gen Xers have lost faith in the mystery of life itself.

Accordingly, as Gen-X scholar Geoffrey T. Holtz noted, the nihilistic attitude that pervades *The Matrix* is far from anomalous:

> In many ways [Gen Xers] have absorbed the ever-growing fatalistic attitude of society in general. There is, to be sure, a vein of hopelessness that runs through this generation. One college professor who has been teaching English composition for more than twenty years recently noted a marked difference between the plots of her students' fiction today and those of previous students. In the past, she observed, "students plotted their stories so that all kinds of terrible things would happen to their protagonists, but in the end [...] everyone, alone or together, would work their way out of danger and get on with their lives." Today, however, "violence enters the story without benefit of plot, as if by metaphysical caprice. Not a caprice of the student writers but of forces way beyond their control."[1]

12

Where Do We Go from Here?

"Who am I, and where do I belong?"

The young adults who comprise Generation X are not the first wave of chronological peers to collectively wrestle with this question, and they won't be the last. But certain aspects of Generation X's past and present make their quest interesting and timely. As has been noted throughout this study, Gen Xers grew up in the shadow of one of the most discussed, celebrated, and, arguably, self-centered generations in American history, the boomers. Like a young child trying to declare his or her own identity while an older sibling gets all of mom's and dad's attention, Gen Xers have faced an uphill battle since birth to find a place in a world that is in many ways of, by, and for the millions upon millions of boomers.

Moreover, the peculiar aspects of the decades during which Gen Xers came of age colored their perspectives. The oldest members of this generation were mature enough to at least somewhat grasp the importance of Watergate, the end of the Vietnam War, and the countless other schisms that sliced through American society in the 1970s. And virtually all Gen Xers were privy (some would say victim) to the changes in education, government, and popular culture that forced youths of the late 1960s through the early 1980s to grow up faster than almost any of their predecessors. While it might be overstating things to say that Gen Xers raised in a period of cynicism, self-involvement, marital disharmony, and political upheaval lost their innocence as quickly as they first tasted it, it's not an overstatement to say that Gen Xers, by and large, were faced with adult choices and quandaries well before they became adults.

This accelerated maturation led to a severe disconnect in this generation's upbringing: Since Gen Xers were asked to come of age before they actually came of age, it's no surprise that so many of them seem to be stuck in prolonged adolescence. They were never allowed to just be children, but were in some cases withheld the rights and responsibilities of adults, so they are a hybrid of different phases of human growth.

For many members of this peculiar generation, the confusion about the roles they are supposed to play in society is exacerbated by the darkest social factors of the periods in which they were raised. Divorce, experiments in hands-off education, the use of medication as a parenting tool, the corporatization of the American workplace, mixed messages from the post-Watergate political establishment, and the homogenization of popular culture all contributed to an environment in which young people felt at least like cogs in some great machine and at worst like disposable accessories to their parents' lifestyles. While not every Gen Xer was touched by every one of these factors (even though those who weren't heard about the social upheavals from friends and the media), the onslaught of changes to American society during Generation X's formative years led to a cheapening of life in this country, and led countless youths to feel unwanted or even betrayed by the institutions that comprise the bedrock of existence in the United States.

For that reason, it makes all the sense in the world that Gen-Xers took the "tune in, turn on, drop out" ethos of the boomers to a new, almost nihilistic extreme. For instead of removing themselves from mainstream culture in order to join an alternative culture fueled by new ideas of positivity and harmony, the Gen Xers most deeply affected by social change removed themselves from mainstream culture in order to join an alternative non-culture fueled by disdain for everything they were expected to take seriously. Irony and disenfranchisement and contempt combined into an all-purpose psyche that produced its own aesthetic, language, and, to a degree, belief system. The most cynical Gen Xers perceived society as having abandoned them, so they fought back by abandoning society.

This led older Americans, and even members of Generation X who felt stronger ties to conventional society, to dismiss slackers and other disenfranchised Gen Xers as avatars of narcissism and sloth. The most stinging accusations hurled at Gen Xers pointed out that Generation X grew up in an era of comparative peace — notwithstanding skirmishes in Grenada, Panama, and the Persian Gulf, there was no war during Generation X's youth, and there certainly was no conflict that promised to erupt into anything as divisive and destructive as Vietnam. Furthermore, skeptics of Generation X's malaise noted, slackers and their ilk didn't propose a new societal model to replace the old one. A generation before, hippies withdrew from polite society and tried to found a new collective called, among other names, the Woodstock Nation. Where, doubters asked, was the grand idea of Generation X? If the youths of the late twentieth century were so fed up with the culture handed to them by their parents, what changes did they propose for making the culture better?

One place in which to look for some answers to these haunting questions is the cinema of Generation X. Even in the earliest films in this wildly varied body of work — Steven Soderbergh's introspective *sex, lies, and videotape*, Richard Linklater's seminal *Slacker*, John Singleton's charged *Boyz N the Hood*—a common theme begins to emerge. All three pictures challenge presumptions about society.

Soderbergh's film portrays a soulful drifter who videotapes women sharing their most private experiences, masturbates instead of actually having contact with women, and breaks up his friend's marriage. Yet in the topsy-turvy world of Gen-X cinema, this character is a sympathetic protagonist. Linklater's movie shows aimless youths wandering through their existences, exploring the wilds of intellectualism and philosophy, but not really living lives by any conventional standard. And Singleton's picture puts human faces on a segment of society many would rather dismiss with epithets, thereby proving that even the most brutal gun-toting "gangsta" in South Central Los Angeles has a story to tell. The characters around whom these pioneering Gen-X directors chose to build their first movies are crucially important windows into the cinema of Generation X, which is largely a cinema of the misunderstood, the eccentric, the disenfranchised, and the lost.

As Gen-X filmmakers matured, they expanded their worldview to include more than misfits and malcontents. So while Quentin Tarantino spent the first few years of his career examining the psyches of criminals, Rod Lurie used his first two films to explore issues relating to the American presidency, surely the ultimate icon of traditional American culture. There's room in the Gen-X mix for angry directors, contemplative directors, ironic directors, subversive directors. There's room in the mix for stories about love, work, religion, drugs, sex, and countless other topics. There's even room for stories about war, a subject few Gen Xers can discuss from a first-hand perspective: Michael Bay directed the glossy epic *Pearl Harbor*; Keith Gordon helmed a reflective combat film set in World War II, *A Midnight Clear*, as well as thoughtful movie set partly during the Vietnam era, *Waking the Dead*; and even actor-director Emilio Estevez entered the fray with a Vietnam-related film called *The War at Home*.

Perhaps because war is among the most polarizing aspects of human behavior, the messages in Gen-X war movies are among the clearest sent by any directors of this generation: *Pearl Harbor*, for instance, is a jingoistic celebration of America's might. Gordon's war-related films, however, are infused with ambiguity and ambivalence. His work is far more characteristic of Generation X than Bay's: In films made by this generation that grew up in confusing times, there are no easy answers, and there often are no absolute answers at all. Traditional concepts of right and wrong became so clouded during this generation's youth that taking a distinct stand on any topic seems hypocritical.

It will be interesting to see how Gen Xers react to the massive changes in the geopolitical landscape that took shape after the devastating terrorist attacks on New York City and Washington in 2001, and it also will be interesting to see how youths of the next generation react to the mixed messages brought on by the destruction of the World Trade Center and the attack on the Pentagon. While some might react to these incomprehensible events by retreating into cynicism, others might be caught up in the wave of nationalism that was felt following the attacks. In a sad way, perhaps the unprecedented manner in which evil was visited upon the civilian population of the United States might help the Americans of Generation Y feel more connected to their country than Generation X ever did during their youth.

In the few instances when a polarizing Gen-X film takes a distinct stand on a social issue, that stand generally defies the status quo. Soderbergh's *Traffic* flat out says that America's war on drugs is a folly that should be replaced by intervention and treatment. Yet even this assertion is to some degree anomalous, for directors belonging to this generation seem far more concerned with questions than with answers. They seem driven to encourage others to understand, and perhaps even emulate, their introspective ways.

Look at the way young characters interact with their parents in *Reality Bites* and other Gen-X movies about family: The kids speak a different language than their parents, who scratch their heads in confusion when trying to understand their children's refusal to embrace traditional goals. Sure, generational clashes are nothing new, but the most peculiar aspect of how Generation X relates to its elders is that Gen Xers don't want to challenge their parents' culture in order to replace it with one of their own. In moments like Troy's sobering soliloquy in *Reality Bites*, Gen Xers challenge their parents' culture as a way of explaining why they don't wish to participate in society at all.

Sometimes, this ennui turns into positive energy: The rebel characters in *The Matrix* undermine the sterile society in which they were raised, and in so doing become actualized. Neo learns that he has spent his entire life in a tiny pod, fed intravenously and doped into contentment by an oppressive establishment. Isn't that imagery a hyperbolic representation of a typical Gen Xer languishing on a couch, loading himself with junk food, and numbing himself with images on television? Therefore, doesn't Neo's choice to free himself from his pod and fight the powers that be represent a Gen Xer departing the couch to become involved in society, instead of just providing commentary from the sidelines?

Gen-X directors rarely take such extreme measures to dramatize the value of participation in society, but they often encourage social change in more personal ways. Kimberly Peirce railed against intolerance with her passionate story about modern gender roles, *Boys Don't Cry*. Alexander Payne and Wes Anderson skewered the notion that ambition equals spiritual happiness by showing driven characters driving their acquaintances crazy in *Election* and *Rushmore*. And M. Night Shyamalan offered reassuring messages about people, both living and undead, taking control of their lives in *The Sixth Sense* and *Unbreakable*.

Gen-X directors seem to want their audiences to participate in life, but they take unusual routes toward dramatizing their calls to action, as if the concept of a traditional hero has lost so much credibility that it's no longer a storytelling option. At the same time, heroes, albeit haunted ones, show up in myriad Gen-X movies. In the cinema of Generation X, there are no absolutes: Just when it seems the directors in this group have given up on traditional ideas of good and evil, along comes a morally righteous filmmaker such as Singleton or Shyamalan. As Charlie Kaufman, the screenwriter of *Being John Malkovich*, noted:

> I really don't have any solutions and I don't like movies that do. I want to create situations that give people something to think about. I hate a movie that will end by telling you that the first thing you should do is love yourself. That is so insulting and condescending, and so meaningless. My characters don't learn to love each other or themselves.[1]

Despite the mixed messages that permeate Gen-X movies, the filmmakers of this generation have racked up spectacular accomplishments.

Robert Rodriguez became a folk hero for countless would-be filmmakers by shooting his debut film, *El Mariachi*, for a meager $7,000. Kevin Smith achieved similar stature by turning an amateurish story shot in a convenience store, *Clerks*, into the launching pad of a celebrated career. Steven Soderbergh was anointed the poster boy for contemporary independent cinema when *sex, lies, and videotape* outperformed all expectations by earning $28 million at the box office. A decade later, the same director won a slot in history by earning twin Oscar nominations for helming *Erin Brockovich* and *Traffic*. Larry and Andy Wachowski broke new

Still searching: Texas-based independent Richard Linklater, shown rehearsing Ethan Hawke and Julie Delpy for their roles in *Before Sunrise*, is one of the many Gen-X filmmakers who build on their success by experimenting with new storytelling techniques (Castle Rock Entertainment).

cinematic ground by integrating "bullet-time" photography into *The Matrix*, and the mind-bending effect was so influential that it was mimicked in subsequent movies ranging from *Scary Movie* to *Charlie's Angels* to *Shrek*.

And then there's Tarantino. The second Gen-X director to gain notoriety as the exemplar of a new wave of filmmakers, he introduced a pop-culture-drenched, fast-moving, ultraviolent storytelling style that influenced independent cinema, and even infiltrated mainstream movies, for most of the 1990s and beyond. Just as the movie brats of the previous generation had, Tarantino slapped contemporary cinema in the face and forced it to change with the times. Movies had been fast and violent before *Reservoir Dogs* and *Pulp Fiction* came along, but thereafter, they had to be fast and violent *and* hip *and* smart *and* ironic, or run the risk of seeming passé.

Tarantino's influence was not entirely positive, but the best aftershock of his gate-crashing was that it so deeply changed financiers' and audiences' ideas of what good movies could look and sound like that other daring Gen Xers — Spike Jonze, David Fincher, the Wachowski brothers, and many more — were able to bring offbeat projects into the marketplace.

There's much more to come, of course. Soderbergh, Linklater, Singleton, Tarantino, though already established talents, probably have yet to make their best movies. In 2001, Linklater released *Waking Life*, an experimental movie for which shots of real actors were painted over, frame-by-frame, to create a dreamlike brand of reality-based animation. In the same year, Soderbergh juggled such diverse projects as an action-oriented remake of the Rat Pack film *Ocean's Eleven*, a sequel to *sex, lies, and videotape*, and a remake of an obscure Russian science-fiction movie called *Solaris*. Even as they secure lasting places in the cinematic firmament, these filmmakers continue to experiment with new forms, new ideas, new subjects, and new techniques.

And in the future, it won't just be the established Gen-X directors who are doing interesting work. Sofia Coppola, the youngest director discussed in this book, has made only one feature film as of this writing, so the question of whether she will create a body of work as lasting as that created by her father, Francis Ford Coppola, remains unanswered. More importantly, who knows what to expect from the numerous Gen-X filmmakers who have yet to storm the gates of Hollywood? At the end of the twentieth century, a revolution in filmmaking was facilitated by the emergence of affordable digital-video cameras capable of capturing professional-quality images with minimal investments of time, money, and personnel. Film festivals around the world have opened their doors to digital movies, and the Internet provides unprecedented distribution options that could democratize the film industry. So not only have we yet to discover every Gen Xer with an important cinematic statement to share, we have yet to discover every means by which the wunderkinds of this and subsequent generations will share such statements.

So far, the cinema of Generation X has been driven by a thirst for knowledge: Characters in Gen-X movies question who they are, how the past shaped them, what options await them in the future, and why they should spend their time doing work of which corporations will be the beneficiaries. The cinema of Generation X may well be a narcissistic cinema — Gen-X characters often spend so much time analyzing their own lives and troubles that they sometimes are blinded to the world around them — but there's a good reason for that focus on the self.

The members of Generation X seem bound by disappointment in the culture that birthed them, and wary of their ability to create a culture that's any better. Gen Xers are on a quest for knowledge, but they're ambivalent about whether they really want answers to their questions. Hence the prevalence not only of slacker characters, but of characters who numb their pain with drugs. As Darren Aronofsky, the challenging director of *Pi* and *Requiem for a Dream*, said: "Maybe the price of knowledge is pain."[2]

James Mangold's *Girl Interrupted*, a drama about a privileged young woman who spends nearly two years in a psychiatric hospital after formless malaise drives her to attempt suicide, attacks the quandary of young people frightened by the roles they may be asked to play once they become adults. Although protagonist Susannah (Winona Ryder) is shown in the early 1970s, her nebulous angst about the modern world strongly echoes the ennui expressed by Ryder's character and her peers in *Reality Bites*. Tellingly, not everyone has sympathy for Susannah's plight: Long-suffering nurse Valerie Owens (Whoopi Goldberg) has seen too many truly sick people pass through the hospital's doors to have patience for young people hiding from life. "You're a lazy, self-indulgent little girl who is driving herself crazy," the nurse barks.

Similar barbs have been shot at countless Gen Xers, whom skeptics believe retreat from life because they are daunted by hard work. But as this study has shown, Generation X's stance is informed by much more than sloth. The characters created by Gen-X filmmakers withdraw from society because they want nothing to do with a society capable of untold cruelty. That, finally, is one answer to the burning question of "Who am I, and where do I belong?"— I am an afterthought of society, and if nothing else, I know where I do not belong.

While poignant, this answer does not address one last question: If Gen Xers know where they don't belong, do they know where they do? Are the destined to assimilate into the society about which they have such paralyzing doubts, or will they, like the rebel heroes of *The Matrix*, extract themselves from the cocoon of contemporary culture to look for a better place? The resolution to that conundrum will be revealed in the future, so for now, it's best to live inside the question — to inhabit the ambiguity that suffuses the cinema of Generation X, thereby understanding how this eclectic body of work relates to what has come before, and what has yet to come. That said, there could be no more appropriate parting thought than the opening scene of *Reality Bites*, which dramatizes the desire for meaning that burns deep in the heart of this confused, confusing generation.

In the scene, Lelaina (Ryder) takes the podium at a college graduation ceremony to deliver her valedictory address. As her speech nears its crescendo, she realizes she's missing the card on which her closing thoughts were written. How she chooses to disguise her error speaks volumes.

> LELAINA: And they wonder why those of us in our 20s refuse to work an 80-hour week just so we can afford to buy their BMWs. Why we aren't interested in the counterculture that they invented, as if we did not seize and disembowel their revolution for a pair of running shoes. But the question remains: What are we going to do now? How are we going to repair all of the damage we inherited? Fellow graduates, the answer is simple.... The answer is "I don't know."

Appendix One:
Key Generation X
Filmmakers

Affleck, Ben (b. 1972) and **Matt Damon** (b. 1970) Affleck, who technically is a year too young to be included in this study, and his childhood friend Damon cowrote *Good Will Hunting*, the Oscar-winning film that was a breakthrough for both of their acting careers. The in-demand thespians have yet to write another film together or separately, although they did assist the writer-director who won a contest called Project Greenlight. Affleck is known for heartthrob roles in *Armageddon* and *Pearl Harbor*, Damon for nuanced work in *The Talented Mr. Ripley* and *Courage Under Fire*, and each has an extensive acting résumé.

FILMOGRAPHY (as screenwriters): *Good Will Hunting* (1997)

Anderson, Paul Thomas (b. 1970) Anderson is one of the most sophisticated storytellers of his generation, perhaps because he grew up close to the movies: His father worked on television as a late-night horror-movie host called Ghoulari, and Anderson was born in Studio City, California, right at the heart of the entertainment industry. He began his career as a production assistant on television movies, game shows, music videos, and small independent films, working both in Los Angeles and New York City. His five-minute short film, *Cigarettes and Coffee*, won him entrance into the Sundance Institute, at which he developed the story that became his first feature, *Hard Eight*.

Anderson's movies generally are dramas featuring dark story lines that are deftly intertwined in a novelistic manner, and his literary bent also shows in the torrents of words that often spew from his characters. Although Anderson frequently gets carried away by his own audacity — the frogs that rained from the sky at the end of *Magnolia* were a love-hate proposition for audiences — his mature, knowing looks at sexuality, obsession, the quest for fame, and the dissipation of American families have been well-served by his bravura camerawork and dazzling editing.

FILMOGRAPHY: *Hard Eight* (1997), *Boogie Nights* (1997), *Magnolia* (1999), *Punchdrunk Knuckle Love* (2002)

Anderson, Wes (b. 1969) A bold voice whose irreverence is mostly devoid of the mean-spirited edge that makes much ironic Gen-X cinema off-putting,

Anderson has gained the admiration of such notables as James L. Brooks and Martin Scorsese by making offbeat movies that mix sly comedy with gentle character insights. A Texas native, he got a degree in philosophy from the University of Texas at Austin, at which he met writer-actor Owen Wilson. (Wilson, born in Dallas in 1968 and known for roles in such films as *Armageddon* and *Meet the Parents*, is Anderson's writing partner.) With chops honed by making numerous Super-8 movies during his youth, Anderson was accepted into the graduate film program at Columbia University, but opted instead to make a 1994 short film called *Bottle Rocket*, which was succeeded by a feature of the same name. Like James Mangold, Anderson seems particularly interested in misfits, and he generally puts across a positive, if somewhat weird, worldview.

FILMOGRAPHY: *Bottle Rocket* (1996), *Rushmore* (1998), *The Royal Tenenbaums* (2001)

Aronofksy, Darren (b. 1969) A provocateur of the first order, Aronofsky filled his early films with confrontational stylistic devices that suited his intense subject matter. After graduating from high school, the Brooklyn native bummed around Europe briefly before entering Harvard University, at which he studied live-action filmmaking and animation. His senior thesis project, *Supermarket Sweep*, was a finalist for the 1991 Student Academy Awards, and in 1994, he received a master's in directing from the American Film Institute. Aronofsky funded his challenging debut film, *Pi*, with $100 investments from relatives and friends. Although *Pi* positioned Aronofsky as a paranoid intellectual, he quickly shunted to more accessible material, even while retaining his tendency to make moviegoers squirm by pummeling them with disturbing sensations and by showing characters enduring horrific ordeals.

FILMOGRAPHY: *Pi* (1998), *Requiem for a Dream* (2000)

Arteta, Miguel (b. 1970) Born and raised in Puerto Rico, Arteta graduated from Wesleyan University in 1989, then received an master's from the American Film Institute in 1993. While at AFI, Arteta made a musical short called *Every Day Is a Beautiful Day*, which was nominated for a Student Academy Award. His sensitivity and his offbeat taste in material won him a slot in the Sundance Institute in 1996, as well as jobs writing for the television shows *Homicide: Life on the Street*, *Freaks and Geeks*, and *Snoops*.

FILMOGRAPHY: *Star Maps* (1997), *Chuck & Buck* (2000)

Avary, Roger (b. 1965) Although he won an Oscar for cowriting *Pulp Fiction* with Quentin Tarantino, Avary's solo output has been, to put it generously, negligible: His films are at best draped in second-hand style and at worst incomprehensible. The Canadian filmmaker met Tarantino when they both worked at Imperial Entertainment, a Los Angeles video store.

FILMOGRAPHY: *Killing Zoe* (1994), *Pulp Fiction* (screenplay only, 1994), *Mr. Stitch* (1995)

Bay, Michael (b. 1965) Under the tutelage of veteran producer Jerry Bruckheimer, music-video and TV-commercial specialist Bay became the preeminent director of overpriced shoot-em-ups at the end of the 1990s. His visual style, in which every image is caressed with lighting and lens filters and special effects until it's as pristine and attractive as a postcard, is a shallow echo of the aesthetic perfected by British stylists of the late 1970s and early 1980s, notably Ridley Scott and

Adrian Lyne. Bay grew up with his adoptive parents in Los Angeles, and studied film at the Art Center College of Design, in Pasadena, California, after attending Wesleyan University. His major student film was a faux Coca-Cola commercial, which prophesied how deeply salesmanship and instant gratification would permeate his features.

FILMOGRAPHY: *Bad Boys* (1995), *The Rock* (1996), *Armageddon* (1998), *Pearl Harbor* (2001)

Black, Shane (b. 1961) Throughout the late 1980s and early 1990s, Black epitomized the gold-rush mentality that overtook screenwriters and would-be screenwriters throughout America, because his scripts, although rooted in simpleminded action concepts and jokey banter, fetched preposterous amounts in bidding wars between studios. *Lethal Weapon* initiated a lucrative franchise and provided a model for many subsequent buddy movies, and *The Last Action Hero* contains some amusing attempts at self-referential humor, even though it was an infamous flop. As of this writing, Black has yet to venture into serious work, and the market for his brand of zippy, grisly action has gone soft.

FILMOGRAPHY (as screenwriter): *The Monster Squad* (1987), *Lethal Weapon* (1987), *The Last Boy Scout* (1991), *The Last Action Hero* (1993), *The Long Kiss Goodnight* (1996), *A.W.O.L.* (1999)

Burns, Edward (b. 1968) Specializing in the kind of gentle, unthreatening interplay that often meets a warmer reception on television than it does in film, Burns has balanced a slight career as a writer-director with acting work in films far more visible than his own, notably Steven Spielberg's 1998 war epic, *Saving Private Ryan*. Born in Queens and raised in Long Island, Burns studied at Oneonta College and the University at Albany before focusing on film while at New York City's Hunter College. His apprenticeship included making short films and working behind the scenes of television shows, and he began writing his first feature while a production assistant on *Entertainment Tonight*. Burns cocreated a TV show called *The Fighting Fitzgeralds*, based loosely on characters in his debut film.

FILMOGRAPHY: *The Brothers McMullen* (1995), *She's the One* (1996), *No Looking Back* (1998), *Sidewalks of New York* (2001)

Christopher, Mark (b. 1961) An Iowa native who studied film at Columbia University and scored at festivals with gay-themed short films including *Alkali, Iowa*, Christopher made an inauspicious debut with a film about famed discotheque Studio 54. The picture featured a terrific performance by Mike Myers, but little else in it made an impression.

FILMOGRAPHY: *54* (1998)

Coppola, Sofia (b. 1971) Before she could walk, Coppola made a noteworthy contribution to American film by playing the child of Michael Corleone in the baptism scene of *The Godfather* (1972), which was directed by her father, Francis Ford Coppola. Her appearance in a 1990 sequel, *The Godfather, Part III*, was widely slammed as a nepotistic indulgence, because Sofia Coppola — who stepped in at the last minute to replace Winona Ryder — was overwhelmed by the movie's operatic style. It was poetic justice, then, when she scored a major critical hit with the first feature she directed, *The Virgin Suicides*.

Following an invaluable apprenticeship during which she traveled the globe with her father during production of his films, Coppola studied painting in California, then explored photography (for *Details* and other publications), acting (in such projects as a Comedy Central series), and fashion (she began her own clothing line) before risking comparisons to her father by becoming a director. She is, incidentally, married to fellow Gen-X filmmaker Spike Jonze.

FILMOGRAPHY: *The Virgin Suicides* (1999)

Damon, Matt see Affleck, Ben

Demme, Ted (b. 1964–d. 2002) The nephew of acclaimed filmmaker Jonathan Demme (*The Silence of the Lambs*), Ted Demme worked steadily as a journeyman director of comedic and dramatic films, displaying an easy touch with comedy and a gift for capturing the interaction among blue-collar urbanites. In addition to his features, Demme — whose real first name was Edward — helmed numerous TV projects. Demme died of a heart attack in January 2002 at age 38.

FILMOGRAPHY: *Who's the Man?* (1993), *The Ref* (1994), *Beautiful Girls* (1996), *Life* (1999), *Monument Avenue* (1999), *Blow* (2001)

Elfont, Harry (b. 1968) and **Deborah Kaplan** These writer-directors, who met while studying film at New York University and work as a team, epitomize their generation's fixation on pop culture, particularly television sitcoms, with their wink-laden, youth-oriented comedies.

FILMOGRAPHY: *A Very Brady Sequel* (screenplay only, 1996), *Can't Hardly Wait* (1998), *The Flintstones in Viva Rock Vegas* (screenplay only, 2000), *Josie and the Pussycats* (2001)

Estevez, Emilio (b. 1962) The son of actor Martin Sheen (whose real name is Ramon Estevez), Emilio Estevez parlayed his success as a member of the "Brat Pack" — a group of young actors who appeared in 1980s youth-oriented films directed by populists including John Hughes — into several directing opportunities. His debut film was a famously overwrought parable, but he later settled into a rhythm of directing minor efforts featuring performances by himself and/or members of his family.

FILMOGRAPHY: *Wisdom* (1987), *Men at Work* (1990), *The War at Home* (1996), *Rated X* (2000)

Eyre, Chris (b. 1969) Eyre earned a place in film history by directing *Smoke Signals*, the first feature written and directed by Native Americans. Of Cheyenne-Arapaho descent, Eyre was born on the Warm Springs Indian Reservation in Oregon, then adopted by white parents and raised in Portland. While attending New York University's graduate film program, he made an award-winning short called *Tenacity*.

FILMOGRAPHY: *Bringing It All Back Home* (documentary, 1997), *Smoke Signals* (1998), *Skins* (2002)

Favreau, Jon (b. 1966) A Queens native who moved to Chicago to study improvisational comedy and theater with the famed Second City troupe, Favreau was discovered by director David Anspaugh, who cast him in the ensemble cast of the football drama *Rudy* (1993). Favreau and another *Rudy* actor, Vince Vaughn, became stars by appearing in the pop-culture-drenched comedy *Swingers*, which Favreau wrote. Favreau continues to balance writing, directing, and acting, and his notable onscreen appearances include a recurring role on the mega-popular sitcom *Friends*.

FILMOGRAPHY: *Swingers* (screenplay only, 1996), *Made* (2001)

Fincher, David (b. 1962) Whereas Michael Bay utilized his background in TV commercials and music videos solely to refine his skill for visual trickery, David Fincher used similar experiences to refine his storytelling. Fincher's award-winning music videos for rock acts including Madonna, Aerosmith, and Don Henley were memorably sensual and provocative, and Fincher brought those same qualities to his features. While he sometimes paints himself into corners by fixating on dank locations and despicable characters, he has created a handful of truly haunting moments, and his tendency to subvert audience expectations makes him one of the least predictable artists of his generation.

A Denver native raised in Marin County, California, and inspired to become a filmmaker, in part, by *Star Wars*, Fincher made movies from age eight. During two years working at *Star Wars* director George Lucas's special-effects firm, Industrial Light and Magic, he worked on pictures including *Return of the Jedi*. Fincher's themes, which have included martyrdom, alienation, and the dehumanization of modern culture, add to his appeal as a serious filmmaker. Furthermore, his embrace of experimental storytelling techniques, to say nothing of a seemingly endless vocabulary of camera tricks and a rigorously consistent aesthetic, position him as Generation X's most adventurous visual stylist.

FILMOGRAPHY: *Alien*³ (1992), *Seven* (1995), *The Game* (1997), *Fight Club* (1999), *The Panic Room* (2002)

Fleming, Andrew One of the few filmmakers to deliberately identify himself as a member of Generation X, Fleming hit Hollywood at the tail end of the 1980s horror craze, and experienced some difficulty proving that he could handle genres other than horror. While studying film at New York University, Fleming made award-winning shorts including *Prisoner*, a clever piece about a man trapped inside a painting. He also has been active as a screenwriter, and seems finally to have established himself as a versatile artist, if not necessarily a distinctive one.

FILMOGRAPHY: *Bad Dreams* (1988), *Every Breath* (screenplay only, 1993), *Threesome* (1994), *The Craft* (1996), *Dick* (1999)

Foster, Jodie (b. 1962) After playing a series of risqué juvenile roles in the 1970s—most notoriously as a teen streetwalker in Martin Scorsese's legendary morality tale *Taxi Driver* (1976)—the woman born Alicia Christian Foster evolved into one of the industry's most compelling adult actors. The precocious maturity of her youthful work led to a signature quality of intense focus and palpable intelligence in mature parts, from the FBI agent in *The Silence of the Lambs* (1990) to the scientist in *Contact* (1997). Foster's directorial efforts have not been as assured as her acting, but in addition to the expected strengths—her attention to acting and character are impressive—she has displayed a deep interest in familial issues.

FILMOGRAPHY: *Little Man Tate* (1991), *Home for the Holidays* (1995)

Freeman, Morgan J. (b. 1969) Freeman, who has the misfortune of sharing a name with a prominent actor to whom he is not related, has shown promise and heart in small-scale films, but has yet to gain the commercial foothold necessary to fund ambitious ventures. A native of Long Beach, California, he studied film at the University of California at Santa Barbara before moving to France, where he worked as a production assistant. He returned to America to get a master's in film from New York University, then made several short films that were received well at festivals. He also developed working relationships with actors including indie-film regular Brendan Sexton III, whom Freeman met while working as an assistant director on the indie comedy *Welcome to the Dollhouse*, in which Sexton appeared. Freeman also has worked on television series including *Dawson's Creek*.

FILMOGRAPHY: *Hurricane Streets* (1998), *Desert Blue* (1999), *American Psycho II* (2002)

Freundlich, Bart (b. 1970) A New York City native, Freundlich graduated from New York University with a double major in cinema studies and film/television production, then made a short film, *Dog Race in Alaska* (1993), and a documentary, *Hired Hands* (1994), before venturing into features. He also studied at Northwestern University and the British Film Institute.

FILMOGRAPHY: *The Myth of Fingerprints* (1997), *World Traveler* (2002)

Gallo, Vincent (b. 1962) A native of Buffalo, New York, whose gaunt, almost deathly looks made him a favorite actor in crime films and a favorite model in ads catering to the "heroin chic" vogue of the early 1990s, Gallo has balanced acting and directing since the beginning of his career, when he helmed and starred in short films such as 1986's *If You Feel Froggy, Jump*. After making a splash in the mid-1990s with his acting in Abel Ferrara's period drama *The Funeral* and with his acclaimed first feature as a director, Gallo mostly kept a low profile, appearing in limited-release films.

FILMOGRAPHY: *Buffalo '66* (1998)

Gomez, Nick (b. 1963) One of countless young filmmakers who emerged in the mid-1990s with hard-hitting crime films that at least seemed to say something profound about urban youths raised around violence, Gomez has worked steadily but not built on his early acclaim. A Massachusetts native, he graduated from the State University of New York at Purchase, then worked in various capacities on several independent films, notably editing Hal Hartley's *Trust* and *Theory of Achievement*. His television work includes episodes of the crime shows *Homicide: Life on the Street*, *Oz*, and *The Sopranos*.

FILMOGRAPHY: *Laws of Gravity* (1992), *New Jersey Drive* (1995), *Illtown* (1996), *Drowning Mona* (2000), *Final Jeopardy* (2001)

Gordon, Keith (b. 1961) Throughout his youth and adolescence in New York City, Gordon immersed himself in films and acting, and his appealing quality as a juvenile performer led to steady work on the New York stage, as well as movie roles including an appearance in 1978's *Jaws 2*. His most visible performance was the male lead in *Christine*, the 1983 adaptation of Stephen King's book about a killer car. Concurrent with his acting, Gordon worked in the film department of the Museum of Modern Art.

Perhaps owing to his long association with the film industry, Gordon has been a mature and serious filmmaker for as long as he's made features. While his work can sometimes be a touch too earnest, his eagerness to explore a wide variety of subjects makes him consistently interesting. He also has directed episodes of intriguing television series, including *Wild Palms*, *Fallen Angels*, and *Homicide: Life on the Street*, and he contributed a short documentary called *Jaws 2: A Portrait by Keith Gordon* to the DVD release of the horror sequel.

FILMOGRAPHY: *The Chocolate War* (1988), *A Midnight Clear* (1991), *Mother Night* (1996), *Waking the Dead* (2000)

Gray, James (b. 1969) A Queens, New York, native who originally wanted to be a painter, Gray studied film at the University of Southern California. His student film *Cowboys and Angels* caught the eye of a producer who encouraged Gray to write a screenplay; the resulting script became Gray's debut picture, *Little Odessa*. In just two movies, the director has established a mournful, serious aesthetic, and displayed extraordinary taste in — and skill with — actors.

FILMOGRAPHY: *Little Odessa* (1994), *The Yards* (2000)

Hawke, Ethan (b. 1970) Arguably the definitive screen representative of slackerdom because of his roles in *Reality Bites*, *Before Sunrise*, and other films, Hawke quickly evolved from a juvenile player in such films as 1985's *Explorers* to the angst-ridden, youthful lead in independent (and occasionally studio) films throughout the 1990s and beyond. By the beginning of the twenty-first century, the seasoned actor had broadened his reach to include work as a novelist and fledgling filmmaker.

FILMOGRAPHY: *Chelsea Walls* (2001)

Haynes, Todd (b. 1961) While some observers have grouped Haynes with other progressive directors who deal with themes relating to gay life, his provocative take on modern sexuality is just part of an expansive worldview. He also comments on popular culture, self-destructive behavior, and the plight of individuals who knowingly remove themselves from the mainstream of society. His reach sometimes exceeds his grasp, but he is nonetheless developing an oeuvre of thought-provoking films.

A California native, Haynes dabbled in filmmaking and painting during childhood, then graduated from Brown University, where he studied art and semiotics. After college, he moved to New York City and made a cult-favorite short film called *Superstar: The Karen Carpenter Story*, which employed Barbie dolls to dramatize the titular singer's battle with an eating disorder. The singer's brother, pianist Richard Carpenter, sued Haynes for illegally using the music the siblings recorded as the Carpenters, so *Superstar* became a cause célèbre disseminated in bootleg form.

Subsequent Haynes pictures have sparked spirited discussions, and despite his reluctance to be ghettoized as a gay filmmaker, his regular treatment of gay-related themes makes him an important voice for a much-misunderstood segment of the population. Still, his strangely alluring movies hold pleasures for adventurous moviegoers of all stripes.

FILMOGRAPHY: *Assassins: A Film Concerning Rimbaud* (1985), *Poison* (1991), *Safe* (1995), *Velvet Goldmine* (1998)

Jenkins, Tamara (b. 1963) An independent spirit whose first film was praised by critics as a fresh satire, Jenkins worked extensively in theater and performance art prior to becoming a feature director. After completing the graduate film program at New York University, Jenkins made several award-winning short films and won the 1995 Guggenheim Fellowship for Filmmaking; the same year, she was accepted into the Sundance Institute, at which she workshopped the script that became her debut feature.

FILMOGRAPHY: *Slums of Beverly Hills* (1998)

Jonze, Spike (b. 1969) While the path that brought Jonze to notoriety is commonplace among Gen-X directors, the acclaim he has enjoyed at every stage of his career is as impressive as his signature combination of wizardry and whimsy is intriguing. Jonze (a stage name for Rockville, Maryland, native Adam Spiegel) got his start directing documentaries and industrials, then began a celebrated run helming commercials and music videos. His slick ads netted awards including the Palme d'Or at the Cannes International Advertising Film Festival, and his arresting imagery and frenetic pacing distinguished videos for prominent musicians including Björk, Puff Daddy, Fatboy Slim, and R.E.M. A clip for the Beastie Boys song "Sabotage," filmed as a cheeky spoof of 1970s cop shows, cemented Jonze's reputation, and paved the way for his famously weird debut film. Jonze also is a noted photographer (for such magazines as *Interview*), an accomplished actor (in such films as *Three Kings*), and a prankster with a tendency to spread playful fictions about himself. He is married to fellow Gen-X director Sofia Coppola.

FILMOGRAPHY: *Being John Malkovich* (1999), *Adaptation* (2002)

Joanou, Phil (b. 1962) A visual stylist whose work suggests an insular perspective informed by movies rather than real life, Joanou has wasted more opportunities than most directors will ever be given. After Steven Spielberg saw one of the student films Joanou made at the University of Southern California, Spielberg hired him for a high-profile television job. The young director parlayed that job into several feature-film assignments, but his movies generally lack individuality and warmth. He's capable of impressive moments, such as suspense sequences, but shallowness bogs down his fictional films, and has even affected some of his documentaries. Joanou's television work includes episodes of the miniseries *Fallen Angels* and *Wild Palms*, and an expensive 3-D sequence for the sitcom *3rd Rock From the Sun*.

FILMOGRAPHY: *Three O'Clock High* (1987), *U2: Rattle and Hum* (documentary, 1988), *State of Grace* (1990), *Age 7 in America* (documentary, 1991), *Final Analysis* (1992), *Heaven's Prisoners* (1996), *14 Up in America* (1998), *Entropy* (1999)

Judge, Mike (b. 1962) Born in Ecuador and raised in New Mexico, Judge didn't set out for a career in the arts. He received a degree in physics from the University of California at San Diego, then got a job working on jet engines. Disturbed that his skills were crafting potential instruments of death, Judge quit and began playing music for a living. A few years later, in 1990, he happened on an animation festival in Dallas, Texas, and caught the filmmaking bug.

He bought a few supplies and taught himself the basics of animation, and one of his first shorts, *Frog Baseball*, introduced a pair of snotty heavy-metal fans named Beavis and Butt-head. The characters found a home on MTV, and the *Beavis and Butt-head* series enjoyed phenomenal success during its 200-episode run. Judge wrote, produced, and directed all of the shows, in addition to providing voice performances. In 1995, Judge launched another successful animated series, *King of the Hill*, which featured only slightly more sophisticated artwork than the crudely rendered *Beavis and Butt-head*.

All of Judge's work rides a fine line between ironic humor and bitter cynicism, and the edgy tension between those extremes leads to outrageous moments that, especially when Beavis and Butt-head are involved, generate controversy as easily as they generate laughter.

FILMOGRAPHY: *Beavis and Butt-head Do America* (animated, 1996), *Office Space* (1999)

Kaplan, Deborah see **Elfont, Harry**

Kaufman, Charlie Like Andrew Kevin Walker and the Wachowski brothers, the witty Kaufman keeps details of his biography private, but it's a matter of public record that prior to making his break into features, he contributed to TV shows including *The Dana Carvey Show* and *Get a Life* (a cult favorite featuring David Letterman crony Chris Elliot). He seems dedicated to justifying his reputation as a postmodern rascal.

FILMOGRAPHY (as screenwriter): *Being John Malkovich* (1999), *Adaptation* (2002)

Kusama, Karyn (b. 1968) St. Louis native Kusama studied film at New York University, and her senior thesis film, *Sleeping Beauties*, received a Mobil Award. She entered the movie industry as an assistant to acclaimed independent filmmaker John Sayles, and Sayles helped fund Kusama's feature debut, which scored at festivals and with critics.

FILMOGRAPHY: *Girlfight* (2000)

LaBute, Neil (b. 1963) No Gen-X filmmaker has more brazenly entered the front lines of the battle between the sexes than LaBute, whose early work contained such violently macho male characters that the filmmaker himself often was perceived as a misogynist. (He undercut that criticism by featuring strong female protagonists in his third and fourth movies.) The erudite LaBute, who was born in Detroit, Michigan, studied at Brigham Young University and the University of Kansas before enrolling in New York University's graduate dramatic writing program. At the tail end of his college career, LaBute won a fellowship to study at the Royal Court Theater in London, and he later was admitted into the Sundance Institute.

LaBute's extensive education shows in his startling dialogue — which ranges from the shockingly stylized to the warmly realistic — and his unusual characters, who often defy audience expectations by revealing hidden qualities, both dark and light. The grand theme of LaBute's work, at least as seen in his early films, seems to be how people are held accountable for their participation in society and their treatment of others. He also has a deep interest in how people get derailed by fate and by petty desires. LaBute's numerous theatrical creations include a trilogy of one-acts called *bash, latterday plays*, which was taped for television in 2000.

FILMOGRAPHY: *In the Company of Men* (1997), *Your Friends and Neighbors* (1998), *Nurse Betty* (2000), *Possession* (2002)

Lemmons, Kasi (b. 1961) Lemmons studied acting at New York University and history at the University of California at Los Angeles, but her writing was limited to scenes that she wrote for actor friends to use at auditions. After achieving moderate success in acting — she played the roommate of FBI agent Clarice Starling (Jodie Foster) in *The Silence of the Lambs*— Lemmons followed the encouragement of comedian-producer Bill Cosby and developed her writing skills.

When she tried to set up her first feature project, *Eve's Bayou*, the reception in Hollywood for an untried black female director was predictably tentative, so a producer suggested that Lemmons prove herself by filming part of the script. The resulting short, *Dr. Hugo*, enticed actor Samuel L. Jackson to become involved in the project, and he also starred in Lemmons's second movie. Her films feature exotic imagery and vivid performances, but her interest in mysticism and dream-like story lines has made marketing her work to general audiences difficult.

FILMOGRAPHY: *Eve's Bayou* (1997), *The Caveman's Valentine* (2000)

Liman, Doug (b. 1966) A stylist with a great eye for composition and a brisk approach to storytelling, Liman is arguably the best of the post-Tarantino hipster directors. He made films while in high school, and studied at both the International Center of Photography, in New York City, and Brown University. At Brown, Liman founded a student-run TV station, which led to his establishment of the National Association of College Broadcasters. While studying film at the University of Southern California's graduate program, Liman was recruited to direct a straight-to-video movie, which started his career in features. In addition to directing *Swingers*, he photographed the film.

FILMOGRAPHY: *Getting In* (1994), *Swingers* (1996), *Go* (1999), *The Bourne Identity* (2002)

Linklater, Richard (b. 1961) While firmly entrenched as a cult figure regarded highly by other indie filmmakers, Linklater has steered an unsteady course because of his erratic taste in material and his seemingly contradictory impulses. His best films are small and iconoclastic, so *The Newton Boys*, his attempt at a star-driven action vehicle, has for years been his personal albatross.

Born in Houston, Linklater studied literature and drama in college before dropping out, like one of his characters, then getting a job on an oil rig in the Gulf of Mexico. Linklater became interested in film during his post-collegiate period, and moved to Austin, where he began experimenting with movies. The self-taught director, who founded the Austin Film Society (and remains an influential figure in the city's cutting-edge cinema underground), debuted with a 1988 film shot on Super-8 and funded with a scant $3,000.

Despite his peculiar trajectory, Linklater has retained the qualities that made him interesting in the first place: A devotion to investigating the ideas and emotions that fuel human relationships, and a devotion to telling stories with a minimum of extraneous style.

FILMOGRAPHY: *It's Impossible to Learn to Plow by Reading Books* (1988), *Slacker* (1991), *Dazed and Confused* (1993), *Before Sunrise* (1995), *SubUrbia* (1996), *The Newton Boys* (1998), *Tape* (2001), *Waking Life* (2001)

Lonergan, Kenneth (b. 1963) Lonergan wrote one of the most celebrated stories about Gen Xers trying to find their identities—but not as a movie. His play *This Is Our Youth*, which garnered numerous awards and rave reviews during its off-Broadway run, dramatizes a day in the lives of two listless twentysomethings living in New York. Lonergan's one-act play *You Can Count on Me* evolved into his Oscar-nominated directorial debut, which was coproduced by Martin Scorsese. A Bronx native, Lonergan studied play writing at New York University, and he also has notable acting skills: Lonergan appears as a priest in one of *You Can Count on Me*'s funniest scenes.

FILMOGRAPHY: *Analyze This* (screenplay only, 1999), *The Adventures of Rocky & Bullwinkle* (screenplay only, 2000), *You Can Count on Me* (2000), *Gangs of New York* (screenplay only, 2002)

Luhrmann, Baz (b. 1962) A shrewd self-promoter whose pretensions sometimes outpace his inarguable talent, Luhrmann has a theatrical approach to filmmaking. He adores intricate sets, glamorous costumes, romantic movement (both by characters and the camera), and brash anachronisms. In 1986, while a student at the National Institute of Dramatic Arts in his native Australia, Luhrmann cocreated a stage show called *Strictly Ballroom* (which he later adapted into a film of the same name). The show launched a theater career that earned Luhrmann numerous awards, as well as a six-year tenure as artistic director of the Old Company Theater Group. Luhrmann's other accomplishments include directing several acclaimed opera productions and releasing a 1999 pop album that spawned a major novelty hit, "The Sunscreen Song."

FILMOGRAPHY: *Strictly Ballroom* (1992), *William Shakespeare's Romeo + Juliet* (1996), *Moulin Rouge!* (2001)

Lurie, Rod (b. 1962) Lurie is peculiar among his peers for at least two reasons: He enjoyed a successful career as a movie critic before becoming a director, and he has a distinct political bent. Dedicated to the kind of humanistic governance often derided as "bleeding-heart liberalism," Lurie famously alienated actor Gary Oldman by painting Oldman's character in *The Contender* as a villain; the right-wing actor saw his character as hero.

Educated at West Point, Lurie spent four years in the U.S. Army before commencing his journalistic exploits. He wrote about movies for *Premiere* and *Movieline*, among other outlets, prior to his five-year tenure as critic, investigative reporter, and contributing editor at *Los Angeles* magazine. His next job was a four-year run hosting a top-rated Los Angeles radio show, on which he interviewed notables including Tom Hanks and James Cameron. Lurie's first short film, *Four Second Delay*, won several awards, and he is the author of a 1995 book called *Once Upon a Time in Hollywood.*

FILMOGRAPHY: *Deterrence* (1999), *The Contender* (2000), *The Last Castle* (2001)

Mangold, James (b. 1964) A sensitive director of actors, and a competent visual stylist, Mangold makes films that seem out of step with contemporary cinema, because his focus on character and story recall American movies of the 1970s. While Mangold's interest in misfits—and characters who perceive themselves as misfits—is both consistent and touching, his films rarely reach the level of emotionalism that his stories (and his characters) deserve. Should he mature sufficiently to maximize his skills, however, he could become a world-class filmmaker.

Mangold first gained notice while a student at the California Institute of the Arts, in Valencia, when one of his short films was chosen as a finalist for the 1982 Student Academy Awards. His success led to work writing TV and theatrical films, but Mangold boldly returned to school even though he was on the way to a steady, if unspectacular, career. In 1991, Mangold completed his studies at Columbia University's film school (where he was mentored by Milos Forman) by making the thirty-minute drama *Victor*. He developed his second feature, *Cop Land*, at the Sundance Institute.

FILMOGRAPHY: *Oliver and Company* (animated, screenplay only, 1989), *Heavy* (1995), *Cop Land* (1997), *Girl, Interrupted* (1999), *Kate & Leopold* (2001)

McQuarrie, Christopher (b. 1968) Best known for his Oscar-winning screenplay *The Usual Suspects*, McQuarrie attended high school with *Suspects* director Bryan Singer in Princeton Junction, New Jersey. McQuarrie spent four years working in a detective agency prior to entering the film world via Singer's request that McQuarrie help write *Public Access*. While clever with structure and dialogue, McQuarrie has yet to expand upon his initial success. When he became a director, he succumbed to pressure to helm a crime film, *The Way of the Gun*, an angry movie that alienated audiences.

FILMOGRAPHY (as screenwriter): *Public Access* (1993), *The Usual Suspects* (1995), *The Way of the Gun* (also director, 2000)

Mendes, Sam (b. 1965) An Englishman who scored major commercial and critical hits in theaters on both sides of the Atlantic, Mendes drew comparisons to Orson Welles by bringing an assured touch to his first film, despite never having handled a camera previously. Thus far, his most visible projects have been boosted by provocative material and outstanding collaborators, so it remains to be seen whether Mendes can be more than brash and bold. He was educated at Cambridge University, and after tenures with the Chichester Festival Theatre and the Royal Shakespeare Company, he became artistic director of London's Donmar Warehouse. His stage hits in England included a revival of *Cabaret* and the initial run of *The Rise and Fall of Little Voice* (later adapted into a film called *Little Voice*); on Broadway, his *Cabaret* production won four Tony awards, and his risqué staging of *The Blue Room* was a cause célèbre.

FILMOGRAPHY: *American Beauty* (1999), *The Road to Perdition* (2002)

Merhige, E. Elias (b. 1964) A former special-effects cameraman who studied film at the State University of New York at Purchase, Brooklyn-born Merhige lingered on the fringes of the indie-cinema scene until actor Nicolas Cage decided to co-produce *Shadow of the Vampire*, which was stronger in conception than execution, notwithstanding an extraordinary performance by Willem Dafoe.

FILMOGRAPHY: *Begotten* (1991), *Shadow of the Vampire* (2000)

Myrick, Daniel (b. 1964) and **Eduardo Sánchez** (b. 1969) Native Floridian Myrick and Cuban-born Sánchez met at the University of Central Florida, and each developed solid résumés before hitting the big time. Myrick's apprenticeship included work as an editor and cinematographer on several low-budget features, and Sánchez's included directing a feature-length picture shot on 16-millimeter film, the unreleased *Gabriel's Dream*. With some studio tweaking and a masterful marketing campaign, their first major collaboration became a phenomenon.

FILMOGRAPHY: *The Blair Witch Project* (1999)

Nelson, Tim Blake (b. 1965) Although Nelson seemed to appear from nowhere when he costarred in the 2000 hit *O Brother, Where Art Thou?*, directed by Joel Coen, the Tulsa, Oklahoma, native actually had accrued several theatrical and film credits prior to his breakthrough role. He also had written plays including *Eye of God*, the film version of which Nelson wrote and directed to a favorable reaction at several festivals. His second film was mired in controversy because its depiction of adolescent violence was filmed during a period of horrific school shootings, and his third was an adaptation of another of his plays.

FILMOGRAPHY: *Eye of God* (1997), *O* (2001), *The Grey Zone* (2002)

Niccol, Andrew (b. 1964) New Zealand native Niccol made his name with a masterful screenplay, *The Truman Show*, and showed tremendous ingenuity by maximizing the small budget and seemingly mundane locations of his first directorial effort. While it's tempting to light upon the paranoia that pervades Niccol's work, it's probably more accurate to say that he's an adroit social commentator with a keen eye on the future and a deep fear of dehumanizing trends in culture and science.

FILMOGRAPHY: *Gattaca* (1997), *The Truman Show* (screenplay only, 1998), *Simone* (2002)

Nolan, Christopher (b. 1970) A London native who began making short films at the age of seven, Nolan studied English literature at University College of London, where he continued making short films. One of his shorts was shown on public television in 1989, and Nolan's sophomore feature, based on a story written by his brother, was a major critical hit that also surpassed box-office expectations. Nolan's first two features indicated a deep devotion to noir style and intricate plotting, as well as a canny understanding of the human capacity for duplicity and delusion.

FILMOGRAPHY: *Following* (1998), *Memento* (2000), *Insomnia* (2002)

Norton, Edward (b. 1970) Maryland-born Norton acted off-Broadway before making his film debut as a disturbed murder suspect in *Primal Fear* (1996), which garnered him a well-deserved Oscar nomination for Best Supporting Actor. An unusually consistent and inventive actor, Norton has stood his ground opposite such powerful costars as Robert De Niro and Marlon Brando. The Columbia-educated Norton's behind-the-scenes inclinations became clear during a post-production squabble surrounding the incendiary drama *American History X* (1998): At the behest of the film's producers, Norton supervised a re-edit of the film that infuriated enfant terrible director Tony Kaye.

FILMOGRAPHY: *Keeping the Faith* (2000)

O'Connor, Gavin A graduate of the University of Pennsylvania, O'Connor entered the film industry as the writer and producer of *The Bet*, a 1992 short directed by Ted Demme. O'Connor then directed a short called *American Standoff*, which was shown on PBS, and a little-seen feature about drugs. His breakthrough was *Tumbleweeds*, a well-observed drama about family that features O'Connor in an impressive acting performance as a loutish boyfriend.

FILMOGRAPHY: *Comfortably Numb* (1995), *Tumbleweeds* (1999)

Payne, Alexander (b. 1961) An adept observer of contemporary society, Payne is poised to become one of the leading lights of his generation, because he has exhibited a skillful approach to satire and an aggressive directorial style. A native of Omaha, Nebraska, Payne studied history and Spanish literature at Stanford University; attended the University of Salamanca, in Spain; and received his master's in film from the University of California at Los Angeles. His thesis film, *The Passion of Martin*, was a festival hit that paved the way for his feature career. Payne's most important filmmaking ally so far is screenwriter Jim Taylor, who contributed to Payne's first three features.

FILMOGRAPHY: *Inside Out* (director, "My Secret Moments" segment, 1992), *Citizen Ruth* (1996), *Election* (1999), *About Schmidt* (2002)

Peirce, Kimberly (b. 1967) A noted photographer who holds degrees in English and Japanese literature (from the University of Chicago) and film (from Columbia University), Peirce entered the film industry with an award-winning short, 1994's *The Last Good Breath*. The director, who lived in Kobe, Japan, for two years, developed her screenplay about doomed cross-dresser Teena Brandon while at Columbia.

FILMOGRAPHY: *Boys Don't Cry* (1999)

Proyas, Alex (b. 1965) Born in Egypt but raised in Australia, Proyas is a visual stylist with a dark vision that, while rooted in the work of many previous filmmakers, could easily mature into something individualistic and sharp. His features tend to have a comic-book feel, but this allows him to employ outlandish special effects and stage outrageous action. He entered the Australian Film and Television School at age seventeen, and one of his early short films, *Groping* (1982), won a number of international awards. For several years, Proyas worked as director-for-hire of music videos and TV commercials, sharpening his skills for telling succinct visual stories while also creating images that entice both the mind and the eye.

FILMOGRAPHY: *Spirits of the Air, Gremlins of the Clouds* (1989), *The Crow* (1994), *Dark City* (1998), *Garage Days* (2002)

Ratner, Brett (b. 1970) A Miami native with a crowd-pleasing comic touch, Ratner entered New York University's film school at age sixteen, and won attention with his 1990 short *Whatever Happened to Mason Reese?*, an odd mix of documentary and fiction about a former child actor who appeared in TV commercials during the 1970s. Ratner established his reputation by making industrial films, commercials, and more than 100 music videos, including an award-winning clip for Madonna's "Beautiful Stranger," which features Mike Myers mugging as his character Austin Powers. Ratner's comedies have enjoyed tremendous financial success, due largely to the magnetism of funnyman Chris Tucker.

FILMOGRAPHY: *Money Talks* (1997), *Rush Hour* (1998), *The Family Man* (2000), *Rush Hour 2* (2001), *Red Dragon* (2002)

Rodriguez, Robert (b. 1968) Rodriguez's ascension is a tale of luck and pluck. His ingenuity is legend — he shot his first feature for $7,000 by building his script around available props, locations, and actors — and his films generally have production values that far exceed their moderate budgets. Yet he also has the good fortune to make connections with powerful people, and to score a hit just when detractors think his reputation has suffered too many body blows. Born in San Antonio, Texas, and educated at the University of Texas at Austin, Rodriguez began making films while a teenager, and has such an innate understanding of film technology that he often shoots and edits his pictures.

Despite his talent and opportunities, Rodriguez has yet to make any truly memorable films: His biggest commercial and critical hits are overpowering spectacles in which cinematic razzle-dazzle hides thin and/or nonsensical stories. He has been closely allied with Quentin Tarantino, and is one of the subjects of the 1997 documentary *Full Tilt Boogie*, which tracks the production of *From Dusk Till Dawn*. Rodriguez wrote a popular behind-the-scenes book called *Rebel Without a Crew: Or How a 23-Year-Old Filmmaker With $7,000 Became a Hollywood Player*.

FILMOGRAPHY: *El Mariachi* (1992), *Roadracers* (1994), *Desperado* (1995), *Four Rooms* (director, "The Misbehavers" segment, 1995), *From Dusk Till Dawn* (1996), *The Faculty* (1998), *Spy Kids* (2001), *Once Upon a Time in Mexico* (2002), *Spy Kids 2* (2002)

Rosenberg, Scott (b. 1964) A Boston native who originally wanted to be novelist, Rosenberg moved to Los Angeles after graduating from Boston University, then got a job as a production assistant and began writing scripts. His benefactor was action-movie producer Joel Silver, who bought a Rosenberg script called *Love Lies Bleeding* and hired the writer to work on his *Tales from the Crypt* series. Like Kevin Williamson and Quentin Tarantino, Rosenberg writes stylized, ironic, hip, super-articulate dialogue that rarely sounds natural but is often catchy and fun. Depth is not the quality for which he is known.

FILMOGRAPHY (as screenwriter): *Things To Do in Denver When You're Dead* (1995), *Beautiful Girls* (1996), *Con Air* (1997), *Disturbing Behavior* (1998), *High Fidelity* (2000), *Gone in 60 Seconds* (2000), *Highway* (2001), *Impostor* (2002), *Down & Under* (2002)

Sánchez, Eduardo see **Myrick, Daniel**

Schaeffer, Eric (b. 1962) A peculiar figure on the New York indie-cinema scene who apparently fancies himself a Gen-X Woody Allen — he writes, directs, and stars in movies about neurotic men who attract beautiful women but have trouble relating to them — Schaeffer made several unmemorable romantic comedies and cocreated a short-lived TV show called *Too Something*. Schaeffer's decision to also make films in which he does not star was wise, and his stamina in the face of public indifference is impressive.

FILMOGRAPHY: *My Life's in Turnaround* (codirected with Donal Lardner Ward, 1993), *If Lucy Fell* (1996), *Fall* (1997), *Wirey Spindell* (1999), *Never Again* (2001)

Shyamalan, M. Night (b. 1970) If only because of his willingness to defy the instant-gratification aesthetic slavishly adhered to by most mainstream directors of the late twentieth century, Manoj Nelliyatta Shyamalan has exhibited the makings of a unique, if not necessarily great, filmmaker. His tendency in interviews to equate box-office success with artistic fulfillment, and to boast about his ability to become the next Steven Spielberg, are distasteful only because they reveal the crass showman lurking not very deep beneath the surface of this talented artist.

Shyamalan was born in India and raised in a Philadelphia family dominated by doctors, including his parents. He was expected to continue the family tradition, but an omen that he wouldn't was his decision, at age ten, to start making movies with his father's home-video camera. At age sixteen, by which point he had forty-five shorts to his credit, he told his parents that he planned to attend film school, not medical school. While studying at New York University, Shyamalan wrote a picture called *Praying With Anger*, which he shot, in India, as his first feature. The picture was named Debut Film of the Year by the American Film Institute.

Shyamalan's thematic concerns — spirituality, personal responsibility, the supernatural — suggest that if he continues in the vein of his breakthrough work, he will one day need to prove that he can excel without the safety net of genre expectations.

FILMOGRAPHY: *Praying With Anger* (1992), *Wide Awake* (1998), *The Sixth Sense* (1999), *Stuart Little* (screenplay only, 1999), *Unbreakable* (2000), *Signs* (2002)

Singer, Bryan (b. 1966) A skillful director of actors who also has visual flair, Singer shares with Steven Soderbergh an inclination to dramatically shift gears between projects, which could lead to career longevity — but which also could, in the worst possible scenario, lead to his becoming a hack. Certainly the number of cinema purists who looked down on Singer's pulpy comic-book movie *X-Men* indicates that he's not held in such esteem that he'll be forgiven for playing to the crowd when he's capable of digging deeper.

As a teen growing up in New Jersey (where he attended high school with future collaborator Christopher McQuarrie), Singer made short films with an 8-millimeter camera. He studied at the School of Visual Arts, in New York City, then got a degree in critical studies from the University of Southern California. An award-winning short film featuring Gen-X stalwart Ethan Hawke, *Lion's Den*, paved the way for Singer's work in features — a trajectory that has taken him from low-budget indies to megabudget studio spectacles.

FILMOGRAPHY: *Public Access* (1993), *The Usual Suspects* (1995), *Apt Pupil* (1998), *X-Men* (2000)

Singh, Tarsem (b. 1962) An Indian native whose travels brought him from boarding school in the Himalayas to business school at Harvard to film school at the Art Center, in Pasadena, California, Singh (who bills himself simply as "Tarsem") established his reputation for creating memorable imagery by directing award-winning commercials and music videos. Some of his ads are in the permanent collection of the Museum of Modern Art, and his clip for R.E.M.'s song "Losing My Religion" is a widely imitated bit of enigmatic mood-setting.

FILMOGRAPHY: *The Cell* (2000)

Singleton, John (b. 1968) For the time being, Singleton enjoys a place in movie history as the youngest person ever nominated for a Best Director Oscar. His permanent slot in history is that he was the first African-American ever nominated for the prize. The picture that won him such acclaim, *Boyz N the Hood*, remains an important cultural reference point more than a decade after its release. If much of Singleton's subsequent output pales by comparison, it's as much a reflection of *Boyz N the Hood*'s significance as an indication of the other pictures' shortcomings.

Singleton — who was born and raised in Los Angeles, and who studied film writing at the University of Southern California — gracefully bears the burden of being his generation's most prominent black filmmaker, and his explorations of race-related issues range from the provocative to the attitudinal. In addition to his skill at handling drama, Singleton has shown an affinity for action scenes, even going so far as to launch a possible franchise by reimagining the 1970s movie *Shaft* as a twenty-first-century shoot-em-up.

FILMOGRAPHY: *Boyz N the Hood* (1991), *Poetic Justice* (1993), *Higher Learning* (1995), *Rosewood* (1997), *Shaft* (2000), *Baby Boy* (2001)

Smith, Kevin (b. 1970) A brash, opinionated, sometimes combative filmmaker whose roots in independent cinema are seen in his often-risqué subjects, his consistently amateurish visuals, and his prolix screenplays, Smith seems utterly satisfied with his status as a cult figure, and devotes much of his energy to communicating with his network of devoted fans. His movies are frustrating, because while Smith is capable of riotous humor and thought-provoking drama, he regularly succumbs to his lesser instincts. The insouciance with which he does so, however, gives him the air of a likable brat.

After seeing Richard Linklater's *Slacker*, which opened Smith's eyes to the concept that scruffy and inexpensive films could affect audiences, the New Jersey native used enterprising means to fund his debut feature. (His first short film, 1992's *Mae Day: The Crumbling of a Documentary*, was a tongue-in-cheek record of its own making.) Having worked at a Garden State concern called Quick Stop Groceries for about four years, he wrote a script about a day in the life of a convenience-store clerk. Smith then signed up for a course at the New School for Social Research in New York City in order to get a student ID, which he used to buy 16-millimeter film at a student discount. After making the purchase, he promptly withdrew from the course.

Educated at Brookdale Community College, the hyper-articulate Smith also has cultivated a career as a comic-book writer, scripting best-selling runs of titles including *Daredevil* and *Green Arrow*. (He's a vocal fan of the superhero medium, and owns a comic store in New Jersey.) Smith has appeared in all of his films as a character named Silent Bob, and the character recurred in *Clerks* comic books and the short-lived *Clerks* animated TV series.

FILMOGRAPHY: *Clerks* (1994), *Mallrats* (1995), *Chasing Amy* (1997), *Dogma* (1999), *Jay and Silent Bob Strike Back* (2001)

Soderbergh, Steven (b. 1963) Soderbergh has never been the flashiest director of his generation, nor the most controversial. But by making huge artistic leaps from picture to picture, by honing a personal style and then setting it aside when appropriate, and by embracing a wide variety of subjects, he quietly established himself as the most important Gen-X filmmaker. He has said in interviews that the filmmaker whose career he most wishes to emulate is John Huston, and given that the prolific Huston prided himself on having a unseen directorial hand, Soderbergh seems well-positioned to make good on his ambition.

While a great deal has been said about the director's technical aptitude — he has edited several of his own films, and by the end of the 1990s, he was his own cinematographer — all of his clever intercutting and image manipulation would be for naught if he didn't have good story sense. He does, and he also has a good sense of which stories will last: *King of the Hill* is a timeless story about family; *Schizopolis*, an arthouse lark in which the director stars as a funhouse-mirror version of himself, is a wild experiment that can be returned to again and again; *Erin Brockovich* is a crowd-pleaser with a long shelf life; and so on. Whereas other Gen-X filmmakers have hurt themselves by clinging too tightly to particular genres or styles, Soderbergh has moved around enough, both artistically and thematically, that he can truly call himself a Huston-like chameleon.

Soderbergh's father, a college professor who wrote about movies, moved around the south throughout the director's childhood, and the family lived longest in Baton Rouge, Louisiana. Because the young Soderbergh showed artistic flair, his father enrolled him in an animation class at Louisiana State University while he was still a high schooler. Soderbergh freed the camera from the animation stand and shot live-action shorts, laying the groundwork for his eventual move to Los Angeles. Soderbergh got work as an editor, winning a Grammy for a concert video featuring the progressive-rock band Yes, but while cutting other people's projects, he wrote several screenplays in the hopes that one would create an opportunity to direct. The script that did it was *sex, lies, and videotape*.

Soderbergh published his journal about making his first movie as a book with the same title as the film, and in 1999 published a second book, the whimsically self-deprecating *Getting Away with It or: The Further Adventures of the Luckiest Bastard You Ever Saw*. For television, he directed a 1993 episode of the film noir anthology series *Fallen Angels*.

FILMOGRAPHY: *sex, lies, and videotape* (1989), *Kafka* (1991), *King of the Hill* (1993), *The Underneath* (1995), *Gray's Anatomy* (1996), *Schizopolis* (1997), *Nightwatch* (screenplay only, 1998), *Out of Sight* (1998), *The Limey* (1999), *Erin Brockovich* (2000), *Traffic* (2000), *Ocean's Eleven* (2001), *Full Frontal* (2002)

Sommers, Stephen (b. 1962) Although he was one of the first Gen Xers to direct a feature, Sommers is among the least notable filmmakers of his generation, not so much because he's a style-over-substance populist, but because he so shamelessly apes the crowd-pleasing style of Steven Spielberg. Sommers showed flashes of wit in some of his early pictures, but once he broke into the big time with his *Mummy* franchise, he became a slave to empty spectacle. Educated at St. John's University and the University of Seville, in Spain, Sommers spent four years performing in theater groups and managing rock bands in Europe. He then returned to America, received a master's from the University of Southern California's film school, and made an award-winning short film called *Perfect Alibi*.

FILMOGRAPHY: *Terror Eyes* (1987), *Catch Me ... If You Can* (1989), *The Adventures of Huck Finn* (1993), *Gunmen* (screenplay only, 1994), *Rudyard Kipling's Jungle Book* (1994), *Tom and Huck* (screenplay only, 1995), *Deep Rising* (1998), *The Mummy* (1999), *The Mummy Returns* (2001), *The Scorpion King* (screenplay only, 2002)

Stiller, Ben (b. 1965) The son of comics Ben Stiller and Anne Meara, Stiller is accomplished as an actor and as a director. Onscreen, he has perfected an offbeat mix of irony, sweetness, neurosis, and pop-culture references that make him among the most unmistakably Gen-X talents in Hollywood. While his comedy often is stinging — particularly when he turns his gaze toward such easy targets as Hollywood and the fashion industry — he generally remains likable. Some find his tic-laden performances annoying, however, recalling how Woody Allen's acting work is an acquired taste.

Stiller studied film at the University of California at Los Angeles, and made his mark in the early 1990s with *The Ben Stiller Show*, a short-lived but critically adored variety show that often contained merciless satires of movie trends. He truly arrived in 1994, with the seminal Gen-X flick *Reality Bites*. He has since concentrated more on acting than directing, but by scoring a major hit as the star of the 2000 comedy *Meet the Parents*, he won himself the opportunity to develop projects he could both direct and act in. At worst, Stiller's comedy — whether on TV or the big screen — is a knee-jerk response to popular culture. At best, it's pointed and human.

FILMOGRAPHY: *Reality Bites* (1994), *The Cable Guy* (1996), *Zoolander* (2001)

Stockwell, John (b. 1961) Like Keith Gordon, Stockwell has been involved in the film industry for two decades as an actor. His screen appearances date back to 1981, and the Texas native acted in such prominent films as *Top Gun* and *Nixon*, not to mention a slew of rank-and-file movies. He also has worked throughout his career as a screenwriter. Stockwell's directing career came of age at the beginning of the twenty-first century, first with a well-received telefilm called *Cheaters* and then with a sensitive theatrical feature about an interracial love affair between teenagers, *crazy/beautiful*.

FILMOGRAPHY: *Dangerously Close* (screenplay only, 1986), *Under Cover* (1987), *Breast Men* (teleplay only, 1997), *Cheaters* (2000), *crazy/beautiful* (2001), *Rock Star* (screenplay only, 2001)

Tarantino, Quentin (b. 1963) Knoxville, Tennessee, native Tarantino moved to Los Angeles with his divorced mother while he was a child. A high-school dropout, he nurtured his obsessive love of movies while working in a video store called Imperial Entertainment, at which he became notorious for steering customers toward obscure exploitation films and underrated B-pictures. Connections that he made with video-store customers who worked in the film industry led to his entrance into the business.

Although he was trained as an actor, and had enjoyed such dubious successes as playing an Elvis impersonator on the senior-themed sitcom *Golden Girls*, Tarantino first gained notice as a writer, selling his script *True Romance* while still an industry outsider. The nascent filmmaker's only proper education in helming movies came during a ten-day workshop at the Sundance Institute, where he was mentored by an impressive roster of Hollywood talents, among them Sydney Pollack and Monte Hellman (who executive-produced Tarantino's first movie).

Tarantino's movies are filled with caffeinated energy, mellifluous language, and ironic pop-culture references. His stories mix film-noir violence, old-Hollywood romanticism, unexpected plot twists, and, often, disjointed time into a fast-moving, smart, and euphoric kind of entertainment that sometimes feels more substantial than it actually is. His wiseacre devices are crutches, and his writerly affection for character and dialogue are distinct strengths. Tarantino's visual approach alternates between 1970s-style realism and 1940s-style noir affection; his editing alternates between meditative patience and full-throttle aggression.

Obsessed with crime and Hollywood's portrayal of it, Tarantino often builds morality tales around the price criminals pay for their lifestyles. In some cases, criminals who adhere to their own moral code are allowed to escape with the spoils of their lawlessness; in others, criminals who violate their own moral code, or too carelessly violate the trust between criminals, pay for their mistakes with their lives. Despite the incessant violence and salacious language of his pictures, Tarantino consistently displays a strong, if skewed, sense of right and wrong. He also allies himself strongly with characters who have personal authenticity, putting poseurs, impostors, and wannabes into humiliating situations.

A final note about Tarantino: As have Edward Burns, Ben Stiller, and other Gen-X directors, Tarantino has nurtured an intriguing career as an actor in addition to his directorial efforts, sometimes appearing as a jokey version of himself (as in Spike Lee's *Girl 6*) and sometimes giving fully rounded performances (as in Robert Rodriguez's *From Dusk Till Dawn.*). He is one of the subjects of a 1997 documentary called *Full Tilt Boogie*, which depicts the making of *From Dusk Till Dawn*, and in 1995, he directed an episode of the top-rated TV medical drama *ER*.

FILMOGRAPHY: *Reservoir Dogs* (1992), *Killing Zoe* (executive producer only, 1993), *True Romance* (screenplay only, 1993), *Natural Born Killers* (story only, 1994), *Pulp Fiction* (1994), *Crimson Tide* (uncredited screenwriting only, 1995), *Four Rooms* (director, "The Man from Hollywood" segment, 1995), *From Dusk Till Dawn* (executive producer, writer, and actor only, 1996), *Jackie Brown* (1997)

Tillman, George Jr. After growing up in Milwaukee, Wisconsin — where he made short experimental films and created a show called *Spice of Life* for a public-access TV station — Tillman studied film and video at Columbia College, in Chicago. While there, he made a thirty-minute short called *Paula*, which won the Midwestern Student Academy Award. The director built on this success by gathering $150,000 from private investors to make his first feature, *Scenes for the Soul*, which was purchased by Savoy Pictures for $1 million, but never released because Savoy went under. Tillman, whose pictures balance accessible discussions of social issues with crowd-pleasing entertainment, rebounded from the demise of *Scenes for the Soul* by writing a script called *Soul Food*, then requiring that whomever bought the screenplay would also hire him to direct. The resulting film was the basis for a series broadcast on the Showtime cable channel.

FILMOGRAPHY: *Scenes for the Soul* (unreleased, 1995), *Soul Food* (1997), *Men of Honor* (2000)

Walker, Andrew Kevin (b. 1964) A smart writer whose work seethes with anger and violence, Walker has clouded his biography by giving cryptic interviews and by allowing a myth to arise about how the screenplay of *Seven* came to be produced. Born in Altoona, Pennsylvania, and educated at Pennsylvania State University, Walker has in the course of only a few projects written everything from scathing social commentary to tepid escapism. He runs the risk of getting marginalized because of his fascination with dark subject matter, and his work seems to be degenerating back to the level of the *Tales From the Crypt* episodes he wrote before scoring with *Seven*. In 2001, Walker contributed scripts to a high-profile series of Internet-only short films designed to advertise BMW vehicles.

FILMOGRAPHY (as screenwriter): *Brainscan* (1994), *Hideaway* (1995), *Seven* (1995), *8mm* (1999), *Sleepy Hollow* (1999)

Wachowski, Andy (b. 1967) and **Larry Wachowski** (b. 1965) Often billed collectively as The Wachowski Brothers, this fraternal writing-directing team has gone out of their way to withhold details of their background, choosing instead to put the focus on their work. Their shared biography in press materials for *The Matrix*, for instance, concludes with this cryptic phrase: "Little else is known about them." What is known about them is that the Chicago-born brothers are deeply informed by pulpy entertainment, from comic books to martial-arts movies to Japanese animation to *Star Wars*.

While others of their generation have regurgitated similar influences as disposable entertainment, the Wachowskis seem to have sufficient interest in, and insight into, human relations to tell memorable stories. Their work also is boosted by technical wizardry; an affinity for stylistic settings, glamorous actors, and whiz-bang action; and a playful approach to issues of morality and perception.

FILMOGRAPHY: *Assassins* (screenplay only, 1995), *Bound* (1996), *The Matrix* (1999), *The Matrix Reloaded* (2003)

Wachowski, Larry see **Wachowski, Andy**

Weitz, Chris (b. 1970) and **Paul Weitz** (b. 1966) The writing and directing fraternity behind *American Pie*, a sleeper hit filled with raunchy comedy, the Weitz brothers have exhibited only the most rudimentary filmmaking skills, but in a peculiar turn of events, both contributed terrific performances to the edgy indie

Chuck & Buck: Chris played Chuck, a straightlaced professional dogged by a stalker, and Paul played an inept actor. Their comedy is effective, but their affinity for crass sexual and scatological jokes is a weakness. The brothers produced the 2001 sequel *American Pie 2*, but did not write or direct the film.

FILMOGRAPHY: *Antz* (animated, screenplay only, 1998), *Clockstoppers* (screenplay only, 1999), *American Pie* (1999), *Nutty Professor II: The Klumps* (screenplay only, 2000), *Down to Earth* (2001)

Weitz, Paul see Weitz, Chris

Wells, Audrey (b. 1961) Wells's output as a screenwriter has been slight but entertaining, and it appears that her directorial output will be more substantial, while retaining the accessible style that distinguishes her screenplays. She seems particularly interested in how men and women relate to each other, and revels in seeing how odd matches can produce lasting affection. She received her master's in film from the University of Southern California at Los Angeles, and set out to become a documentarian. That ambition gave way to a desire to write screenplays, but her work failed to reach the screen until 1996; her first produced screenplay was inspired, in part, by the three years she spent as a disc jockey in her native San Francisco.

FILMOGRAPHY (as screenwriter): *The Truth About Cats & Dogs* (1996), *George of the Jungle* (1997), *Guinevere* (also director, 1999), *Disney's The Kid* (2000)

West, Simon (b. 1961) A British filmmaker who began his career as an apprentice film editor at the BBC, West enjoyed a highly successful career directing television commercials before graduating to features. He has so far proven himself to be a highly capable technician, but seems utterly without soul. His second picture, *The General's Daughter*, was among the most vile movies of the 1990s, in part because of its exploitive shots of a woman's naked corpse, so it was surprising that West later attached himself to a potential franchise featuring an empowered female protagonist.

FILMOGRAPHY: *Con Air* (1997), *The General's Daughter* (1999), *Lara Croft: Tomb Raider* (2001)

Whaley, Frank (b. 1963) A charming actor from Syracuse, New York, who played leads in pictures including a hormone-driven comedy (1991's *Career Opportunities*) and a vicious Hollywood satire (1994's *Swimming With Sharks*), Whaley showcased the sensitivity that was only rarely utilized by his directors when he became a filmmaker himself. The respectful reception afforded his debut suggests he made the most of opportunities to learn from peers including Keith Gordon, for whom Whaley acted in *A Midnight Clear*, and Quentin Tarantino, for whom Whaley acted in *Pulp Fiction*.

FILMOGRAPHY: *Joe the King* (1999), *The Jimmy Show* (2002)

Whedon, Joss (b. 1964) Like Mike Judge and Kevin Williamson, Whedon has enjoyed tremendous success on television in addition to his feature work: He's the creator of *Buffy the Vampire Slayer*, a cult-favorite show that mixes supernatural action and ironic humor. The series was Whedon's way of correcting what he saw as another filmmaker's mistakes, because the Buffy character was introduced in a flop movie before she hit the small screen. Whedon, who has directed numerous Buffy episodes but, as yet, no features, comes from a line of writers: His grandfather penned episodes of *The Donna Reed Show* and *Leave It to Beaver*, and his father wrote installments of *Alice* and *Benson*. Whedon got his start in television, most notably as a story editor and writer on the successful sitcom *Roseanne*, and has balanced high-profile feature work with his deep commitment to TV. *Angel*, a spin-off of *Buffy*, was another success.

FILMOGRAPHY (as screenwriter): *Buffy the Vampire Slayer* (1992), *Toy Story* (animated, 1995), *Alien Resurrection* (1997), *Titan: A.E.* (animated, 2000), *Atlantis: The Lost Empire* (animated, 2001)

Williamson, Kevin (b. 1965) A native of New Bern, North Carolina, educated in theater and film at East Carolina University, Williamson started his career as a New York City actor, winning small roles in stage productions and TV shows. Trying another tack, Williamson relocated to Los Angeles and worked as an assistant to a music-video director while developing screenplays. The first screenplay he sold, a revenge tale set in high school and titled *Killing Mrs. Tingle*, got him into the door of the industry but was not produced until years later (with the new title *Teaching Mrs. Tingle*).

His first produced screenplay sparked a phenomenon. *Scream* appealed to young adults who grew up watching the 1980s slasher flicks that *Scream* satirized, as well as younger viewers eager to catch the new wave of horror films. Williamson quickly became a name-brand writer stuck in the ghetto of teen-horror films, but he branched out by creating a successful TV drama called *Dawson's Creek*, which shares with his screenplays an irreverent attitude toward popular culture, a fixation on youthful sexuality, and dialogue so labored and precocious that it's like a secret language. Williamson's second TV series, *Wasteland*, did not enjoy the success of its predecessor. His third series, *Glory Days*, debuted in 2002.

FILMOGRAPHY (as screenwriter): *Scream* (1996), *I Know What You Did Last Summer* (1997), *Scream 2* (1997), *The Faculty* (1998), *Teaching Mrs. Tingle* (also director, 1999), *Scream 3* (producer only, 2000)

Yakin, Boaz (b. 1966) Native New Yorker Yakin plugged away as a screenwriter for several years before making his first film, *Fresh*, a hard-hitting indie about a twelve-year-old drug runner. Whereas his screenplays written for hire generally contain violent escapism, his directorial efforts tackle serious subjects in an intelligent manner. His mainstream work, however, lacks the vigor of his smaller efforts.

FILMOGRAPHY: *The Punisher* (screenplay only, 1989), *The Rookie* (screenplay only, 1990), *Fresh* (1994), *A Price Above Rubies* (1998), *From Dusk Till Dawn 2: Texas Blood Money* (screenplay only, 1999), *Remember the Titans* (2000)

Appendix Two:
Notable Generation X Films

About Schmidt (2002) Directed by Alexander Payne. Written by Payne and Jim Taylor.

Adaptation (2002) Directed by Spike Jonze. Written by Charlie Kaufman.

The Adventures of Huck Finn (1993) Written and directed by Stephen Sommers. Based on the novel *The Adventures of Huckleberry Finn* by Mark Twain. 108 min.

Alien³ (1992) Directed by David Fincher. Written by Larry Ferguson, David Giler, and Walter Hill. Story by Vincent Ward. 115 min.

American Beauty (1999) Directed by Sam Mendes. Written by Alan Ball. 122 min.

American Pie (1999) Directed by Paul Weitz. Written by Adam Herz. 96 min. (Note: Weitz did not direct 2001's *American Pie 2*.)

Apt Pupil (1997) Directed by Bryan Singer. Written by Brandon Boyce. Based on the novella by Stephen King. 111 min.

Armageddon (1998) Directed by Michael Bay. Written by J. J. Abrams, Tony Gilroy, Jonathan Hensleigh, Robert Roy Pool, and Shane Salerno. 150 min.

Baby Boy (2001) Written and directed by John Singleton. 130 min.

Bad Boys (1995) Directed by Michael Bay. Written by Michael Barrie, Jim Mulholland, and Doug Richardson. Story by George Gallo. 118 min.

Bad Dreams (1988) Directed by Andrew Fleming. Written by Fleming and Steven E. de Souza. 84 min.

Before Sunrise (1995) Directed by Richard Linklater. Written by Linklater and Kim Krizan. 101 min.

Beautiful Girls (1996) Directed by Ted Demme. Written by Scott Rosenberg. 107 min.

Being John Malkovich (1999) Directed by Spike Jonze. Written by Charlie Kaufman. 112 min.

Beavis & Butt-head Do America (1996) Directed by Mike Judge. Written by Judge and Joe Stillman. 80 min.

The Blair Witch Project (1998) Written and directed by Daniel Myrick and Eduardo Sánchez. 81 min. (Note: 2000's *Book of Shadows: Blair Witch 2* was not directed by Myrick and/or Sánchez.)

Blow (2001) Directed by Ted Demme. Written by Nick Cassavetes and David McKenna. Based on the book by Bruce Porter. 124 min.

Boogie Nights (1997) Written and directed by Paul Thomas Anderson. 156 min.

Bottle Rocket (1996) Directed by Wes Anderson. Written by Anderson and Owen Wilson. 95 min.

Bound (1996) Written and directed by Andy and Larry Wachowski. 108 min.

The Bourne Identity (2002) Directed by Doug Liman. Written by Tony Gilroy, W. Blake Herron, and David Self. Based on the novel by Robert Ludlum.

Boys Don't Cry (1999) Directed by Kimberly Peirce. Written by Andy Bienen and Peirce. 118 min.

Boyz N the Hood (1991) Written and directed by John Singleton. 112 min.

The Brothers McMullen (1995) Written and directed by Edward Burns. 118 min.

Buffalo '66 (1998) Directed by Vincent Gallo. Written by Alison Bagnall and Gallo. 112 min.

Buffy the Vampire Slayer (1992) Directed by Fran Rubel Kuzui. Written by Joss Whedon. 94 min.

The Cable Guy (1996) Directed by Ben Stiller. Written by Lou Holtz, Jr. 96 min.

Can't Hardly Wait (1998) Written and directed by Harry Elfont and Deborah Kaplan. 98 min.

The Caveman's Valentine (2001) Directed by Kasi Lemmons. Written by George Dawes Green, from his novel. 105 min.

The Cell (2000) Directed by Tarsem Singh. Written by Mark Protosevich. 107 min.

Chasing Amy (1997) Written and directed by Kevin Smith. 111 min.

Chelsea Walls (2001) Directed by Ethan Hawke. Written by Nicole Burdette, from her play.

The Chocolate War (1988) Written and directed by Keith Gordon. Based on the novel by Robert Cormier. 95 min.

Chuck & Buck (2000) Directed by Miguel Arteta. Written by Mike White. 95 min.

Citizen Ruth (1996) Directed by Alexander Payne. Written by Payne and Jim Taylor. 102 min.

Clerks (1994) Written and directed by Kevin Smith. 103 min.

Con Air (1997) Directed by Simon West. Written by Scott Rosenberg. 115 min.

The Contender (2000) Written and directed by Rod Lurie. 126 min.

Cop Land (1997) Written and directed by James Mangold. 105 min.

The Craft (1996) Directed by Andrew Fleming. Written by Fleming and Peter Pilardi. 100 min.

crazy/beautiful (2001) Directed by John Stockwell. Written by Phil Hay, Matt Manfredi, Stockwell, and Lizzy Weiss. 95 min.

The Crow (1994) Directed by Alex Proyas. Written by David J. Schow and John Shirley. Based on the comic book by James O'Barr. 101 min. (Note: Proyas was not involved with spin-off properties including sequels and a television series.)

Dark City (1998) Directed by Alex Proyas. Written by Lemm Dobbs, David S. Goyer, and Proyas. 101 min.

Dazed and Confused (1993) Written and directed by Richard Linklater. 102 min.

Deep Rising (1998) Written and directed by Stephen Sommers. 106 min.

Desert Blue (1999) Written and directed by Morgan J. Freeman. 90 min.

Desperado (1995) Written and directed by Robert Rodriguez. 105 min.

Deterrence (1999) Written and directed by Rod Lurie. 101 min.

Dick (1999) Directed by Andrew Fleming. Written by Fleming and Sheryl Longin. 94 min.

Dogma (1999) Written and directed by Kevin Smith. 135 min.

8mm (1999) Directed by Joel Schumacher. Written by Andrew Kevin Walker. 119 min.

Election (1999) Directed by Alexander Payne. Written by Payne and Jim Taylor. Based on the novel by Tom Perrotta. 103 min.

El Mariachi (1992) Written and directed by Robert Rodriguez. 81 min.

Entropy (1999) Written and directed by Phil Joanou. 104 min.

Erin Brockovich (2000) Directed by Steven Soderbergh. Written by Susannah Grant. 132 min.

Eve's Bayou (1997) Written and directed by Kasi Lemmons. 108 min.

The Family Man (2000) Directed by Brett Ratner. Written by David Diamond and David Weissman. 125 min.

The Faculty (1998) Directed by Robert Rodriguez. Written by Kevin Williamson. Story by David Wechter, Bruce Kimmel. 102 min.

54 (1998) Written and directed by Mark Christopher. 92 min.

Fight Club (1999) Directed by David Fincher. Written by Jim Uhls. Based on the novel by Chuck Palahniuk. 139 min.

Final Analysis (1992) Directed by Phil Joanou. Screenplay by Wesley Strick. Story by Robert Berger and Strick. 124 min.

Four Rooms (1995) "The Man from Hollywood" segment written and directed by Quentin Tarantino. "The Misbehavers" segment written and directed by Robert Rodriguez. "The Missing Ingredient" segment written and directed by Alison Anders. "The Wrong Man" segment written and directed by Alexandre Rockwell. 97 min.

Fresh (1994) Written and directed by Boaz Yakin. 112 min.

From Dusk Till Dawn (1996) Directed by Robert Rodriguez. Written by Quentin Tarantino. Story by Robert Kurtzman. 108 min. (Note: Rodriguez and Tarantino produced, but did not write or direct, this film's sequels.)

Full Frontal (2002) Written and directed by Steven Soderbergh. (Note: This film is a pseudo-sequel to Soderbergh's *sex, lies, and videotape*.)

The Game (1997) Directed by David Fincher. Written by John Brancato and Michael Ferris. 128 min.

Garage Days (2002) Directed by Alex Proyas. Written by Proyas, Michael Udesky, and Dave Warner.

Gattaca (1997) Written and directed by Andrew Niccol. 106 min.

The General's Daughter (1999) Directed by Simon West. Written by Christopher Bertolini and William Goldman. Based on the novel by Nelson DeMille. 116 min.

Girlfight (2000) Written and directed by Karyn Kusama. 110 min.

Girl, Interrupted (1999) Directed by James Mangold. Written by Lisa Looner, Mangold, and Anna Hamilton Phelan. Based on the memoir by Sussanah Kaysen. 127 min.

Go (1999) Directed by Doug Liman. Written by John August. 103 min.

Good Will Hunting (1997) Directed by Gus Van Sant. Written by Ben Affleck and Matt Damon. 126 min.

Gray's Anatomy (1996) Directed by Steven Soderbergh. Written by Spalding Gray, from his monologue. 80 min.

The Grey Zone (2002) Written and directed by Tim Blake Nelson, from his play.

Guinevere (1999) Written and directed by Audrey Wells. 104 min.

Hard Eight (1997) Written and directed by Paul Thomas Anderson. 101 min.

Heaven's Prisoners (1996) Directed by Phil Joanou. Screenplay by Scott Frank and Harley Peyton. Based on the novel by James Lee Burke. 132 min.

Heavy (1995) Written and directed by James Mangold. 103 min.

Higher Learning (1995) Written and directed by John Singleton. 127 min.

Home for the Holidays (1995) Directed by Jodie Foster. Written by W.D. Richter. Story by Chris Radant. 103 min.

Hurricane Streets (1998) Written and directed by Morgan J. Freeman. 88 min.

I Know What You Did Last Summer (1997) Directed by Jim Gillespie. Written by Kevin Williamson. Based on the novel by Lois Duncan. 101 min. (Note: Williamson did not write the 1998 sequel *I Still Know What You Did Last Summer*.)

Illtown (1996) Written and directed by Nick Gomez. Based on the book *The Cocaine Kids* by Terry Williams. 103 min.

In the Company of Men (1997) Written and directed by Neil LaBute. 97 min.

Jackie Brown (1997) Written and directed by Quentin Tarantino. Based on the novel *Rum Punch* by Elmore Leonard. 155 min.

Jay and Silent Bob Strike Back (2001) Written and directed by Kevin Smith. 104 min.

The Jimmy Show (2002) Written and directed by Frank Whaley. Based on the play by Jonathan Marc Sherman.

Joe the King (1999) Written and directed by Frank Whaley. 93 min.

Josie and the Pussycats (2001) Written and directed by Harry Elfont and Deboarah Kaplan. Based on the Harvey Comics characters. 98 min.

Jungle Book see *Rudyard Kipling's Jungle Book*

Kafka (1991) Directed by Steven Soderbergh. Written by Lem Dobbs. 98 min.

Kate & Leopold (2001) Directed by James Mangold. Written by Andy Fleming, Mangold, and Steven Rogers. 121 min.

Keeping the Faith (2000) Directed by Edward Norton. Written by Stuart Blumberg. 128 min.

Killing Zoe (1993) Written and directed by Roger Avary. 96 min.

King of the Hill (1993) Written and directed by Steven Soderbergh. Based on the memoir by A.E. Hotchner. 102 min.

Lara Croft: Tomb Raider (2001) Directed by Simon West. Written by Patrick Massett and John Zinman. Adaptation by West. Story by Michael Colleary, Sara B. Cooper, and Mike Werb. Based on the Eidos Interactive character. 100 min.

The Last Castle (2001) Directed by Rod Lurie. Written by David Scarpa and Graham Yost. 131 min.

Laws of Gravity (1992) Written and directed Nick Gomez. 98 min.

The Limey (1999) Directed by Steven Soderbergh. Written by Lem Dobbs. 90 min.

Little Man Tate (1991) Directed by Jodie Foster. Written by Scott Frank. 99 min.

Little Odessa (1994) Written and directed by James Gray. 98 min.

Made (2001) Written and directed by Jon Favreau. 94 min.

Magnolia (1999) Written and directed by Paul Thomas Anderson. 188 min.

Mallrats (1995) Written and directed by Kevin Smith. 108 min.

The Matrix (1999) Written and directed by Andy and Larry Wachowski. 136 min.

The Matrix Reloaded (2003) Written and directed by Andy and Larry Wachowski.

Memento (2000) Written and directed by Christopher Nolan. Based on a story by Jonathan Nolan. 113 min.

Men of Honor (2000) Directed by George Tillman, Jr. Written by Scott Marshall Smith. 128 min.

A Midnight Clear (1991) Written and directed by Keith Gordon. Based on the novel by William Wharton. 107 min.

Money Talks (1997) Directed by Brett Ratner. Written by Joel Cohen and Alec Sokolow. 96 min.

Mother Night (1996) Directed by Keith Gordon. Written by Robert B. Weide. Based on the novel by Kurt Vonnegut, Jr. 110 min.

Moulin Rouge! (2001) Directed by Baz Luhrmann. Written by Luhrmann and Craig Pearce. 127 min.

The Mummy (1999) Written and directed by Stephen Sommers. 124 min.

The Mummy Returns (2001) Written and directed by Stephen Sommers. 129 min.

My Life's in Turnaround (1993) Written and directed by Eric Schaeffer and Donal Lardner Ward. 84 min.

The Myth of Fingerprints (1997) Written and directed by Bart Freundlich. 90 min.

New Jersey Drive (1995) Written and directed by Nick Gomez. 95 min.

The Newton Boys (1998) Directed by Richard Linklater. Screenplay by Linklater, Claude Stanush, and Clark Lee Walker, from Stanush's book. 122 min.

No Looking Back (1998) Written and directed by Edward Burns. 96 min.

Nurse Betty (2000) Directed by Neil LaBute. Written by James Flamberg and John C. Richards. Story by Richards. 112 min.

O (2001) Directed by Tim Blake Nelson. Written by Brad Kaaya. Based on the play *Othello* by William Shakespeare. 95 min.

Ocean's Eleven (2001) Directed by Steven Soderbergh. Written by Steve Carpenter and Ted Griffin. Based on the 1960 movie *Ocean's Eleven*, written by Harry Brown and Charles Lederer (screenplay) and George Clayton Johnson and Jack Golden Russell (story). 116 min.

Office Space (1999) Written and directed by Mike Judge. 90 min.

Once Upon a Time in Mexico (2002) Written and directed by Robert Rodriguez.

Out of Sight (1998) Directed by Steven Soderbergh. Written by Scott Frank. Based on the novel by Elmore Leonard. 123 min.

The Panic Room (2002) Directed by David Fincher. Written by David Koepp.

Pearl Harbor (2001) Directed by Michael Bay. Written by Randall Wallace. 182 min.

Pi (1998) Written and directed by Darren Aronofsky. 85 min.

Poetic Justice (1993) Written and directed by John Singleton. 109 min.

Poison (1990) Written and directed by Todd Haynes. 85 min.

Possession (2002) Directed by Neil LaBute. Written by David Henry Hwang, Laura Jones, and LaBute. Based on the novel by A. S. Byatt.

A Price Above Rubies (1998) Written and directed by Boaz Yakin. 116 min.

Public Access (1993) Directed by Bryan Singer. Written by Michael Feit Dougan, Christopher McQuarrie, and Singer. 87 min.

Pulp Fiction (1994) Written and directed by Quentin Tarantino. Stories by Roger Avary and Tarantino. 153 min.

Punchdrunk Knuckle Love (2002) Written and directed by Paul Thomas Anderson. 89 min.

Reality Bites (1994) Directed by Ben Stiller. Written by Helen Childress. 99 min.

Red Dragon (2002) Directed by Brett Ratner. Written by Ted Tally. Based on the novel by Thomas Harris.

The Ref (1994) Directed by Ted Demme. Written by Richard LaGravenese and Marie Weiss. 93 min.

Remember the Titans (2000) Directed by Boaz Yakin. Written by Gregory Allen Howard. 113 min.

Requiem for a Dream (2000) Directed by Darren Aronofsky. Written by Aronofsky and Hubert Selby, Jr. Based on the novel by Selby. 100 min.

Reservoir Dogs (1992) Written and directed by Quentin Tarantino. 99 min.

The Road to Perdition (2002) Directed by Sam Mendes. Written by David Self. Based on the graphic novel by Max Allan Collins, Patrick Marber, and Richard Piers Rayner.

The Rock (1996) Directed by Michael Bay. Written by Douglas S. Cook, Mark Rosner, and David Weisberg. 136 min.

Rosewood (1997) Directed by John Singleton. Written by Gregory Poirier. 140 min.

The Royal Tenenbaums (2001) Directed by Wes Anderson. Written by Anderson and Owen Wilson. 109 min.

Rudyard Kipling's Jungle Book (1994) Directed by Stephen Sommers. Written by Mark D. Geldman, Sommers, and Ronald Yanover. Based on the novel *The Jungle Book* by Rudyard Kipling. 111 min.

Rush Hour (1998) Directed by Brett Ratner. Written by Jim Kouf and Ross Lamanna. 98 min.

Rush Hour 2 (2001) Directed by Brett Ratner. Written by Jeff Nathanson. Based on characters created by Ross Lamanna. 90 min.

Rushmore (1998) Directed by Wes Anderson. Written by Anderson and Owen Wilson. 93 min.

Safe (1995) Written and directed by Todd Haynes. 118 min.

Schizopolis (1997) Written and directed by Steven Soderbergh. 96 min.

Scream (1996) Directed by Wes Craven. Written by Kevin Williamson. 110 min.

Scream 2 (1997) Directed by Wes Craven. Written by Kevin Williamson. 116 min. (Note: Williamson did not write 2000's *Scream 3*.)

Seven (1995) Directed by David Fincher. Written by Andrew Kevin Walker. 127 min.

sex, lies, and videotape (1989) Written and directed by Steven Soderbergh. 100 min. (Note: This film was followed by the 2002 pseudo-sequel *Full Frontal*.)

Shadow of the Vampire (2000) Directed by E. Elias Merhige. Written by Steven Katz. 92 min.

Shaft (2000) Directed by John Singleton. Written by Richard Prince, Shane Salerno, and Singleton. Story by Salerno and Singleton. Based on the novel by Ernest Tidyman. 99 min.

She's the One (1996) Written and directed by Edward Burns. 96 min.

Sidewalks of New York (2001) Written and directed by Edward Burns. 107 min.

Signs (2002) Written and directed by M. Night Shyamalan.

Simone (2002) Written and directed by Andrew Niccol.

The Sixth Sense (1999) Written and directed by M. Night Shyamalan. 107 min.

Skins (2002) Directed by Chris Eyre. Based on the novel by Adrian C. Louis.

Slacker (1991) Written and directed by Richard Linklater. 97 min.

Slums of Beverly Hills (1998) Written and directed by Tamara Jenkins. 90 min.

Smoke Signals (1998) Directed by Chris Eyre. Written by Sherman Alexie, from his book *The Lone Ranger and Tonto Fistfight in Heaven*. 88 min.

Soul Food (1997) Written and directed by George Tillman, Jr. 114 min.

Spy Kids (2001) Written and directed by Robert Rodriguez. 88 min. (Rodriguez also wrote and directed the 2002 sequel *Spy Kids 2*.)

Star Maps (1997) Directed by Miguel Arteta. Written by Arteta and Matthew Greenfield. 86 min.

State of Grace (1990) Directed by Phil Joanou. Written by Dennis McIntyre. 134 min.

Strictly Ballroom (1992) Directed by Baz Luhrmann. Written by Luhrmann and Craig Pearce. Story by Luhrmann and Andrew Bowell, based on Luhrmann's stage production, which was devised by its original cast. 94 min.

SubUrbia (1996) Directed by Richard Linklater. Written by Eric Bogosian, from his play. 121 min.

Swingers (1996) Directed by Doug Liman. Written by Jon Favreau. 96 min.

Tape (2001) Directed by Richard Linklater. Written by Stephen Belber, from his play. 86 min.

Teaching Mrs. Tingle (1999) Written and directed by Kevin Williamson. 96 min.

Things to Do in Denver When You're Dead (1995) Directed by Gary Fleder. Written by Scott Rosenberg. 114 min.

Three O'Clock High (1987) Directed by Phil Joanou. Written by Richard Christian Matheson and Thomas Szollosi. 101 min.

Threesome (1994) Written and directed by Andrew Fleming. 93 min.

Tomb Raider see *Lara Croft: Tomb Raider*

Traffic (2000) Directed by Steven Soderbergh. Written by Stephen Gaghan. Based on the 1989 British miniseries *Traffik*, written by Simon Moore. 147 minutes.

True Romance (1993) Directed by Tony Scott. Written by Quentin Tarantino. 119 min.

The Truman Show (1998) Directed by Peter Weir. Written by Andrew Niccol. 103 min.

The Truth About Cats & Dogs (1996) Directed by Michael Lehmann. Written by Audrey Wells. 97 min.

Tumbleweeds (1999) Directed by Gavin O'Connor. Written by O'Connor and Angela Shelton, from Shelton's unpublished memoir. 102 min.

Unbreakable (2000) Written and directed by M. Night Shyamalan. 106 min.

The Underneath (1995) Directed by Steven Soderbergh. Written by Daniel Fuchs and Sam Lowry. 100 min.

The Usual Suspects (1995) Directed by Bryan Singer. Written by Christopher McQuarrie. 105 min.

Velvet Goldmine (1998) Written and directed by Todd Haynes. 123 min.

The Virgin Suicides (1999) Written and directed by Sofia Coppola. Based on the novel by Jeffrey Eugenides. 97 min.

Waking Life (2001) Written and directed by Richard Linklater.

Waking the Dead (2000) Directed by Keith Gordon. Written by Scott Spencer. Based on the novel by Robert Dillon. 105 min.

The War at Home (1996) Directed by Emilio Estevez. Written by James Duff, based on his play *Homefront*. 119 min.

The Way of the Gun (2000) Written and directed by Christopher McQuarrie. 119 min.

Wide Awake (1998) Written and directed by M. Night Shyamalan. 88 min.

William Shakespeare's Romeo + Juliet (1996) Directed by Baz Luhrmann. Written by Luhrmann and Craig Pearce. Based on the play *Romeo and Juliet* by William Shakespeare. 120 min.

Wisdom (1986) Written and directed by Emilio Estevez. 109 min.

World Traveler (2002) Written and directed by Bart Freundlich. 103 min.

X-Men (2000) Directed by Bryan Singer. Screenplay by David Hayter. Story by Tom DeSanto and Hayter. Based on the Marvel Comics characters. 104 min.

The Yards (2000) Directed by James Gray. Written by Gray and Matt Reeves. 115 min.

You Can Count on Me (2000) Written and directed by Kenneth Lonergan. 109 min.

Your Friends and Neighbors (1998) Written and directed by Neil LaBute. 99 min.

Zoolander (2001) Directed by Ben Stiller. Written by John Hamburg, Drake Sather, and Stiller. Story by Sather and Stiller. 89 min.

Notes

Chapter 2

1. Geoffrey T. Holtz, *Welcome to the Jungle* (New York: St. Martin's Griffin, 1995), p. 27.

Chapter 3

1. Mark Salisbury, "Thanks for No Memories" (*Premiere*, April 2001), pp. 42, 46–47.
2. Jeff Gordinier, "1999: The Year That Changed Movies" (*Entertainment Weekly*, November 26, 1999), pp. 38–49.
3. Geoffrey T. Holtz, *Welcome to the Jungle* (New York: St. Martin's Griffin, 1995), p. 200.
4. Michael Sragow, "Being Charlie Kaufman" (Salon.com, November 11, 1999).

Chapter 4

1. Geoffrey T. Holtz, *Welcome to the Jungle* (New York: St. Martin's Griffin, 1995), p. 114.

Chapter 5

1. Johanna Schneller, "Crunch! Pow!" (*Premiere*, August 1999), pp. 68–73, 100.
2. Richard Linklater and Kim Krizan, *Before Sunrise* (New York: St. Martin's Griffin, 1995), p. vi.

Chapter 7

1. Geoffrey T. Holtz, *Welcome to the Jungle* (New York: St. Martin's Griffin, 1995), p. 182.

Chapter 8

1. Geoffrey T. Holtz, *Welcome to the Jungle* (New York: St. Martin's Griffin, 1995), p. 68.
2. Ibid., p. 86.
3. Rick Lyman, "Gritty Portrayal of the Abyss from a Survivor" (*New York Times*, February 5, 2001), p. E1, E3.
4. Mark Salisbury, "'Requiem' in Excelsis" (*Premiere*, October 2000), p. 54.
5. Holtz, *Welcome to the Jungle*, p. 77.
6. Trish Deitch Rohrer, "Two Flew Over the Cuckoo's Nest" (*Premiere*, October 1999), pp. 78–83.

Chapter 9

1. Lynn Hirschberg, "The Man Who Changed Everything" (*New York Times Magazine*, November 16, 1997), pp. 112–116.
2. Gary Whitta and Chris Gore, "Leonard Shelby is the Man with the Photographic Memory" (*Total Movie*, April 2001), pp. 66–69.
3. Todd Lippy, "Writing *The Usual Suspects*" (*Scenario*, Summer 1995), pp. 50–53, 191–196.

Chapter 10

1. Annie Nocenti, "Writing and Directing *Eve's Bayou*" (*Scenario*, Summer 1998), p. 198.
2. "Vanguard Dialogue: Chris Rock & Kevin Smith" (*Premiere*, October 1999), p. 98.

Chapter 11

1. Geoffrey T. Holtz, *Welcome to the Jungle* (New York: St. Martin's Griffin, 1995), p. 196.

Chapter 12

1. Michael Sragow, "Being Charlie Kaufman" (Salon.com, November 11, 1999).
2. Annie Nocenti, "Writing and Directing *Pi*" (*Scenario*, Summer 1998), p. 202.

Bibliography

Ahrens, Frank. "The Cyber-Saga of the 'Sunscreen' Song." *The Washington Post.* March 18, 1999, C1.

Alexandria, Michelle. "George Tillman, Jr. A Director on a Mission." Eclipse Magazine.com (www.eclipsemagazine.com). Accessed August 23, 2001.

Allen, Harry. "Can You Digit?" *Premiere.* November 1999, 93–103.

Bernstein, Jill. "The Education of M. Night Shyamalan." *Premiere.* November 2000, 57–60.

_____. "Tough Love." *Premiere.* October 2000, 76.

Brown, Gene. *Movie Time.* New York: Macmillan (1995).

Connors, Martin, and Jim Craddock, eds. *VideoHound's Golden Movie Retriever 1998.* Detroit, Michigan: Visible Ink (1998).

Coupland, Douglas. *Generation X: Tales for an Accelerated Culture.* New York: St. Martin's (1991).

Cowan, Alison Leigh, and Christopher S. Wren. "Dealing in Reality: A Film's Depiction of Drugs." *New York Times.* January 18, 2001, E1, E12.

"The Fifty Most Important Independent Films." *Filmmaker.* Fall 1996, 41–59.

Gordinier, Jeff. "1999: The Year That Changed Movies." *Entertainment Weekly.* November 26, 1999, 1, 38–49.

Hirschberg, Lynn. "The Man Who Changed Everything." *New York Times Magazine.* November 19, 1997, 112–116.

_____. "The Screenwriters: Shane Black and Harmony Korine." *New York Times Magazine.* November 19, 1997, 136–137.

Holtz, Geoffrey T. *Welcome to the Jungle: The Why Behind "Generation X."* New York: St. Martin's Griffin (1995).

Horn, John. "McTeer's Year." *Premiere.* March 2000, 57.

Jensen, Jeff. "First Tango in Paris." *Entertainment Weekly.* May 25, 2001, 30–39.

Katz, Ephraim. Revised by Fred Klein and Ronald Dean Nolen. *The Film Encyclopedia: Fourth Edition.* New York: HarperCollins (2001).

Koppelman, Brian. "The Anxiety of Tarantino." *Premiere.* February 2001, 38–39.

Lewin, Alex. "Arrested Development." *Premiere.* August 2000, 53.

Linklater, Richard, and Kim Krizan. *Before Sunrise.* New York: St. Martin's Griffin (1995).

Lippy, Todd. "Writing and Directing *Heavy.*" *Scenario.* Summer 1995, 98–101, 196–201.

_____. "Writing and Directing *Safe.*" *Scenario.* Summer 1995, 184–191.

_____. "Writing *The Usual Suspects.*" *Scenario.* Summer 1995, 50–53, 191–196.
Lyman, Rick. "Gritty Portrayal of the Abyss from a Survivor." *New York Times.* February 5, 2001, E1, E3.
Mayo, Mike. *VideoHound's Video Premieres.* Detroit, Michigan: Visible Ink (1997).
Nashawaty, Chris. "Spying Young." *Entertainment Weekly.* April 6, 2001, 25–26.
Niccol, Andrew. *The Truman Show: The Shooting Script.* New York: Newmarket (1998).
Nocenti, Annie. "Adapting *Out of Sight.*" *Scenario.* Summer 1998, 57–60, 199–202.
_____. "Steven Soderbergh on *Out of Sight.*" *Scenario.* Summer 1998, 61, 202.
_____. "Writing and Directing *Eve's Bayou.*" *Scenario.* Summer 1998, 192–199.
_____. "Writing and Directing *Pi.*" *Scenario.* Summer 1998, 91–95, 202–204.
Patterson, Troy. "The Gang's All Here." *Entertainment Weekly,* July 13, 2001, 90.
Puig, Claudia. "Soderbergh Flashes Forward." *USA Today,* January 2, 2001, D1–D2
Rohrer, Trish Dietch. "Two Flew Over the Cuckoo's Nest." *Premiere,* October 1999, 78–83.
Russo, Tom. "007 (Going on Eight)." *Total Movie.* April 2001, 36.
Salisbury, Mark. "'Requiem' in Excelsis." *Premiere.* October 2000, 54.
_____. "Thanks for No Memories." *Premiere.* April 2001, 42, 46–47.
Schneller, Johanna. "Crunch! Pow!" *Premiere.* August 1999, 68–73, 100.
Soderbergh, Steven. *sex, lies, and videotape.* New York: Harper & Row (1990).
Spines, Christine. "In Love and War." *Premiere.* May 2001. 46–53, 106–107.
_____. "Sofia's Choice." *Premiere.* March 2000, 90–93.
Sragow, Michael. "Being Charlie Kaufman." Salon.com (www.salon.com). November 11, 1999.
Sterngold, James. "Art and Reality." *New York Times.* June 12, 1998, E10.
_____. "The Low-Budget Realities of Making Indie Films." *New York Times.* April 15, 1999, E1, E8.
Sullivan, Monica. *VideoHound's Independent Film Guide.* Detroit, Michigan: Visible Ink (1998).
Svetkey, Benjamin. "Blood, Sweat & Fears." *Entertainment Weekly,* October 15, 1999, 24–31.
Tarantino, Quentin. *Pulp Fiction.* New York: Hyperion (1994).
Thompson, Anne. "Cinema Purité." *Premiere.* August 2000, 78–80, 90.
_____. "The Filmmaker Series: Steven Soderbergh." *Premiere,* October 2000, 59–65.
"Vanguard Dialogue: Chris Rock & Kevin Smith." *Premiere.* October 1999, 98.
"Vanguard Dialogue: Sarah Polley & Audrey Wells." *Premiere.* October 1999, 94.
Walker, John, ed. *Halliwell's Film and Video Guide 2001.* New York: HarperCollins (2000).
Whitta, Gary, and Chris Gere. "Leonard Shelby Is the Man with the Photographic Memory." *Total Movie.* April 2001, 66–69.

Online Sources

All-Movie Guide. www.allmovie.com. October 1999–September 2001.
Hollywood.Com. www.hollywood.com. August 2001.
Internet Movie Data Base. www.imdb.com. October 1999–September 2001.

Supplemental Sources

In addition to sources cited in the Bibliography, press kits and official Web sites for many of the films cited in the book were consulted, as were the unpublished screenplays of several films.

Index